THE DOG
WENT OVER THE
MOUNTAIN

For Wayne,

THE DOG WENT OVER THE MOUNTAIN

TRAVELS WITH ALBIE: AN AMERICAN JOURNEY

Stay on the high road!

Peter Zheutlin

1-1-2020

PETER ZHEUTLIN

PEGASUS BOOKS
NEW YORK LONDON

THE DOG WENT OVER THE MOUNTAIN

Pegasus Books Ltd.
148 W 37th Street, 13th Floor
New York, NY 10018

First Pegasus Books edition September 2019

Interior design by Maria Fernandez

The author is grateful to BringFido for their
generous support of the author's book tour.

DO RE MI
Words and Music by Woody Guthrie
WGP/TRO © Copyright 1961 (Renewed) 1963 (Renewed) Woody Guthrie
Publications, Inc. and Ludlow Music, Inc., New York, NY
Administered by Ludlow Music, Inc.
International Copyright Secured   Made in U.S.A.
All Rights Reserved Including Performance for Profit
Used by Permission

Library of Congress Cataloging-in-Publication Data is available.

ISBN: 978-1-64313-201-3

10 9 8 7 6 5 4 3 2 1

Printed in the United States of America
Distributed by W. W. Norton & Company

In memory of my late mother Baila, a caring parent,
voracious reader, and passionate advocate for education,
social justice, and equality for all . . .

. . . and for Albie, with whom every moment is precious.

Contents

Author's Note

I n the course of our travels, Albie and I met and talked with a lot of people. Only a few visits and conversations were planned in advance. For example, we stayed in Sacramento with my old friend and colleague Bill Monning. Bill is a lawyer who worked for many years with Cesar Chavez and the United Farm Workers of America and later California Rural Legal Assistance seeking justice for the hard-working immigrants and migrant workers who harvest our fruits and vegetables throughout California's Central Valley. He's now the majority leader of the California State Senate. In New Orleans, I arranged to sit down with 79-year-old JoAnn Clevenger, the legendary proprietor of Upperline, named best restaurant in the city by the *New Orleans Times-Picayune* in 2017. Clevenger's remarkable life in the city has given her keen insight into what makes New Orleans, in my view, the country's most unique city.

During some of these conversations, with JoAnn, for example, I took contemporaneous notes. But since most of our conversations were the result of chance encounters we had with strangers, some brief and some that lasted hours, I relied on memory until I could write them down, to the best of my recollection, later that day or evening. Nothing kills a spontaneous conversation like asking someone if they can wait while you get a pad of paper and a pen or, even worse, turn on a voice recorder and stick it in their face. The presence of any recording device tends to inhibit open, unguarded dialogue. I have worked hard to be faithful to the substance of all the conversations recounted in this book and believe the rendering of them to be true and accurate, even if not all are reported verbatim.

Albie and I were on a road trip. We never lingered long enough in any one place to immerse ourselves fully in the life of a community as, say, an anthropologist or sociologist would. What a traveler has to share are impressions, snapshots if you will, created from random encounters and chance events. Thus, the view offered here is kaleidoscopic and panoramic rather than microscopic. I don't pretend to speak with authority on any of the communities we passed through. Doing that would require settling into a place, observing the rhythms of life over weeks or months, and getting to know many people well. The best the traveler can do is to be observant and aware of his or her own prejudices and preconceptions as impressions take form, impressions that are, ultimately, completely subjective. Some places impressed me favorably, some did not, and I'll be the first to admit some of my impressions are based on limited evidence and may not be entirely fair. Maybe if we'd spent more time in Pampa, Texas, for example, I'd have loved it. But I doubt it. Albie is a less discerning traveler. He seemed to be pretty happy wherever we went, especially if there were squirrels.

Introduction

On a mild, rainy night in the spring of 2018, I patted the mattress of the bed in the dog-friendly inn where Albie and I were spending the night in Bennington, Vermont. Albie is the soulful yellow Lab and golden retriever mix our family had adopted six years before, when I was fifty-eight and he was, our vet surmised, about three. Albie hopped up on the bed and laid his head in the crook of my arm. As I had every night during our travels, I gently stroked his head, told him where we were, where we would be going tomorrow, and what a good guy he was. This night I told him we would, after nearly six weeks on the road, be going home. And I told him I loved him.

He looked at me with his deep, dark brown eyes, rolled slightly on his side to rest his body against mine, and sighed. I knew he didn't understand. I could have been reading him *"The Road Not Taken"* by Robert Frost, or sections of the Internal Revenue Code, it didn't really matter. He also didn't know where we were or why. What mattered was the sound of my voice, that he was safe and sound, and that we were together.

The safe and sound part is important. Albie had been picked up as a thin and frightened stray, a lost soul, on a country road in rural Louisiana in February of 2012, and impounded at a shelter where nearly nine of every ten dogs are "euthanized," a bland euphemism for "killed in a gas chamber." Against all odds, and thanks to a shelter volunteer who took a shine to him, Albie survived for five months until we found him online and vowed, without ever laying eyes on him, to set his world right. *

That night in Bennington we had nearly 9,000 miles behind us and just a couple of hundred more to go. The next night, after a stop in southern Maine, we'd be sleeping in our own beds, reunited with my wife Judy, and our two other rescue dogs, also from Louisiana, Salina and Jambalaya (Jamba for short).

During the nearly six weeks we'd been on the road, Albie and I had watched a full moon rise over the Sangre de Cristo Mountains in New Mexico, snow showers sweep across the Grand Canyon, and bison walking along the road in Yellowstone. We'd driven by massive stockyards in the Texas panhandle, through endless orange groves in California's Central Valley, and alongside vast fields of onions in eastern Oregon. Travel around America and you'll see where most of your food comes from.

We'd stood on the spot where the great explorer Meriwether Lewis took his life along the Natchez Trace in Tennessee, spent time in front of the hardware store in Tupelo, Mississippi, where Elvis's mother bought his first guitar (for $7.90), and walked

---

* Albie inspired my last two books: *Rescue Road: One Man, Thirty Thousand Dogs, and a Million Miles on the Last Hope Highway* (Sourcebooks, 2015) and *Rescued: What Second-Chance Dogs Teach Us About Living with Purpose, Loving with Abandon, and Finding Joy in the Little Things* (TarcherPerigee, 2017).

up and down the streets that shaped the conscience of Woody Guthrie in Okemah, Oklahoma. Albie had posed for pictures standing on a corner in Winslow, Arizona, and with curious Chinese tourists in Yosemite Valley. We'd driven through sun-splashed corridors of wild rhododendrons and dogwoods blooming along the Blue Ridge Parkway in North Carolina, in rain so heavy it was bringing down trees in Mississippi, and along remnants of old Route 66 in Texas, New Mexico, and Arizona. And along the way we'd met many characters, each of whom enriched our lives in some way: restaurateurs, politicians, veterans, musicians, shopkeepers, and itinerant travelers also in search of America.

So—why did we go and how did we get to Bennington on this rainy spring night?

In 1960, as he was approaching the beginning of his seventh decade, the writer John Steinbeck hit the road with his French poodle, Charley. Steinbeck was the acclaimed author of some of the greatest works ever penned by an American writer—*Of Mice and Men*, *The Grapes of Wrath*, and *East of Eden* to name just a few. But in the twilight of his life he "discovered that I did not know my own country. I, an American writer, writing about America, was working from memory, and the memory is at best a faulty, warpy reservoir . . . I had not felt the country for twenty-five years. In short, I was writing of something I did not know about." Steinbeck deemed this lapse "criminal" and set out to right this writer's wrong.

So, he mounted a small camper on the back of a pick-up truck, called the rig *Rocinante* after Don Quixote's horse, and, with Charley as his wingman, spent three months driving from his Long Island home to his native California and back. Among his provisions were the tools of his trade. To a modern-day writer most sound downright quaint: "paper, carbon, typewriter, pencils, notebooks and not only those but dictionaries, a compact encyclopedia, and a dozen other reference books, heavy ones." Oh, and maps, the old-fashioned paper kind you spread wide on a table and then attempt, in frustration, to fold back into their original form.

The result of Steinbeck's wanderings was a widely beloved book, *Travels with Charley*, which became a number one *New York Times* best seller. By the time Steinbeck died in 1968 it had sold more than two and a half million copies, including one to a teenage boy from Paramus, New Jersey. At ninety-five cents, it was a bargain for a trip that would take me, or more precisely my imagination, through dozens of states along backroads, byways, and highways. During the summer of 2017, at age sixty-three, I reread that very same copy of *Travels with Charley*, yellowed with age, barely intact, and held together with Scotch tape.

Over the years, the veracity of some of Steinbeck's account has been questioned. Though his wife is barely mentioned as a road companion—she met him briefly in Chicago and again in Texas for Thanksgiving, he wrote—she apparently joined Steinbeck for several weeks during the journey. He purportedly spent many more nights in fine hotels than one would be led to believe. Some of his encounters along the way were with people who were more likely the product of his fertile imagination than of biological parents, or composites of several people. The introduction to the fiftieth anniversary edition of *Travels with Charley* cautioned readers not to take the book too literally; Steinbeck was first and foremost a novelist.

When I first read *Travels with Charley*, I *did* take all of it literally. When I reread it nearly half a century later I was a little bit more the wiser, but it didn't dim the experience. Maybe the gumption and imagination required to undertake such an odyssey are the same qualities that cause the journeyman, or woman, to embellish from time to time. After all, an epic journey is supposed to be the stuff of legend and no one wants to come home empty-handed.

I am no stranger to the traveler on an epic journey who takes liberties with the literal truth. From 2003 to 2007, I labored to resurrect the long-lost story of my great-grandaunt, Annie Cohen Kopchovsky, who from 1894 to 1895 endeavored to become the first woman to circumnavigate the world by bicycle. A married mother of three and traveling under an assumed name ("Annie Londonderry," adopted from the first of her many corporate sponsors),* she left Boston alone carrying only a change of underwear, a pearl-handled revolver and a hyperactive imagination. She was, quite simply, a fabulist with a casual relationship with the truth.** Though she cycled about 9,000 miles, many of the things she claimed to have done and seen were conjured while safely ensconced in the cabin of a steamship or the sleeping compartment of a train.

Like my own Aunt Annie's partly apocryphal tale, *Travels with Charley* may not be literally true in every particular, but it remains a beautiful, witty, evocative, and quintessentially American story. A story need not be literally true in whole or in part to contain *Truth*.

---

* The Londonderry Lithia Spring Water Company of Nashua, New Hampshire, paid her $100 to affix an advertising placard on her bike that simply said "Londonderry" in a stylized script that was widely familiar from the company's ubiquitous print advertising.

** This journey became the subject of my first book, *Around the World on Two Wheels: Annie Londonderry's Extraordinary Ride* (Citadel Press, 2007).

❖

As I reread *Travels with Charley* at age sixty-three, it occurred to me how I should spend at least part of my year at sixty-four: traveling America, roughly along Steinbeck's route, with Albie.

When we adopted him, Albie, at about three years old, was a canine teenager. But because dogs mature on a different timetable than humans, by the time I had turned sixty-four we had arrived on the cusp of old age together. Both of us were squarely in the autumn of our lives. Perhaps, I thought, we two aging gentlemen should, like Steinbeck and Charley, reacquaint ourselves with America.

"A dog," Steinbeck wrote in *Travels with Charley*, "is a bond between strangers. Many conversations en route began with, 'what degree of dog is that?'"

Like Charley, Albie would be my calling card. I would count on him to attract passersby and ease me into conversations with strangers without them thinking I was deranged, dangerous, or slightly daft. He proved to be very much up to the task, endearing himself to countless people with his winsome good looks and his willingness to be touched and petted by everyone and anyone.

One goal of the trip was to rediscover the country I'd lived in for more than sixty-four years, but one that seemed to have slipped its moorings and drifted into dangerous waters. My intention in writing about the experience was not to embellish, as Steinbeck occasionally did, or conjure stories out of whole cloth as my great-grandaunt Annie often did, but to render a faithful accounting of my travels with Albie and what they revealed—about the country, about myself, and about my ever-deepening bond with Albie. There was no particular agenda, and there were no specific questions to answer. The premise, really, was no more complex than that in the old children's ditty about the bear that went over the mountain. We went over the mountain, metaphorically speaking, to see what we could see.

I had last crossed the country by automobile in 1977 with my brother, Michael. Elvis died while we were somewhere in the wide-open spaces of Wyoming. More than forty years later, as for millions and millions of us, the romance of the Great American Road Trip still beckoned.

In a September 2, 2017, piece in the *Wall Street Journal*, the renowned travel writer Paul Theroux recounted the origins of the Great American Road Trip beginning with F. Scott and Zelda Fitzgerald's experience in 1920, a trip that resulted in F. Scott's *The Cruise of the Rolling Junk.*[*] In my more ambitious moments I hoped to write a book as *avant garde* as Jack Kerouac's *On the Road*, as laugh-out-loud funny as Bill Bryson's *The Lost Continent*, as meditative as William Least Heat-Moon's *Blue Highways*, and as enduring as Steinbeck's *Travels with Charley*—all Great American Road Trip books. I'd also like to play basketball like LeBron James, baseball like Babe Ruth, football like Tom Brady, and golf like Arnold Palmer. In my more realistic moments I just hoped man and dog would return home in one piece (well, two), and with enough material for a good book.

Though, like Steinbeck, I wanted to better understand and know the country, this was *not* a mission to discover some verity about Donald Trump's America and what had led us to this

---

* The book was a compilation of journalistic pieces originally written for *Motor* magazine describing a journey from Connecticut to Alabama in a car Fitzgerald called the "Rolling Junk."

peculiar and precarious moment in our history. Many other writers and pundits have taken a serious swing at those questions, and it's been discussed and argued about *ad nauseum* in the media and over kitchen tables for nearly three years. There wasn't much to add that would be new or revelatory, but one could not travel America in 2018 and not brush up against those questions at some point.

When there were discussions of politics, and it was inevitable, they happened organically. When it came up, usually I was not the one to raise the subject, something my family and friends might find downright unbelievable. And there were moments that shed some light for me on what was afoot, politically speaking, in the country. I wasn't going to avoid the subject, not on the trip or in my book, but it wasn't the core mission. As a news junkie who has obsessively followed national politics for decades, frankly, I needed a break from the headlines that were delivering me into a state of greater and greater despair on a daily basis. Indeed, within a couple of days on the road and with less exposure to the daily onslaught of dispiriting headlines (and Facebook) I began to relax and found my relative news blackout copacetic and mildly therapeutic.

By taking you on this journey with us, my aim is to offer a bit of a respite from the dark and depressing state of our national politics—to share a more lighthearted, heartfelt, and dog-friendly tour of America and, in the process, remind us what remains wonderful and grand and good about it, even as it seems the country is coming apart at the seams. I didn't come home more hopeful about the future; our divide seems to be growing, not retreating, and the breakdown of civility and democracy seems to be accelerating. But I did come home feeling that most Americans, wherever they live, are fundamentally decent and less at each other's throats than one might believe from spending time on social media or watching television where the extremes dominate our national conversation. Perhaps we will one day leverage this common decency to restore a sense of national unity. There are no easy answers for what ails us, but I did, I think, gain some insight into lives very different than my own.

Not every trip we take is life-altering or results in a profound epiphany. But an observant traveler—observant not only of what is around him (or her) but of his own feelings and responses to what is seen, heard, and experienced—can't help but be changed in ways that may be subtle and small but nevertheless meaningful. Our journey fell squarely into this category. When we returned home, I didn't walk into the house and announce to Judy and the dogs that we were moving to Maui to seek enlightenment through meditation or psychedelics, decide to become vegan, or resolve to buy a camper so we could drive to Alaska and gaze at the northern lights, though I would someday love to see them. I did, however, become much more aware of the biases, preconceptions, and prejudices I had packed like my toothbrush and razor. And, I came back with a better understanding of why so many Americans feel left behind and forgotten in a fast-changing world and are susceptible to the appeals of demagogues who promise to make them winners again and provide them with convenient scapegoats.

Ultimately, however, our journey was simply a personal one, no more and no less. I wanted to take in the country one more time in a single big sweep, to regain a measure of its staggering grandeur and breadth and to do so in the company of Albie, a genial and loving canine companion. That boy makes my heart leap every single day. Not only was he a passport to conversations with strangers, being with him twenty-four hours a day for six weeks forced me to be more attuned to what *he* was experiencing as the miles went by and to try to appreciate the world a bit more as he sees and feels and *smells* it.

More than mere curiosity about what lay over the mountain animated the journey, however. Though in good health and feeling no different really than in 1977 when I last crossed the country by car, this trip, I thought, might be a kind of last hurrah, a curtain call, a victory lap (celebrating what victory is unclear), a final big adventure, if not for Albie then certainly for me. Who knew if I'd ever get another chance to undertake a grand tour of America?

Born in 1953, I am squarely in the middle of the baby boom generation. We are the generation that was supposed to remain forever young. But now that we are staring down the barrel of our own mortality, who is there to sue for breach of that contract?

We try to escape the reality that our days are numbered but know we cannot. It is a time in life when we are forced to reckon with the inevitable, to take stock of our lives and the measure of our days. Each is a piece of valuable currency precisely because the supply is finite.

Perhaps the trip would help me, once and for all, wrestle to the ground, or at least to a draw, a dread of mortality that has gnawed at me for as long as I can remember, simmering like a low-grade fever. My feelings about mortality are, somewhat paradoxically, a bit like those of Samuel Hamilton, one of the principal characters in Steinbeck's *East of Eden*, who rapidly descended into old age after the death of a daughter:

> Samuel may have thought and played and philoso-
> phized about death, but he really didn't believe in it.

His world did not have death as a member. He, and all around him, were immortal. When real death came it was an outrage, a denial of the immortality he deeply felt, and the one crack in his wall caused the whole structure to crash. I think he thought he could always argue himself out of death. It was a personal opponent and one he could lick.

Expecting to come home completely at peace with the reality that there was far more sand in the bottom of my hourglass than the top was probably unrealistic; I just hoped it might help a little. Just months from signing up for Medicare, perhaps something about dropping out of my day-to-day routine, rarely seeing a familiar face, and living with nothing but my own thoughts and Albie for company would lead to a place of acceptance about aging. Albie would be there not just to pave the way for social interaction but also as a constant source of perspective and no small amount of joy. I am pretty much convinced that dogs cannot contemplate their own mortality. They may sense and react to threats and fight for survival if need be, but they don't navel gaze as humans do. That's why dogs are very present in the moment and why their joy can be so complete. I aspire to be more like Albie in that way and hoped that after spending several weeks on the road alone with him some of his *sangfroid* would rub off.

It didn't. But I did come back with a much keener appreciation for home, both in the literal and figurative sense, and that's no small matter, as anodyne as it sounds. I had missed all the little things—the garden, the white picket fence, the climbing hydrangea that grows more than fifty feet up the large oak, the way the sun sets over the backyard—and the big things—my good-natured, bighearted wife; the other dogs; our rather large village of down-to-earth, warm, and caring friends; and the old stone walls and craggy coastline of New England. Having radically altered my life and Albie's for six weeks, I came to appreciate more keenly the life I had, rather haphazardly, managed to create by age sixty-four. And maybe that is the best we can hope for in coping with mortality: to do things that enhance our appreciation of the here and now and to be mindful about living in the present without dreading the future. Much easier said than done. Much.

Like Steinbeck, I brought notebooks along. (I take notes the old-fashioned way.) But we were otherwise differently equipped. Steinbeck had his typewriter and typing paper; I had my laptop. My cell phone served as my stereo, my reference books, my camera, my navigator and, oh yes, as my phone. One of the big advantages of Google Maps is that they don't need to be folded. I brought a road atlas and referred to it several times, but those maps are not nearly detailed enough to help you navigate when you end up well off the beaten path because of a road closure or because you missed a turn and didn't realize it until miles later. With Google Maps, if you have a network connection, you know exactly where you are within a matter of inches. But you don't always have a connection, hence the road atlas.

When Steinbeck and Charley made their trip, the Interstate Highway System was in its infancy, but Steinbeck made a keen observation about these roads he called "thruways." "When we get these thruways across the whole country," he wrote, "it will be possible to drive from New York to California without seeing a single thing." Albie and I traveled as much as we practically could along secondary roads, for there is little to be seen, heard, or learned at a rest stop along Interstate 90 in Ohio or Indiana that can't be seen, heard, or learned at a rest stop along the same highway in Massachusetts or Montana. I wasn't so much interested in driving *across* the country as I was in *diving into* it.

We drove some of the country's most scenic roads. Some I'd driven before, such as Virginia's Skyline Drive, which runs down the spine of the Blue Ridge Mountains and above the Shenandoah Valley. But others were new to me, such as the Natchez Trace Parkway, which runs from just south of Nashville for over 440 miles to Natchez, Mississippi, and U.S. 20, which took us across much of Idaho. With a few deviations, some for practical reasons (I couldn't afford to be away long enough to noodle around northern Maine and New Hampshire for two weeks as Steinbeck had) and others sentimental (I wanted to see the Oklahoma birthplace of my childhood hero, Woody Guthrie, and had arranged for Albie to have a reunion with the two women in central Louisiana who saved his life), we mostly stayed true to Steinbeck's route with Charley. Steinbeck rarely identified the specific roads he traveled, but his approximate route can be plotted by the place names he mentions. However, unlike Steinbeck, who traveled west through the northern part of the United States and then east though the southern states, we reversed the order because of the time of year. Steinbeck traveled in autumn and we traveled in spring. For Albie's sake, I wanted the weather to be as mild as possible, not too hot or too cold, for as much of the trip as possible and that meant heading south first.

Any road trip, of course, traces a single, very narrow line, and none can lay claim to taking you anywhere near the entire country, even one that covers more than 9,000 coast-to-coast-to-coast miles. You'd have to drive up and down and back and forth like you were trying to fill in an entire Etch A Sketch to do that.* But by driving over 9,000 miles you can acquaint yourself with much more of the country than you can by flying or, aside from walking or biking, by any other means.

Though my travels with Albie were inspired by Steinbeck's *Travels with Charley*, our aim was *not* an authentic re-creation of Steinbeck's journey with Charley. What would be the point? Steinbeck had already written that book and done a damned fine job of it, too. Even if we had wanted to, no journey can truly be replicated, for every journey, as Steinbeck himself wrote, is one of a kind. Had Albie and I left Boston one day earlier, or one day later, we might have met an entirely different cast of characters. Instead of arriving at the Grand Canyon and finding several inches of fresh, wet snow on the ground and dense fog obscuring the view, we might have arrived on a perfectly warm, sunny day. It would have been a similar, but different, trip.

There were still other differences. Steinbeck's conveyance was a camper and ours a convertible. By the time he made his trip, Steinbeck was married to his third wife; I am still married to

---

*   For younger readers, the Etch A Sketch, introduced in 1960, is a mechanical drawing toy comprising a thin box housed in a red plastic frame with two white dials, one on the bottom left and another on the bottom right. The frame holds a clear plastic screen and inside the Etch A Sketch is aluminum powder that clings to the screen until, using the dials that mechanically control a pointed metal stylus (the left control moves the stylus horizontally, and the right one moves it vertically) causes a trace of the powder to fall into the box as the stylus traverses the underside of the screen. These traces allow you to draw pictures, the image created by the voids where the powder once was. When you are done with your picture you can begin again by shaking the box which causes the powder to again cling to the screen. Some of us, those with a little OCD, often make it a practice to clear the entire screen by meticulously tracing lines up and down and across many hundreds of times.

my first. Steinbeck was nationally famous and worried he'd be recognized wherever he went (he wasn't); to say I had no such concern would be a vast understatement.

Even if we *had* tried to faithfully re-create Steinbeck's journey in every possible detail, someone would surely have chimed in, "But Albie's a Lab and Charley was a poodle!" So, the goal wasn't a re-creation of Steinbeck's trip, but to use his journey as a touchstone for our own.

We went over the mountain just to see what we could see, and this is what we saw.

THE DOG WENT OVER THE MOUNTAIN

PART ONE

From Here . . .

ONE

Outward Bound*

I t sounds simple: pack a suitcase and some dog food, fill up
the car with gas, and drive. Fat chance. No, a trip like this,
especially with a dog, required some planning, some foresight,
and some imagination about what might go wrong.

In the weeks before our departure, as supplies—notebooks,
maps, flashlights, a tent, batteries, dog food, and a hundred
other odds and ends—began to pile up in my small home
office, little piles of anxiety began to accumulate in my head,
too, mostly at night as I lay in bed thinking ahead to the trip.

My biggest worry was Albie. What if something happened
to me? What if I got really sick, or was injured and had to go to

---

* "Outward Bound" was a song written by the folk singer Tom Paxton and
released in 1966.

an emergency room, or worse? Who would take care of Albie? How would I make sure he was safe? Would he somehow find his way home again? Right before we left I took a small adhesive mailing label and wrote, "In case of emergency please contact my wife," added her name and cell phone number, and affixed it to the back of my driver's license. I didn't tell Judy I'd done this; not because it would have alarmed her, but because I'm always trying to convince her I'm not as neurotic as she thinks I am.

My concern about Albie wasn't just limited to what would happen if I got sick or was injured. He was never consulted about my plan and there was no way of explaining it to him. Like most dogs, open a car door and Albie will happily leap in. He doesn't know if we're going around the corner, heading out for a three-hour trip, or driving two days from Boston to South Carolina as we've done several times. How would he fare traveling for six weeks? Would he get depressed and miss Judy and the other dogs? Would he get enough exercise? Would he act out in some way, or become aggressive toward other dogs and people? Was this entire venture fair to *him*?

As glamorous as the whole trip sounded—and everyone who knew about it seemed to envy me for it to one degree or another—I am a confirmed homebody and a creature of habit, so I was unsettled on many counts. But being unsettled was part of the point. Another six weeks of the usual routine didn't promise to make much of an impact on my life, lead to any new insights, create any new memories, or change my perspective on anything. One of my hopes for this trip was to rattle my own cage a bit.

I knew nights spent in cheap motels (I was on a budget) would often feel lonely and dispiriting. Sleeping on a bed shared by thousands of itinerant strangers in bland rooms designed only to meet the basic demands of human existence is inherently depressing. In towns where nobody knows your name, and no one really cares, hours in a generic motel room can make you feel like a character in a Eugene O'Neill play. "Life is for each man a solitary cell whose walls are mirrors," O'Neill wrote. Oy.

Right on cue, the anxiety that kept me awake at night started to infiltrate my increasingly rare sleep, too. Three weeks before we left, dreams about the trip took form.

In the first I was back in college but living out of my car. It was so hard to stay organized in that little space that I had no idea when or where my classes were meeting and couldn't find the schedule. I was supposed to be in class but was stuck in my car not knowing where to go or when. Panic about flunking out gripped me. Then, my roommate (my real-life college roommate, Jerry), who seemed oddly detached, got in the passenger seat and a stranger got into the driver's seat and claimed it was *his* car and *he* was driving it home. When asked for proof of ownership he told me the car was registered to Lululemon, the clothing company. I know; it didn't make any sense to me either.

In the next dream, I'd ridden my bike across the country and was in Cannon Beach, Oregon, where we had vacationed in real life for twenty years as our kids were growing up. Just as I was about to head back East, a bunch of children started harassing me, my front tire went flat, and I was totally flummoxed by how my cell phone operated. When I woke up the next morning, I added Eric Clapton and Steve Winwood's haunting 2009 rendition of "Can't Find My Way Home" to my trip playlist.

Initially, my plan was to make the trip in summer. Isn't that the American dream? Driving the open road when the sun shines and the air is warm? But it's also the worst time to travel by car with a dog. There would inevitably be times when I'd need to run into a grocery store, visit a restroom, or spend an hour in a laundromat, places Albie might not be allowed to go. He's perfectly fine waiting in the car when it's cool outside, but the inside of a car can heat up to dangerous levels within minutes on a hot day, even with the windows at half-mast. For his sake, making the trip in spring, when cooler weather prevailed, made more sense. Though he didn't say so, perhaps the same considerations are what led Steinbeck to make his trip in autumn.

The decision to go in spring made sense for another reason: Why travel when everyone else is, when kids are out of school and millions of families are hitting the road for summer vacation? The roads would be less congested in spring, the competition for space in state and national parks far less keen (or so I thought) and hotels, motels, and restaurants would be less crowded (that proved to be true).

These were the practical, prosaic reasons for traveling in spring, but there was a more sentimental, maybe poetic reason, too. Given my obsession with mortality, maybe this little odyssey would be a spring-like rebirth, as I entered what was almost certain to be the last decade or two of my life. There's no flipping the hourglass back over, but maybe, *just maybe*, this adventure would be a new beginning of sorts.

So, just days after deciding I should spend part of my "summer of 64" traveling with Albie, I reconsidered. Spring, for reasons practical and symbolic, it would be. Since we would be traveling with the special dispensation of my wife, Judy, who was suspiciously enthusiastic about my being away for a good stretch and who would remain at home with Salina and Jamba, we couldn't be away *indefinitely*. Six weeks seemed about right. We chose, or I chose, April 15 as the day for our departure, not because an astrologer said it would be an auspicious date to leave, but because the calendar said that if we left on April 15 and traveled for six weeks we'd be home by Memorial Day weekend, the unofficial start of the busy summer travel season.

The plan was to try and average a reasonable two hundred miles a day, a distance we could easily cover between breakfast and early afternoon, giving us the rest of each day and evening to take long walks and soak up the local atmosphere of wherever we happened to stop that day. Averaging two hundred miles a day we could make it to the West Coast—to Steinbeck's hometown of Salinas, California—and then back to New England in six weeks, enough time for everything at home to fall apart. Judy isn't exactly what you'd call skilled in the housekeeping arts—I'm the compulsive, organized, neat one that stands between order and chaos, the guardian of our galaxy—and it might take her weeks to realize a pipe had sprung a leak in the basement or that she'd left the oven on for eight days, if ever. Judy often has many things on her mind at once and has been known to put the orange juice away in the microwave thinking it was the fridge, only to be discovered days later. So, on top of the anxiety of making a cross-country trip with a large dog, there was the fear that we might return home a few weeks hence with no habitable place to live.*

For nearly a year, on and off, I pondered the logistics of a road trip with a seventy-five-pound yellow Lab. Nothing was more vexing than the challenge of making the most of very little space. The trunk of my small car is, well, small, even more so

---

* Things were pretty much in order when we did return home, except that Judy forgot to pay one bill: our mortgage.

with the top down because that's where it's stored when you're traveling topless, so to speak. There is a back seat but it, too, is small and Albie would be occupying the back seat, both because it's safer and because he could lie down comfortably there. Everything would have to fit either in the trunk (accounting for top-down travel) or in the front passenger seat.

I planned on one small travel-size suitcase, a day pack, and a sleeping bag for me; a small tent for both us; a five-gallon jug for water; and a large container to keep his food fresh. This wasn't going to be a camping trip—we planned to stay mostly in dog-friendly motels and occasionally with friends and family—but I hoped to camp at Grand Canyon. Other necessities were food and water bowls, poop bags, a cooler, several pairs of shoes, jackets for all weather, and the hundred and one last minute must-haves that always come to mind as you're about to back out of the driveway—a first aid kit, an extra fleece, a spare leash, that second pair of sneakers.

Giving my rig, such as it was, a name as if it were a yacht, as Steinbeck did, seemed a wee bit pretentious so, after careful deliberation, I decided to refer to it as "the car."

Normally, April 15 in New England can somewhat safely be called spring. In 2018, the Boston Marathon was to be held the next day, April 16 (it's always on the third Monday in April), and it's often run in warm, even hot weather, though cool and rainy is possible, too. Visions of leaving with the sun shining in our faces and the wind riffling our hair or, in Albie's case, his fur, filled my head. I'd even planned a very detailed route from our Massachusetts home all the way to Wilkes-Barre, Pennsylvania, that would take us on scenic backroads through Connecticut and along the Delaware River outside of Port Jervis, New York.

But the spring had so far been a bust. One early-April day, several inches of snow fell, and throughout the first part of the month the temperatures struggled to escape the forties. Before our scheduled departure the forecast got worse with each passing day. By Friday, April 13, the forecast for Sunday, April 15, was miserable: a high temperature of thirty-five with wind and freezing rain. Never mind putting the top down, without snow tires my car is an adventure in wintry weather. Farther south, in the places we expected to be within a few days—Virginia and North Carolina—the weather looked perfect for cruising the Skyline Drive and the Blue Ridge Parkway. Having lived in Charlottesville, Virginia, for a year in the early 1980s, I knew the exquisite beauty and intoxicating air of an Appalachian spring and was eager to get there.

We hadn't even backed out of the driveway and already our plans were in disarray. I'd booked dog-friendly motel rooms for the first five nights and now had to decide whether to leave a day early to beat the freezing rain, a day or two later and have to rebook all the reservations and lose some deposits, or stick with the original plan and hope for the best. The best laid plans, especially when planning a trip, are often pointless. Steinbeck himself had warned me.

"When the virus of restlessness begins to take possession of a wayward man," he wrote in the introduction to *Travels with Charley*, "and the road away from Here seems broad and straight and sweet, the victim must first find in himself a good a sufficient reason for going." That I had done. "Next he must plan his trip in time and space, choose a direction and a destination." That, too, I had done. "And last he must implement the journey. How to go, what to take, how long to stay. . . . Once a journey is designed, equipped, and put in process, a new factor enters and takes over.

A trip . . . is an entity, different from all other journeys. It has personality, temperament, individuality, uniqueness. A journey is a person in itself; no two are alike and all plans, safeguards, policing and coercion are fruitless . . . we do not take a trip; a trip takes us. Tour masters, schedules, reservations, brass-bound and inevitable, dash themselves to wreckage on the personality of the trip. Only when this is recognized can the blown-in-the-glass bum relax and go along with it. Only then do the frustrations fall away. In this a journey is like a marriage. The certain way to be wrong is to think you control it."

Thus, on the morning of April 14, I decided we should leave that afternoon, a day earlier than planned, and hope that by getting just a bit south, even to Connecticut, we would avoid the freezing rain forecast for Boston and stay on schedule. But since the forecast for the Northeast in general looked pretty dismal for the next couple of days, we scrapped the scenic route to Pennsylvania I had so meticulously written out on index cards. We'd head down to coastal Connecticut via the Interstate, have dinner with my younger son, Noah, who lives in Pound Ridge, New York, and spend the first night in nearby Norwalk, Connecticut. On the second day, the fifteenth, we'd drive through northern New Jersey and into Pennsylvania, again on the Interstate, all in an effort to hasten our way to fairer weather.

So, at about two o'clock on afternoon of the fourteeneth, after nearly a year of anticipation, hours of packing and repacking, several hours of house maintenance instructions for Judy, and last-minute trips to Petco, CVS, and my therapist, I hugged Judy and each of the other dogs goodbye, hustled Albie into the car, took a deep breath, and put the key in the ignition.

TWO

Jersey Boys

For more than sixty years I've been wearing out the roads of Connecticut. While growing up in northern New Jersey, we were always making car trips to Boston to visit my grandparents and other relatives. My mother was born and raised in Brookline, Massachusetts, and her entire family was still in the Boston area. When I went off to college in Amherst, Massachusetts, and later to Boston College Law School, I traveled to and from home in New Jersey via Connecticut countless times. Then Judy, who also grew up in northern Jersey, and I were married and had kids, and both sets of grandparents lived in New Jersey. Actually, more than two sets since her parents were divorced as were mine and all lived in New Jersey either with second spouses, companions or, in my mother's case, alone. That's a lot of trips to see Grandma and Grandpa and Ellen and Papa

Gus and Helen and Nana and Poppy. So, to say I am familiar with the drive through Connecticut is like saying Yo-Yo Ma is familiar with the cello. I can visualize almost every mile of Interstate 84 from Union to Danbury.

It was disappointing that we'd be unable to drive my well-planned scenic route along the backroads of Connecticut and into New York State, but those are the breaks. The consolation was that we'd have a chance to see Noah. Less than a year out of college, he was working his dream job in the virtual and augmented reality labs at IBM Research in Yorktown Heights, New York, about an hour north of New York City. That, in itself, was something of a miracle since the kid never even prepared a résumé and might never have gotten around to it anyway. IBM found *him* after he posted a short video about his senior project in virtual reality on Reddit, a social media site. Talk about a break!

Because the roads we traveled that afternoon were so familiar, and we were only driving about three hours, it didn't feel at all like we were at the beginning of a long journey. If, after dinner with Noah, I'd gotten cold feet, we could have been home well before midnight. As Steinbeck wrote in *Travels with Charley*, "In long-range planning for a trip, I think there is a private conviction that it won't happen." Amen to that.

Saturday, April 14, was overcast and cool and the trees along the Massachusetts Turnpike to Sturbridge were brown and bare. What a stingy spring it had been. But as we crossed into Connecticut a little south of Sturbridge, the skies brightened briefly, and the temperatures rose from the low forties to about fifty. Just fifty miles west and a little south of Boston there were a few, *but just a few*, signs of spring. A handful of roadside forsythia were starting to bloom, and we spotted a few daffodils and hyacinth, even a few green buds on some of the trees. This wasn't entirely surprising; it's often just a tad warmer inland.

As we neared New Haven and drove through the town of Hamden to try and get around some traffic on the Wilbur Cross Parkway, I caught a brief glimpse of a very elderly man at the end of a driveway, turning back toward his house. He was shuffling slowly along using a walker. A few wisps of unruly white hair strayed from his scalp and his clothing was rumpled and ill-fitting. He was in view for just a few seconds, but the image of this old man, clearly near the end of his days, stayed with me throughout the trip. I can still see him quite clearly. Wasn't this, after all, why we were taking to the road to begin with? To have at least one more big adventure while we still could, before all the sand in our hourglass had just about run out?

I have often wondered how people stay sane when they reach a state of decrepitude. Unless dementia has robbed you of your self-awareness, how do you get through each day as a shadow of your former self? How do you carry on knowing that your circumstances aren't going to get better? I'm not sure who said it, but my brother told me years ago that someone was once asked, "What's the hardest part of getting older?" and the reply was, "Remembering when I was young."

As I glimpsed this elderly man for a couple of more seconds in my rearview mirror I wondered: who *was* he? What life did he live? Was he happy with it? What goes through his mind as he shuffles slowly up and down his driveway? I would never know. But I do know this: having had a date with cancer in my early fifties, a cancer with a good prognosis but a set of surgical complications that left me wondering what I'd be willing to endure if I'd had a bad one, I don't want to outlive *myself*. In other words, I want to *live*, not just exist, until I die.

Steinbeck, too, had pondered these questions as he considered the trip he was about to take with Charley. "[I]n my own life," he wrote, "I am not willing to trade quality for quantity . . . I see too many men delay their exits with a sickly, slow reluctance to leave the stage. It's bad theater as well as bad living." Words to live by.

Noah has always been one of the most guileless, and dryly funny, people I've ever known. He's six feet four inches tall now and all of about 150 pounds. For years we struggled to separate him from the video screens and computers that were his obsession, thinking he was wasting his time. It was now nearly a year after his college graduation and Judy and I thoroughly expected that he'd be living at home, glued to his computer and sleeping until midafternoon while we harangued him to get his résumé together and look for a job. And that might have happened but for that stroke of incredible luck that led IBM to find *him*.

Noah has always had an unusual turn of mind, a sideways way of looking at the world. When he was in third grade, we were summoned for a conference to discuss some problems he was having in school. The children had been given an evaluation that included answering true or false to fifty statements. Noah only got through the first handful of questions. Why? Because one of those true/false statements was this: "Birds can fly." As Noah explained to us and the special education staff at our meeting, he knew most birds could fly, but he also knew that penguins and ostriches are birds and they *can't* fly. So, he was stuck. Rather than soldier on, he simply stopped, turning the question over and over in his head, unsure how to proceed.

Now, over a pizza supper in New Canaan, Connecticut, and an after-dinner walk the first night of our journey, Noah talked on and on about theoretical physics, the possibility of time travel, the time/space continuum, and other topics that were very far over my head, not to mention Albie's. By evening's end I thought, *This must be what it's like to be in a book group with Stephen Hawking.*

When Albie and I checked into our hotel around eight o'clock it was already dark, and it felt very strange. It all had a "what do we do now?" feeling about it. The hotel was on a major thoroughfare, though there was little traffic, and the neighborhood comprised modern office and apartment buildings. We took a walk but there was nothing appealing about our surroundings and little grass for Albie to explore and hunt for a place to do his business. Could we really do this for the next six weeks? I kept reminding myself to take it a day at a time and not to jump to conclusions. There were bound to be moments like this.

Not for the last time, I wondered again, now that we were on the road at last, if this entire venture was fair to Albie. Earlier in the afternoon he happily jumped into the car, but he's *always* happy to jump in the car. It means we aren't going to be leaving him alone at home with the other dogs for a couple of hours. I actually did explain to him several times before we left that we were going to take a long trip together. I've become one of those slightly daft people who talk out loud to their dogs as if they speak and understand English. I was whisking him away from the home, the routines, the people (mainly Judy), and the other dogs that populate his days and nights. For the next six weeks I'd be hustling him in and out of the car, taking him to strange places with strange smells, a new place almost every night. I would be the only constant and the only connection to the life he'd known for nearly six years. Would he be happy traveling?

Once we had checked in, Albie spent a good five minutes sniffing all around the hotel room. It was, of course, a pet-friendly hotel, as all of the hotels and motels would be, and there were, no doubt, the lingering scents of dozens of dogs who'd been in this room before us that only another dog could detect. He eventually settled down and, to my surprise, chose to lay down on the floor, though I made it clear that he could, as at home, join me on the bed.

Albie woke me up at 6:30 A.M. the next morning the way he usually does—by staring intently at me from a distance of about six inches while making a low groaning sound. He looked a little confused. Where are we? Why are we here? Are we really going to be gone for six weeks? Well, the last question was mine, but I wondered if I was projecting and whether Albie might become a canvas onto which I projected all my feelings as we traveled.

We crossed the Hudson River on Interstate 287 and the new Tappan Zee Bridge, a graceful three-mile span. Two-eighty-seven skirts the New York/New Jersey border for about twenty miles before it plunges south into the Garden State at Mahwah. This was very familiar territory for me: my hometown of Paramus, deep in the bosom of suburbia,* is just fifteen minutes south of Mahwah.

---

* I am borrowing here from an acquaintance of mine growing up in Paramus, singer-songwriter Dean Friedman. In 1977, Friedman had his biggest hit record with the song "Ariel." Ariel was about a girl from Paramus and the song opens this way: *"Way on the other side of the Hudson/ Deep in the bosom of suburbia/I met a young girl she sang mighty fine/Tears on my pillow and Ave Maria/Standing by the water fall in Paramus Park."*

The small hills here are, somewhat generously, called the Ramapo Mountains, and they have always carried an air of mystery and foreboding for me. I can't drive through these parts without thinking of the warnings many of us who grew up near here got as teenagers from our parents about these hills. If we had to go up Route 17 toward Mahwah we were told to stay on the highway and not to go driving on the roads that wind through the hills and hollers. The danger? The people who lived there.

The Ramapo Mountains were, and still are, home to an insular group of mixed-race people we knew growing up as "the Jackson Whites," though they have in more recent years become more integrated into the surrounding towns. The Jackson Whites, as I learned about them, were a mix of Native Americans, African Americans, and German mercenaries (Hessians, who fought alongside the British during the Revolutionary War). It was said that many Jackson Whites could be identified by their tawny skin, blue or slate-gray eyes, and blond hair. Albinism is also common. They kept their contacts with the outside world to a minimum. The children didn't attend local public schools and they ventured into nearby towns only to buy things at local stores. My father once told me about a state game warden who went up into these hills and disappeared, never to be seen again. Rumor was the Jackson Whites were feeble-minded and degenerate. What makes their story so remarkable is that on a clear day you can see the top of the Empire State Building from some of these hills; they're just thirty miles from Manhattan.

The history of these people is so shrouded in layers of fact and myth, some so obscure they can't be traced, that it's virtually impossible to tease out the real origins of the people *or* the

myths. Today, "Jackson White" is considered a racial epithet.*
They prefer to be known as Ramapough Mountain Indians or
the Ramapough Lenape Nation. The State of New Jersey recog-
nizes them as an Indian tribe, but the federal government does
not. The community comprises some 5,000 people in three
primary settlements, in Mahwah and Ringwood, New Jersey,
and Hillburn, New York.

Tales of a primitive race of people living in the Ramapo
Mountains date back to the Revolutionary War. According to an
article in *The New Yorker* by Ben McGrath published in 2010,**
the origins of these people as I learned about them from my
parents dovetails with legends passed along for centuries, but
with a little more detail: the "Jackson Whites" were a mix of
West Indian prostitutes, Hessian deserters, and escaped slaves,
all people who would have had a reason to seek refuge in the
isolation of the hills. More likely, according to McGrath, their
origins are Afro-Dutch.

In any event, as we passed through the Ramapo Mountains
on I-287 the legends and warnings I had heard as a kid about
the people living in these hills automatically leapt to mind.
As McGrath wrote decades after I first learned of the so-called
Jackson Whites, "Area teen-agers, recalling decades-old legends
of unsuspecting people who climbed Stag Hill [the center of
the community] and never returned, dare one another to drive

---

* Though the origins of this community date back to the 18th century, the
term "Jackson Whites" only came into usage in the late 19th century,
and like the people themselves the origin of the term is unclear. The
most commonly accepted explanation is that it derives from the phrase
"jacks and whites," meaning a mixed population of black former slaves,
called "jacks," and white people.

** Ben McGrath, "Strangers on the Mountain," *The New Yorker*, March 1, 2010.

up at night." As I always had before, Albie and I drove through the Ramapo Mountains on the highway and didn't venture into the hills.

A heavy overcast hung over the day and it was chilly, only in the forties. Not what I had imagined for April 15. But at least we'd escaped the threat of freezing rain forecast for this day back home and were on our way. All across New Jersey and into the Lehigh Valley of Pennsylvania clouds and mist clung to the low ridges and settled into the valleys, and it showered on and off.

We drove for four gloomy hours until we pulled off the Interstate in Dickinson, Pennsylvania. I knew people who had attended Dickinson College, but had never seen it, and a college campus seemed like it would offer pleasant surroundings for a long walk with Albie. And it would have, except the skies opened up as soon as we arrived, so we settled for a cold and very wet walk around campus. The magnolias and daffodils were out in full force, but it was hard to enjoy them in the drear. There was nowhere dry to sit outside and get a bite to eat, so I had to leave Albie in the car while I ran into a local pub for a quick sandwich.

We'd booked a motel room in Shippensburg, Pennsylvania, for the night, just a dozen miles down the road. Having planned a backroads route through rural Connecticut, along the Delaware, and into Pennsylvania, it was disappointing, to say the least, to have spent the day thus far on the Interstate. It was only midafternoon and as a consolation prize of sorts we eschewed Interstate 81 and drove to Shippensburg on a two-lane road, Route 11, that paralleled it. Within minutes I was reminded why I had hoped to follow secondary roads as much as possible.

About halfway to Shippensburg we came up behind a traditional Amish horse-drawn buggy—high, square, and black with thin, wagon-wheel-like tires. From our vantage point, all I could see of the horse were its hooves trotting along the highway. It gave the illusion of a vehicle that was part wagon and part horse which, I suppose, is literally true, but to me it looked like the hooves were attached directly to the underside of the buggy. The appearance of this ancient form of conveyance on a paved highway was startling, partly because it seemed like we'd been transported back in time in an episode of *The Twilight Zone* and partly because of my own ignorance. I knew there were Amish communities farther east, near Lancaster, Pennsylvania, but I didn't realize they were present here in central Pennsylvania, as well. In fact, there are Amish communities sprinkled throughout the Midwest, too.

What was the proper road etiquette here? Reluctant to pass for fear of startling the horse, I soon had a half dozen cars behind me. When the car directly behind made a move to go around us both, I assumed it was okay to pass. As we did, I caught a glimpse of the couple in the buggy, he in a black suit, black hat, and full beard (no moustache), and she in a simple dress and bonnet.

This, I thought, will be the reward for traveling the backroads. We'll see things we'd never see on the Interstate. And here was another community of people, the second of the day, like the Ramapough Indians, living as if in another time in the middle of 21st-century America.

Over the next few miles we saw several more horse-drawn Amish wagons making their way at a stately 18th-century pace along the roadway. But the quaint charm of it all quickly dissipated when I noticed that one of the horses was clearly in distress, craning its neck left and right and frothing at the mouth as it trotted down the road.

The simplicity of Amish life has long held appeal for visitors to communities where many Amish live. We imagine the entire town turning out to raise the frame for a neighbor's barn and community suppers held at long tables in the fields. But things are not always as they seem. Recent years have seen a spate of news stories about Amish communities rife with sexual abuse concealed beneath a code of silence. The Amish are also notorious operators of puppy mills that turn out dogs for profit on a large scale, often in cruel and unsanitary conditions. Seeing this horse, clearly suffering, was disturbing and the image stayed with me throughout the rainy night.

Without realizing it, we drove right past the hotel in Shippensburg where we were staying because we fell victim to one of the traps that can ensnare you if you rely too much on technology to guide you. I had opened Google Maps and typed in the hotel's street address on Walnut Bottom Road. Then I had clicked on the first option that popped up. When we arrived it was nothing but an empty field. Perplexed, I double-checked what I'd done. Out hotel was indeed on Walnut Bottom Road—*in Shippensburg*—but we were on Walnut Bottom Road in a little town of the same name. Not that I hadn't all my life wanted to see Walnut Bottom, Pennsylvania, but we'd driven ten miles out of our way before finally landing at our hotel, a forlorn Best Western. The room smelled of cigarette smoke, the weather was still gloomy, and it was now dark. Even if it had been a nice evening for a walk there was nothing nearby that would have beckoned. Again I asked myself, can we really do this for six weeks? It was only our second night on the road, and we hadn't yet reached the point of no return.

With nothing to do, we got back in the car and drove into downtown Shippensburg, nearly deserted on a Sunday night, and then around the campus of Shippensburg University, where there was also virtually no sign of human life. Within half an hour we were back at the hotel. Albie lay down at the foot of the bed and I wondered: can a dog formulate the thought, "I want to go home"?

THREE

Oh, Shenandoah·

W hen does north become south, or more to the point, when does *the North* become *the South*? That was the question I had in mind the next morning. We had a short driving day planned, but one that would take us from Pennsylvania, through short sections of Maryland and West Virginia, and into Virginia. Most Americans would surely consider Pennsylvania a Northern state and Virginia a Southern one, but you can drive from one to the other in under forty-five minutes at their closest points.

---

*   "Oh, Shenandoah," or sometimes just "Shenandoah," is an American folk song of uncertain origin dating to the early 19th century. In one version, the opening lyrics go as follows: *Oh Shenandoah/ I long to see you/ Away you rolling river/ Oh Shenandoah/ I long to see you/ Away, I'm bound away/'Cross the wide Missouri.*

Some might argue that the Mason-Dixon Line, which is also the border between Pennsylvania and Maryland, divides North from South, and there's a widespread misconception that that's precisely why the Mason-Dixon Line exists; that it's a relic of the Civil War. In fact, the line was drawn well before the Civil War, in the 1760s, to settle a land dispute among Pennsylvania, Maryland, and Delaware. Even a sizable chunk of New Jersey lies south of the Mason-Dixon Line, so it's not a good way to separate the North from the South. Besides, I wasn't looking so much for a specific geographic point, but something more ephemeral, a cultural signal or a sensation that would make me say, "Aha, now we're in the South," much as Dorothy turned to Toto when she landed in Oz and said, "Toto, I have a feeling we're not in Kansas anymore."

At home, when the dogs get me up between 6:00 and 6:30 A.M., I just want to roll over and go back to sleep. Waking up in a strange motel room, I was just eager to get going. The night couldn't pass fast enough. At least the car is mine and familiar and once I was behind the wheel I felt I'd regained a little bit of the control and humanity I'd surrendered when we checked into this sad motel in Shippensburg the night before.

On this, our third day, it was yet again cold, windy, wet, and heavily overcast. Except for some brief sunny breaks the first day in Connecticut, this was the weather hand we'd been dealt, and it wasn't doing a lot for my mood. I had envisioned long, leisurely walks through springtime flowers, but our walks were brief, businesslike, and uncomfortable.

We got back on Route 11, a two-lane road that crosses over and under Interstate 81 countless times between Shippensburg and Winchester, Virginia. The two are braided like the caduceus, the traditional symbol of Hermes that features two snakes winding around a staff used as a medical symbol. As we approached the Maryland border there was an auto body shop to the right with a large sign: TODD AUTO BODY: SERVING YOU AND THE LORD. I don't know what kind of wheels the Lord drives, but this would be the first of countless overt manifestations of Christian religiosity we would see across a large swath of America, mainly in the South, where proclamations of religious faith are commonplace and very public. Not once did we see a public display of any other faith.

As we drove from Pennsylvania to Virginia we also passed dozens upon dozens of roadside billboards advertising the services of lawyers, car dealers, mortgage brokers, and real estate agents, with some politicians thrown in, each with a mug shot of the person soliciting business, or votes, from passing motorists. This is truly an odd way to drum up customers (or votes), but it must be effective because so many people seemed to think their face, rendered about twenty times life-size on a billboard, would attract business. But, I wondered, how many people have passed a billboard at sixty miles an hour and suddenly said, "Hey, that's my new lawyer!" or "I should buy a car from that guy, he looks so honest and sincere!" Collectively, if you assembled the pictures of all these people and created one image, it would have looked like a casting call for secondary parts in *The Sopranos*.

Taking Route 11 instead of the interstate would turn a ninety-minute drive from Shippensburg, Pennsylvania, to Winchester, Virginia, into a three-hour drive, but wasn't that the point? To slow down and see the country instead of just watching it pass by at seventy-five miles an hour?

Traveling the backroads here also gave us a chance to have a closer look at West Virginia's panhandle. Now, I don't mean to pick on West Virginia. Goodness knows they have enough problems there, from grinding poverty and the nation's second worst economy and the nation's worst infrastructure, according to a 2017 analysis by *U.S. News and World Report.* But the panhandle was a motley collection of moldering trailers, used car dealers (and I do mean *used*), "gentlemen's clubs," discount stores, and trash-strewn yards. Granted, there are surely beautiful country roads in West Virginia; we just weren't on one. The WELCOME sign we'd passed when we entered the state proclaimed "wild, wonderful West Virginia." Wild? Yes. Wonderful? Based on an admittedly small sample size, not so much. Almost heaven? Lord, I hope not.

We were in West Virginia for all of thirty minutes and I was greatly relieved when I saw the WELCOME TO VIRGINIA sign ahead. I informed Albie we were about to cross into Virginia. He was unfazed; the states smelled the same from inside the car. You wouldn't think an imaginary line separating two states would make any difference, but as soon as we crossed the state line it felt like another world. There was none of the roadside detritus, and everything seemed tidier, less cluttered, *prettier.*

Winchester was just ten miles south. I'd been there just a few months before to give a talk at a local book shop called The Book Gallery and decided we'd stop there for a walk. The weather still wasn't great, but at least it had stopped raining, and downtown Winchester is clean and attractive, with many Colonial era buildings and a pedestrian mall lined with restaurants and shops.

Albie and I walked into The Book Gallery and Christine, the proprietor who had hosted my talk there a few months earlier, was behind the register. You'd have thought I'd just stepped out for a cup of coffee. She seemed utterly unsurprised to see me. I bought a copy of *East of Eden*, to fill an inexcusable gap in my Steinbeck reading, and Albie I walked for about an hour in the chilly, dank weather before I was able to convince a local coffee shop to let Albie sit with me inside for a few minutes while I warmed myself with a mocha latte, my coffee drink of choice. Once inside, many of the staff came over to meet Albie. As I'd hoped, he was proving to be a magnet.

Our destination for the night, Front Royal, was only another twenty miles down Route 522 from Winchester and it wasn't even noon. Along the way I spotted (and it wasn't hard) two life-size dinosaurs, a Tyrannosaurus Rex and a Brontosaurus, by the side of the road in front of a store selling rocks and fossils. (Need I say they were replicas?) Immediately recognizing the photographic possibilities—I was documenting the trip in pictures on Instagram—we pulled over. The wind was blowing up a gale and though Albie seemed indifferent to the monstrous creatures behind him (surprising since little squirrels drive him mad), I managed to get a couple of quick shots. There was also a road sign that indicated that Route 522 was, in these parts, designated "The Patsy Cline Highway," after the country singer, and that's when I knew we had arrived in *the South*. I could be wrong, but I bet you could scour every road in New England, and maybe the entire Northeast, and not find a highway named for a country western singer.

In Front Royal, we found another sign we were in the South—a truck in a parking lot with a bumper sticker that proclaimed, "American by Birth, Southern by the Grace of God," with the words flanked by American and Confederate flags. That clinched it. We were definitively now in another part of the country. And that's why, long before we left home, I had the sense that our trip would begin in earnest here. Though I'd been here before, and in the early 1980s lived in Charlottesville for a year, we were no longer in familiar territory. The preliminaries were over.

Front Royal is the northern terminus of the Skyline Drive, a scenic two-lane road that traces a meandering line for slightly more than one hundred miles through the Shenandoah National Park. In the morning we would continue south through this national treasure.

For the fourth morning in a row it was cold—a raw and unseasonable thirty-nine degrees—and overcast. The sun felt like a distant cousin you never see, the weather like a broken record. This isn't what I had in mind at all and it was getting truly frustrating. Weather is the biggest variable in planning any trip or vacation and it can make or break the experience. It affects mood, activity, and even the scenery and few things are more out of our control. Because the weather was limiting the length of our walks together, I really felt badly for Albie. Surely, he'd have been happier at home, a place he knew and was comfortable in, and with two other dogs to play with, than in this little car in bad weather that limited our activity to rushed bathroom breaks. Maybe we'd left too early. Perhaps we should have started in early May. But here we were, and second-guessing wasn't productive. I comforted myself with the thought that with every mile we'd be farther south and that the weather had to improve and with it would come more physical activity and more opportunity to meet other people and other dogs. There was nothing to do but carry on.

We hadn't been listening to the radio or to music the first few days—I was just kind of enjoying the silence—but this morning as we started down the Skyline Drive I put on a James Taylor playlist. I've listened to James Taylor nearly every day for almost fifty years now and it never gets old. Since we were heading south I, too, had Carolina in my mind.

As the road began to climb up into the Blue Ridge Mountains we saw two large deer, the first of many dozen, just lying by the roadway, unfazed by a passing car. They looked like an old couple sitting on their front porch just watching the day go by.

The seasons seemed to change as the parkway rose and fell. At lower elevations a few trees were showing their spring color, but as we climbed above 3,000 feet the traces of snow we'd seen in the surrounding woods became more of a frosting and there was no sign that the trees up here were ready to abandon their winter hibernation. The temperature dropped into the low thirties. Occasionally, holes opened in the clouds and sent sunlight flooding down onto patches of the valleys and mountain ridges off to the west. It was as if a heavenly spotlight was being aimed at random on the Earth.

Forty miles south we pulled off into a parking area that provided access to some of the hiking trails that crisscross the national park. We hadn't seen more than a dozen cars in forty miles and when we got out of the car the only sound was the wind. When it abated for brief periods we stood in utter and complete silence. Even silence is a sound but one we urbanites and suburbanites rarely experience. We could see the valley floor through the bare trees. Since we had climbed another few hundred feet before parking, the temperature had dropped even further. It was late April in Virginia and twenty-seven degrees. As we walked, we met a hiker getting ready to start down one of the trails.

"I wasn't ready for this," he laughed. "But I'm going to do it." *Same here*, I thought.

❖

The Skyline Drive ends just west of Charlottesville, and since we arrived around lunchtime I decided to find a place I'd loved when I lived here in the early 1980s, Crozet Pizza in the little town of Crozet. As I remembered it, Crozet Pizza sat near some railroad tracks next to a gun and ammo store and little else. Now, suburban subdivisions had been carved out of the rolling fields and farmlands, there was a new gas station and minimart across the street, and Crozet Pizza, once a small, rustic little place, had expanded. The gun and ammo store was gone.

Albie and I walked along some of the surrounding streets. Now that we had descended into the valley spring was very much in evidence. Trees were flowering, there were daffodils and hyacinth in abundance, and I allowed myself to think that perhaps the cold and the gloom were behind us for good.

For all intents and purposes, as far as the motorist is concerned, the Skyline Drive and the Blue Ridge Parkway* comprise one, long contiguous two-lane parkway, but the latter is more than four times as long, 469 miles in all. To begin the drive down the Blue Ridge Parkway we retraced our steps back toward Waynesboro where we'd exited Skyline Drive a short time earlier. We planned to spend the night in Roanoke, about 110 miles southwest.

You could drive from Front Royal, where we began the day, to Roanoke in about three hours on Interstate 81, but the speed

---

* Construction of the Blue Ridge Parkway began in 1936 and was completed, except for one section, in 1966. That final section, the Linn Cove Viaduct, was completed in 1987.

limit on both Skyline Drive and the Blue Ridge Parkway is never greater than forty miles per hour and, especially around some of the more harrowing curves, drops as low as twenty. It would take us nearly ten hours in all, including our stops for lunch and walks, to get from Front Royal to Roanoke.

Together, the two parkways form a kind of Pacific Coast Highway in the sky. The views in every direction are endless, eagles and hawks soar above, and there were times, especially on the Blue Ridge Parkway, that I felt like I was piloting a small plane rather than driving a car. Skyline Drive felt safer because it's straighter, and everywhere there are beautiful stone walls that serve as guard rails. I never felt like I might drive clear off and down a mountainside. That wasn't the case on the Blue Ridge. Not only did it reach elevations in excess of 6,000 feet, it wound through the mountains and over the ridges in what seemed like a never-ending series of curves. If you didn't pay attention there were ample opportunities to plunge to your death over a precipitous drop.

But both are sublime to drive because there are no traffic lights (and we're talking nearly 600 miles of road combined), no traffic, no gas stations, and virtually no restaurants (you need to exit the parkways for that).*

We had both roads virtually to ourselves this day. Being out here, far from home but with the magnificent handiwork of nature all around, time seemed to operate differently. There was no particular time we needed to be in Roanoke and no one waiting on us anywhere.

In the early afternoon, for the first time since leaving home, the skies started to clear and it became alternately sunny and

---

* There was one National Park Service operated hotel and restaurant on the Blue Ridge, as best I recall.

cloudy. Wherever the sunshine struck the Earth it lit it up in sharp contrast to the nearby land that remained in shadow. In the morning we had driven by bare trees and snow-covered ground and walked in subfreezing temperatures. It may as well have been mid-November. The tide was starting to turn at last. Now, later the same day, it finally felt like the trip I had imagined had begun.

As we climbed the mountains and descended into the valleys the seasons again toggled back and forth; it was winter in the mountains and spring in the valleys. As we dropped into the James River Valley the temperature steadily increased until, at the valley floor, it was sixty-two degrees and everything around us was exploding with color (for me) and lush smells (for Albie.).

For the first time since leaving home, we lowered the convertible top. Albie stuck his nose straight up toward the sky, the better to take in all the fragrance of an Appalachian spring. For us humans, sight is our principal way of taking in the world, but for a dog it's smell, and he wanted to "sniff around" just as we would "look around" when confronted with a beautiful sight.

Our top-down celebration was premature, however. Within a few minutes we started to climb again, and the temperature rapidly dropped to a chilly fifty degrees. In the rearview mirror, I could see Albie curled up in a tight ball as far into a corner of the back seat as possible. He was cold and, try as I might, I couldn't persuade myself that I wasn't, too. So, we pulled over and back up went the top. But at least we'd had a taste of what lay ahead as we continued south into what would surely be milder weather.

Though it had taken ten hours to reach Roanoke, it was never boring, and the day passed quickly. There was, for me at least, so much to see and the road commanded my attention. This was not the kind of mindless driving you experience on the interstate; you could ill-afford not to pay attention at any point. The irony is that time driving on such roads passes much more quickly than when you're driving twice as fast on major highways. I've been on two-hour drives that were tedious and seemingly never-ending. When we drive simply to get somewhere we choose the fastest route possible—getting there is the only goal. The time often feels wasted. In our case, this day was not about getting to Roanoke. Roanoke was beside the point, just a place with a motel where we could spend the night. It was about *the going.*

It may be a big country, but it's a small world. Albie came with me into the lobby while I checked into a seedy Motel 6. I had seen the couple ahead of me at check-in get out of their car and noticed the Louisiana license plates. The woman greeted Albie and told me they had three dogs of their own.

"Actually, Albie came from your neck of the woods; he's a rescue from Alexandria, Louisiana," I said.

The husband had been listening, and he turned and said, "We live not far from there."

"He was picked up as a stray in Deville," I added, figuring they might know the area. Deville also happens to be the town where Keri Toth, our adoption coordinator with Labs4rescue, the rescue organization who helped us adopt Albie, is from.

"I'm from Deville!" exclaimed the wife. Naturally, I mentioned Keri's name, and it was familiar to both of them.

"Some of my family go to church with her," said the husband.

I explained that we had a reunion with Keri planned a couple of weeks into our road trip when we would be in Louisiana, and we all marveled at what a small world it was.

The room at the Motel 6 was as Spartan as any we would stay in the entire trip, and I was quickly learning that those first moments after getting into our room were always the worst of the day. It was when I missed home the most. I wondered if Albie felt the same way, especially as he lay down on the hard wood floor. I put a few things away, then lay on the bed with pillows to prop myself up. I invited Albie to join me by patting the mattress next to me, which he did. I can't say for sure, but for Albie I think home is wherever I am. As for me, I was starting to feel like we were on the lam.

FOUR

Gone to Carolina

The next morning, our fourth day on the road, we resumed our passage down the Blue Ridge Parkway. It was sunny (finally!), but cool, too cool to put the top down, especially because it's breezier and colder in the back seat. Up front the driver can blast the heat, and the windshield breaks the wind, but for Albie it would have been very uncomfortable. So he could enjoy the smells of the outdoors, I lowered the back windows a bit and he stuck his nose out toward the passing scenery.

The terrain was less dramatic, the road flatter, than the day before, but the driving was a dream. The pavement was perfectly smooth, and we passed through massive corridors of wild rhododendrons, twenty-five feet high or more. In the first hour only seven cars passed in the other direction. Near midmorning we stopped in a parking area with access to some hiking trails.

It was a beautiful early spring day and we could, at last, after three days of rain and cold, go for a proper walk.

About a quarter mile down a wooded trail we met a hiker and stopped to chat. He told us he was a retired builder and lived nearby in Roanoke.

"Where are you from?" he asked.

"Near Boston," I answered.

"Funny, I met some people hiking here last week from Massachusetts." He pronounced it, as many people who are not from the state do, "Mass-uh-two-shits."

"There's lots of people moving down here from Mass-uh-two-shits, Vermont, and New Jersey," he told us. "They come down here and see what they can buy for so much less and they sell their houses and move down.

"Usually the wildflowers are out by now," he added. It had been a grudging spring all along the East Coast. "Is he an old dog?"

Since we don't know Albie's exact age, I gave the same answer I would give countless times to others along the way: "Well, he's a rescue and they think he was about three when we adopted him six years ago. So, he's about nine, we think."

"Well, he's really well-behaved."

As we talked, Albie just took a seat and watched us patiently, his smiling face turning toward whoever was talking at the moment, as if he was following the conversation. He *was* well-behaved, and had been for the past four days, better, in fact, than at home where the other dogs often get him amped up. He'd been so much more mellow here on the road.

I remarked that the terrain was flatter than what we'd passed through the day before.

"You're on the Blue Ridge Plateau," the hiker explained. "A few miles south and you'll start climbing again."

He directed us to another nearby trail where we could get a great view to the east, and we said goodbye. He didn't steer us wrong. A short walk from where we were, there was an expansive view of gentle green hills with two larger mountain peaks off in the distance. After days of gloomy weather and drear it was a wonderful, uplifting sight.

As the morning passed the air warmed. By 10:30 A.M. it was in the low sixties, and by noon had reached seventy. There wasn't a cloud in the sky. We stopped right on the North Carolina state line to put the top down, and when the top went down, up went Albie's nose, like a periscope, to take in the aromas of spring. I often glanced at him in the rearview mirror and saw him sitting up, eyes closed, and nose tilted into the wind.

A few miles farther south we pulled into at an overlook at High Piney Spur.

A northbound SUV with California license plates pulled in and a couple about my age got out. Albie drew their attention and the husband immediately took out his iPhone to show me a picture of their recently deceased yellow Lab, Honey, also a rescue. The resemblance was striking.

We didn't exchange names, but he told me they were on a two-year journey around America in a large camper. They tow the SUV behind the camper when they're on the move and use the smaller vehicle to explore their surroundings. Every few months they fly home to Fresno to see their children and grandchildren and their doctors and dentists. He recently retired as the city manager of Clovis, California.

"I want to see all the places in America I've never seen before I travel overseas," he said, his own personal "America First" philosophy. He was the first of countless road-trippers we met along the way just wandering about to have a look at their country.

As we chatted, another SUV pulled in, this one towing a camper and headed southbound, with Maine plates. Another couple, also around my age, got out, and soon we were all talking. The couple from Maine told us they *also* had a rescued Lab, but he doesn't like the car and was staying with their daughter. All of us who had reached this point at the same time had rescued Labs; a coincidence that gave us something in common to talk about, in addition to our travel plans. And it gave Albie practice at meeting the countless strangers down the road who were drawn to him and wanted to lay hands on him.

"We have no itinerary," said the woman from Maine. "We just wanted to do all this before we got too old." I understood. We had all come to look for America, as Paul Simon might have said, while we still could.

As we continued south I no longer had a clear fix on what day of the week it was. Differentiating weekdays and weekends no longer mattered. We had nothing on our agenda that required us to be in any particular place on any particular day, so the name for any given day of the week was irrelevant. There were no appointments to miss, no friends waiting for us to show up for coffee or dinner, and no deadlines to make.

One reason the Blue Ridge Parkway is a motorist's dream is that it's impossible to get lost. It's like following the Yellow Brick Road. But the dream was suddenly and abruptly interrupted, about a hundred miles from Asheville. We had planned to stay on the parkway all the way there, but just north of Wilkesboro, a gate, usually used to close the parkway in winter, was drawn across the roadway. The weather was fine so that didn't explain it, and there was nothing to indicate the reason for the closure or even a detour sign. The parkway was simply and indisputably closed.*

We turned onto the short access road that connected the parkway to Highway 18. There was no cell phone reception, so I turned for the first time to the *Rand McNally Road Atlas* I had brought just for such circumstances. But its detail wasn't nearly granular enough to be of help. We'd have to follow Highway 18 until we could get our bearings. For some twenty-odd miles we took the road south, on a long, gradual descent into Wilkesboro. Unsure of how long a section of the Blue Ridge Parkway was closed—could have been a mile, could have been a hundred—and feeling it had been a good run of nearly five hundred miles along these scenic parkways (Skyline Drive and the Blue Ridge), I decided to navigate directly to Asheville, whether it took me back to the parkway or not. Judy and I had been to Asheville a few years before while visiting colleges with Noah. There are many worse places to kill a few extra hours.

As we approached Wilkesboro I looked in the rearview mirror to check on Albie. The top was still down. Earlier he'd been lying on the protective seat cover that hooks behind the two rear headrests and covers both the seat back and seat itself. To escape the wind, he'd managed to work himself *behind* the seat cover to use it as windscreen. All I could see was his smiling

---

* That night, once we had finally reached Asheville, I went online and learned that a seven-mile section, the last section of the parkway completed, the Linn Cove Viaduct, was closed for repairs between March 1 and May 24. It had never occurred to me to check and I wondered why there wasn't signage to that effect at the northern terminus of the parkway where we had entered the day before.

face beaming above the top edge. He seemed utterly delighted with himself for figuring it out. *That is just so cute*, I thought, *and so clever.*

The route to Asheville wound through rural North Carolina for more than fifty miles before connecting with Interstate 40, and as we traveled the backroads I was slightly uneasy.* We were in a BMW convertible with Massachusetts plates and stuck out like a sore thumb (or so I believed) along these very rural backroads and in these very conservative towns. The religious messaging was overt and ubiquitous. We passed dozens of lawn signs that said, simply, "Thank you, Jesus." A sign in front of one church proclaimed, "The Tomb is Empty, so the Church Should be Full." Whether there was any reason to feel uneasy is another question. It's much easier to unpack our suitcases when we travel, than to unpack our biases, anxieties, and preconceptions and the drive was, in the end, uneventful. But it did get me to thinking: what was the root cause of my unease about driving through the rural south?

I am old enough to remember, just months after the assassination of President Kennedy in Dallas, the three young civil rights workers from the North—Mikey Schwerner, James Chaney, and Andrew Goodman—who were murdered in Mississippi in June of 1964, and the impression it made on me at age ten that two of them were Jewish as am I. I clearly remember the assassinations of civil rights advocate Medger Evers near Jackson, Mississippi in 1963, and Dr. Martin Luther King in Memphis in 1968; Governor George Wallace standing defiantly

---

* The forty miles we drove on I-40 to Asheville would be the only interstate driving we would do between Dickinson, Pennsylvania, and New Orleans.

at the entrance to the University of Alabama to block the entrance of its first black student in 1963; images of bombed-out black churches where little children were killed by the Ku Klux Klan; and civil rights marchers set upon by snarling police dogs and high-power fire hoses. The world has changed since then, the number of elected black officials in the South has increased dramatically, voting rights expanded (though still under assault), and the nation has had its first black president, but the resurgence of hate crimes and extremist violence—the murder of nine black members of the Mother Emmanuel A.M.E. Church in Charleston and the chilling march of white supremacists and neo-Nazis in Charlottesville, to name just two—had me wondering if we'd completely backtracked on decades of slow and arduous progress. With no voice of calm and reason at the very top, indeed quite the opposite, and political tribalism intensifying by the day, anything seemed possible and here I was, a liberal Jew* from Massachusetts passing through the deep South in his little red convertible with his rescue dog. Yes, it had been half a century since the events that shaped my early impressions of the South, but the images were indelible.

Once on I-40, I felt a mild sense of relief. Here, cars and trucks from every state blend together in a great, never-ending flow of traffic. It's a melting pot of metal traveling at seventy miles an hour. You become anonymous, just another droplet in a great asphalt river, just one more car rolling down the road. But as conspicuous as I had felt, the whole point of driving as much as possible on secondary roads was to experience the country

---

* I am Jewish by birth and ethnicity, but I'm not religious.

rather than pass it by. After Asheville, we'd get back to business and onto the backroads again.

When we arrived in Asheville around 4:00 P.M., it was ninety-three degrees, a far cry from the twenty-seven degrees during our walk just the day before on Skyline Drive.

Albie and I strolled through downtown, found a coffee shop where he was welcome, and then strolled some more until we found the restaurant where Judy and I had eaten on our previous visit to Asheville that was run by a fellow from Puerto Rico. We took an outdoor table in an alley alongside the restaurant, and for the first time on our trip the weather was nice enough to enjoy a leisurely dinner outside together. Albie lay down on the brick-paved alley by my side, as quiet and calm as could be. He sure was a different dog than he was at home.

When we first adopted him in 2012 we often took Albie with us when we knew we could dine outdoors, and he was always docile and patient. In more recent years, he'd become less predictable in his interactions with both dogs and humans. He sometimes barked or growled at other dogs nearby, or even the server, so we were unable to bring him with us to eat out anymore. I wasn't sure how it was going to go on this trip, but, fortunately, so far at least, he was reverting to his original form. It was a huge relief because it gave us so many more options. I wasn't about to leave him in a strange hotel room while I went out; in fact, on only a couple of occasions during the entire trip would I even leave him briefly in the car while I had a quick bite to eat somewhere, and only because there were no other options and it was cool enough to do so safely. Why he reverted to his old form I don't know; perhaps because I was now the only familiar marker in his life and pleasing me was now his top priority.

After dinner we walked some more and stopped to listen to a fellow with glasses and a dark, neatly trimmed beard playing old-time fiddle tunes at the entrance to an old JC Penney store.

Shane Elliott is an architect in Asheville. In his midforties, he had been taking fiddle lessons for just a year and half, which was remarkable considering he was quite skilled at it. His fiddle-playing style, he told us, is known as Round Peak, a fiddling tradition passed down over many generations and named for a small unincorporated community near Mount Airy, North Carolina. It's a variation on "old time" or mountain string band music with Anglo-Celtic roots. As Shane explained it, there are just a few basic notes involved but with deceptively complicated accent notes added in. "There are countless great fiddle players around here," he told me.

Taking up the fiddle changed Shane's life in a big way. He'd recently married a woman he met who was taking lessons from the same fiddle teacher. They live in a so-called "tiny house," a mere nine by seventeen feet, that his wife designed and built, and her self-reliance and practical skill are something he clearly admired. Originally from eastern Tennessee, Shane studied boat building in Seattle and worked at that craft in Maryland before he moved south and became an architect. As we would learn many times on our trip, most people are eager to share their stories, given the opportunity. Then he asked about Albie and me and I told him we were on a cross-country car trip together.

"Oh," he said, "like *Travels with Charley*!" Shane loves Steinbeck and told me he often read passages from Steinbeck's *Cannery Row* before bed.

"Yes, that's the inspiration," I told him.

"That is *awesome*, dude!" he replied. "I think people should throw everything they have at whatever they do, even if it's stamp collecting. That's great! Where you headed next?"

"Tomorrow we'll stop for night in Maryville, Tennessee," I answered, and pronounced Maryville as you would expect: "mary-ville."

Shane laughed. "You mean Muhr-ville. That's how they pronounce it. Muhr-ville." I'd just had my very own "Mass-uh-two-shits" moment.

Since he was a musician and interested in traditional American music, I wondered if he'd know why we were planning a stop in Okemah, Oklahoma. He paused for a minute, then it hit him.

"Woody Guthrie!" he exclaimed.

"You got it. A hero of mine."

As we got ready to move on, I said, to my own surprise, "Maybe when you're my age you'll make a trip like this." Without meaning to, I must have sounded like some sage, slightly self-involved old man giving the younger man advice. I think most of us in our sixties continue to see people even a generation behind us as "our age" somehow, but at forty-five Shane was young enough to be my son. Maybe I was giving advice to my younger self. I wasn't sure.

The next morning, I noticed for the first time that my car looked and smelled like someone with a dog had been traveling in it for nearly a week. There were strands of yellow fur all over the black dashboard and the carpets. The seat cover Albie had been lying on, or occasionally taking refuge behind, was dirty and smelled of wet dog since it had rained for the first few days, and naturally he was damp after even a short walk.

The trunk, which had been so neatly and carefully packed to make the best use of limited space, was also becoming disorganized. How we pack, and how we use the stuff we pack, don't always align. What worked for making sure everything fit nicely wasn't optimal in terms of what we were using most often. Dog treats, the cans of vegetables added to Albie's kibble, and the can opener needed to open them were buried in the farthest reaches of the trunk which meant practically emptying the trunk every time we needed to get to them. Things we weren't using at all—paper plates, utensils, a tent—were right at my fingertips. Thus began constant tinkering to make life on the road more convenient, especially when I had to manage Albie on the leash and carry what we needed for the night into a hotel. About two days before we finally returned home I had it down to a science.

We rejoined the Blue Ridge Parkway just outside of Asheville. After our brief sojourn on the interstate the day before, it was like returning to an old friend. No more cars and trucks screaming by at high speed along four lanes of traffic. We were back on a graceful, and peaceful, two-lane road. It was bucolic, and I wished it would go on forever.

A road trip is a perfect metaphor for life which may explain why my thoughts turned in this direction. A road, like life, has ups and downs and twists and turns. Sometimes it throws us a curve. But, perhaps more to the point, and most poignantly, all roads have a beginning and an end.* We travel the road of life knowing the final destination. For someone with a persistent dread of mortality, *me*, the notion of a road that goes on forever has a lot of appeal.

---

* OK, there are loop roads, but you get my drift.

As we drive roads like the Blue Ridge Parkway, we tend to take them for granted and give little thought to how they got there. But on this, our second day on the parkway, I began to appreciate the vision behind it and what a Herculean effort went into its creation. Half a century in the making, this beautiful ribbon of asphalt, nearly five hundred miles in all, didn't just materialize.

How many men and women and machines cut paths along and sometimes *through* mountainsides—we drove through twenty-five tunnels one day—to create this road for our pleasure? Who built the bridges and the guardrails and hauled the materials, cut the trees, and graded the earth? Throughout our trip I often saw, in my mind's eye, the entire country being built as if in a time-lapse film; not just this extraordinary piece of roadway engineering meandering over and through the Blue Ridge Mountains, but all the great cities from New York to San Francisco, the small towns from Fort Kent, Maine, to Forks, Washington, the great bridges from the Golden Gate to the George Washington, the tunnels from the Chesapeake Bay to the Lincoln, and all the many thousands, nay millions, of barns, ballparks, and barrooms, factories, fences, and filling stations, and homes, hotels, and high-rises in between. Out of pure wilderness this massive country was, at the most basic level, built and rebuilt brick by brick, plank by plank, and girder by girder and the building never stopped. It's truly something to behold and I would return home with a newfound appreciation for how Americans built America, ever mindful, however, that to do so we forced Native Americans off their land, which they had been stewards and developers of in accordance with their own values, and turned them into third-class citizens, often through bloodshed. It is America's original sin.

We soon returned to the heart-in-your-stomach climbs and curves at high elevation that sometimes had me feeling we were about to sail right off into the wild blue yonder. About thirty miles beyond Asheville we came to the highest point on the parkway, the Richland Balsam Overlook, at 6,053 feet more than mile in the sky. We got out to have a look and when I mentioned to Albie we were more than a mile high he just looked at me and cocked his head slightly as if to ask if he was supposed to be impressed.

Again, spring climbed the mountains like a slow-moving brush fire: it looked like winter at the higher elevations and lush, late spring when we descended to the valley floor and arrived in the town of Cherokee where evidence of our original sin was very much evident.

Over the course of our six weeks on the road, Albie and I saw many forlorn, depressed towns that were shells of their former selves, places that looked like everyone had either left or simply given up. Cherokee was *not* one of them. Indeed, even in mid-April, this town, the heart of the eastern part of the Cherokee Nation and a gateway to the Great Smokey Mountain National Park, was bustling with tourists. * But few places we visited were more dispiriting.

Cherokee's soul seemed to have been sold for the price of a tourist dollar. It was a collection of tawdry amusements, some still shuttered for the winter: mini-golf, bumper cars, water-slides, gem shops where you could ostensibly pan for gold, and Chief Saunooke's Trading Post (with the chief depicted in full

---

* There are Cherokee people across the Southeast and into Oklahoma. Indeed, about two-thirds of the federally recognized tribe's 300,000 people live in Oklahoma. Those in North Carolina are part of the eastern band of the Cherokee people.

Indian headdress), one of about a dozen such "trading posts" selling cheap souvenirs and knickknacks. There was a "medicine man" shop, a "ruby mine," and motels named Warrior, Arrowhead, and Wigwam. Every Native American stereotype seemed to be represented in the town's commercial center.

Well over a century ago we forced these and other native peoples off their land and onto reservations. I wondered: what do the Cherokee who live here make of the tourists, the descendants of those who forced them onto reservations, who come this way? Are they anything other than a cash cow? And can you blame them for exploiting perhaps their most valuable asset, their heritage—or, more precisely, a white man's limited conception of their heritage—to make a living? Is there any other work nearby or work that would be as lucrative? To make money the Cherokee had turned to "trading posts" and "medicine man" shops and other Indian-themed amusements. They had, at least for the benefit of tourists, turned this town, and with it themselves, into a caricature.*

In the middle of town was the Museum of the Cherokee Indian, a heritage center devoted to perpetuating Cherokee history and culture. There was nothing about the town itself that seemed to be doing that other than the street signs which were in both English and Cherokee. The noble history and culture of the Cherokee had been distilled and refined to the point where it could be squeezed inside this box of a building and packaged for consumption by people passing through in their shorts, T-shirts, and sneakers. The museum seemed to invite

---

* I admit that we were in Cherokee only briefly and largely because I found it so unappealing for the reasons stated here. Fair or not, these were my impressions.

people to see the Cherokee as they once *were*, not as they *are*, and that's what was especially disturbing.

As we drove out of town we passed a historical marker that declared the Cherokee reservation had been "created for" the Cherokee people, as if those who created it (powerful white people in Washington, D.C.) were doing something magnanimous for these otherwise forsaken people they'd forced off their land, something they should be grateful for. It spoke to all the hubris, callousness, and racism that white Europeans and their descendants brought to the lives of those who were here long before them. It was the story of colonialism writ small.

The Blue Ridge Parkway was now behind us, and we were once again on lightly traveled state roads. And once again, the feeling of discomfort I experienced the day before around Wilkesboro crept in. Confederate flags were a common sight, the religious messaging on yard and church signs was overt and oppressive, and half the men in their oversized pickup trucks looked as if they were on their way to audition for a ZZ Top tribute band. It was as though I'd defied my parents' admonition not to drive up into the Ramapo Mountains in New Jersey to take my chances with the "Jackson Whites."

These were *my* biases and prejudices, a kind of culturalism akin to racism I suppose. And perhaps all of it was ill-founded for we were never hassled or harassed in any way by anyone in the South or, for that matter, anywhere in the course of our entire 9,000-mile odyssey.

FIVE

Tennessee Waltz

T here are many ways to get from North Carolina into Tennessee, but by far the most terrifying, if you're into that sort of thing, is through Deal's Gap on U.S. 129. Just yards before you enter Tennessee is the start of what's known as the Tail of the Dragon, an eleven-mile stretch of road through mountain terrain into which are packed three hundred and eighteen sharp, steeply pitched turns, and once you're on it, like a roller coaster, there's no way off. If you are at all prone to motion sickness, or simply hope to live to see tomorrow, this is not the road for you.

What makes this short section of roadway doubly terrifying is that it's a magnet for every motorcyclist and sports car enthusiast with a death wish. They come from all over the world for this thrill ride. The parking lot of the Tail of the Dragon Motel, which sits in splendid isolation right at the North Carolina entrance, was filled with them.

As we slowly slalomed our way along the Tail of the Dragon like lost retirees from Florida, a group of racing bikes crawled up our own tail, engines revving, the drivers looking for any opportunity to blow past us. Since there weren't any I had to improvise. Any sudden move by me could mean death for the riders twelve inches behind us, but rather than frustrate them for another ten miles I took a chance and managed to bump to a sudden stop on a tiny crescent of pavement alongside one of the hairpin turns. Three motorcyclists dressed like ninja warriors roared past. To my surprise none of them flipped us the bird.

It wasn't just the bikes and cars behind us, but those coming in the other direction, also at high speed, that were causing second, third, and fourth thoughts about taking this tortuous, nausea-inducing route. Since so many of the motor heads who come here do so to push the limits of their motoring skills and any idiot can give it a go, your life is literally in the hands of people you wouldn't trust to watch your dog for two minutes. Every year since 2004 at least one person has been killed on the Tail of the Dragon, and usually it's more like three or four. It would not have surprised me in the least if these were the daily fatality statistics.

At various points along the way photographers in folding chairs were snapping pictures of every vehicle that passed, a job that must surely have one of the highest mortality rates in America. Next to each was a banner with a website address, which if you had time to glance at it and remember it meant you weren't paying sufficient attention to the road. That's why I'm embarrassed to admit to you that the address was www.129photos.com.

When we finally reached the end and U.S. 129 flattened out, straightened out, and spit us out, we pulled over and I practically had to peel my fingers off the steering wheel. I turned around to check on Albie in the back seat.

"So, Albus," I said, feeling a little green. "Whad'ya think?" I often call him Albus, as in Dumbledore of Harry Potter fame.

He was sitting upright and smiling. He couldn't have seemed happier. I swear the expression on his face seemed to say, "Do it again!"

That evening, once the thrill had worn off and I started to regain my equilibrium, I went to www.129photos.com where you can peruse thousands of photos by date and time, find yours, and, for about $25, order a copy. Now, why anyone would order a still photo of their car on the Tail of the Dragon beats me since they all look like pictures of cars parked at a slight pitch. The motorcycle pictures are infinitely more dramatic since the riders appear as if they are defying both gravity and common sense which, in fact, they are.

I'd chosen Maryville, or Muhr-ville, to spend the afternoon and night based on nothing more than its location on the map. I had no idea, and neither did Albie, if it was a worn-out mountain town, a charming artsy town, or nothing but a strip mall and a gas station. It turned out to be absolutely lovely.

One of the joys of traveling is the pleasant surprise. In 1985, on my first and only trip to Rome, I ditched my maps (iPhones were still in the future) and just walked, for hours, in whatever direction struck my fancy. After a couple of hours, the street opened onto a capacious and magnificent plaza lined with cafés and ornate fountains and filled with children chasing pigeons across the cobblestones. This, I thought, is the reward you get for daring to go off the beaten path; you find a hidden gem no one but the locals know about. Only later did I learn I had walked into the Piazza Navona, one of Rome's most famous, most visited, and picturesque squares.

Because the weather had been so uncooperative for so much of the early days of our trip, I'd been promising Albie a good, long walk at the first opportunity. I wasn't expecting a Piazza Navona in Maryville, but within a few minutes of parking at the town hall we found ourselves on a network of fifteen miles of pleasant walking and bike paths, part of Maryville's "greenway," many of which parallel the gently flowing Pistol Creek. It was a glorious spring afternoon. The temperature was in the sixties, the grass was a deep green, and spring flowers bloomed all around us.

When Steinbeck traveled with Charley he, too, passed through western North Carolina and eastern Tennessee. But our route from here *to* New Orleans would deviate from his as he traveled to these parts *from* the Big Easy.* Our plan was to go farther west in Tennessee, to Nashville, and to take the Natchez Trace Parkway all the way from there, for four hundred and forty-four miles, to Natchez, Mississippi. We would be paralleling Steinbeck across this stretch of the South, but some two hundred miles to the west so we could drive the Natchez Trace.

To reach Nashville from Maryville we hewed to secondary roads that took us through rural Tennessee, squarely in the Bible Belt. Even small towns of a few hundred people often had four or five churches, and almost every one had a religious message posted on a sign board in front. There seemed to be some

* Remember, we were roughly following Steinbeck's route, but in reverse.

friendly, and often quite witty, competition to see who could conjure the most clever way of appealing to God's appreciation of the double entendre:

> *Unlimited Text: Have You Talked to Jesus Today*
> *God Answers Knee Mail*
> *Weather Forecast: God Reigns, Son Shines*
> *The Key to Heaven Was Hung on a Nail*
> *Forbidden Fruits Create Many Jams*

There were dozens of similar messages that helped pass the time. I had gotten so used to trying to puzzle out the meaning of these little ditties that when we passed one that said, "Space to Lease, Time to Plant," it took me a moment to realize we'd just passed a garden center, not a church.

Late in the morning we stopped in Sparta and parked near a marker declaring the town to be the "Home of Lester Flatt," the famed bluegrass musician. In a pleasant square near the courthouse we found the Coffee Collective, a warm, spacious, high-ceilinged coffeehouse with exposed brick walls and a 1960s-era tandem bicycle hanging from the ceiling. Ever since unearthing the story of my great-grandaunt Annie Londonderry, the 'round the world cyclist, I've had an affinity for antique bikes, so I liked the place straight away. Albie was invited in and the owner, Mariangela, and her daughter, Rachel, were friendly and welcoming.

Our conversation began over the bicycle hanging from the ceiling. Rachel is an avid cyclist and since she had her laptop open I showed her the website I'd created about Annie and told her a bit of the story. When I asked about the cycling around

Sparta she told me that on many of the country roads outside town people have posted signs, BICYCLES NOT WELCOME HERE. There seemed to be some cockamamie association between bicycles and undesirables, such as hippies.

Mariangela grew up in the area, but the family lived in San Diego for several years, and moved back recently. In San Diego, Rachel bought a used white Bluebird school bus, on top of which the previous owner had installed a strip of Astroturf from which he could drive golf balls. She drove it back to Tennessee and has been converting it into a mobile home. An aspiring photographer, her plan is to drive it around the country and take photographs.

"Travel is important to open your mind and expand your horizons," she told me. "There's a lot of intolerance here." The NO BICYCLES signs she sees while riding the country roads are just one manifestation of it. Her gumption and her desire, at the tender age of twenty-two, to indulge the wanderlust that seems to be a part of the American DNA is admirable.

As Albie and I started to leave, a wiry older man sitting at a table by the door rose slowly and appeared to have something he wanted to say to us. He looked and dressed like Richard Petty, the race car driver, down to Petty's signature feathered cowboy hat. As he extended his hand to shake mine I mentioned the resemblance and though I could barely understand a word he said, a combination of his being somewhat incoherent and in possession of a southern drawl so thick even individual words were hard for me to parse, he seemed cheered by the comparison. We spoke, or rather *he* spoke, for about three solid minutes. All I was able to glean was that he once played with Flatt and Scruggs (he showed me a laminated photo of himself playing the banjo) and in 2012 suffered a leg injury that required thirty staples to repair, two facts that, as best I could tell, bore no relation to one another. It was tempting, because he was such a character, to sit down and see where the conversation might take us, but for the life of me only five percent of what he was saying was the least bit intelligible. It didn't strike me at the time, but after many such encounters along our way (though more intelligible), I came to realize that everyone has a story to tell and most just want someone to listen, even to a small part of it. They don't necessarily want to be famous or to bare their souls, they just want to be heard and *known* in some small way, even if by a complete stranger. Especially in small towns—Okemah, Oklahoma, would become my exhibit A—people also often appreciated that we'd stopped and took an interest, however fleeting, in the place they call home.*

As we followed Highway 70 west toward Nashville, there was an astonishing number of yard sales in progress. Near Watertown, on both sides of the road, they were nearly wall-to-wall. Clearly this wasn't a coincidence and we stopped to check it out.

It was a Friday afternoon. Albie and I wandered among tables and blankets and old furniture loaded with mountains of what could only be called "junk." As I looked, he sniffed. Well-worn toys, beaten up kitchenware, glassware, utensils, clothing, lawn chairs, dolls, lamps, bad paintings, rusted tricycles, battered suitcases, old baby strollers, and tchotchkes of every imaginable shape and description abounded, the flotsam and jetsam of a thousand lifetimes. Oddly, there was even a fellow with shelves of shampoos, soaps, and deodorants, products you can find at any grocery store or pharmacy. Who shops for toiletries at a yard sale?

---

* *See* Chapter Ten: This Land is Your Land.

An older woman sitting in a lawn chair wearing bilious green velour pants and a plain sleeveless white blouse looked at Albie and said, "He looks like he could use some water." I realized I'd left Albie's water bottle, a clever device with a little fold down plastic trough you squeeze the water into, in the car.

"Oh, yes, thank you. I have some in the car," I said. "I'll give him some soon." I asked her what was going on.

"This is the Watertown Mile Long Yard Sale," she told me. "Every year." She added that homeowners along the highway rent space in their yards for $50 a day so people can set out their wares.

"Can people make money doing this?" I asked.

"Oh, yes!" she replied. "Tomorrow you wouldn't be able to get down this road it's so crowded. We get people come all the way from California for this."

"Really?" I asked, utterly gobsmacked. "All the way from California? You don't say. That's amazing!"

What I was thinking was something entirely different. The notion that people would drive thousands of miles and spend hundreds of dollars on gas and hotels and food to look through pile after pile and mile after mile of worthless junk seemed preposterous. There are forty million people in California. Didn't they produce enough of their own junk to gawk at without having to drive all the way to central Tennessee? It was like people from New Jersey driving to Colorado to buy industrial waste.

Truly, the stuff looked like belongings the impoverished Joad family in *The Grapes of Wrath* deemed too worthless to take with them when they packed their meager possessions into a jalopy and fled the Dust Bowl *for* California. Now people were coming *from* California to Tennessee to repatriate it? Why drive all the way from California just to buy a one-armed Barbie doll when you could have stayed home, bought a new one at Walmart in Fresno, and dismembered it yourself? Ninety-nine percent of the stuff looked like it was either salvaged from a landfill or belonged in one. Actually, one hundred percent of it did but I want to allow for the possibility that I may have missed something, like a previously undiscovered original copy of the Gettysburg Address or Ben Franklin's kite. All this remained unsaid, of course.

"Anyone ever find any treasures here?" I asked the woman in the green pants once the shock wore off. I wasn't sure if ten seconds or ten minutes had passed.

"I knew a woman who bought a necklace for $10 and it turned out to be worth $500," she said. "If I'd bought it, I'd have returned it. But that's just me."

I'll bet it *is* just you, I thought. Wasn't the whole attraction of a yard sale the chance to make a score, or perhaps buy some Head & Shoulders shampoo?

As we continued west it became clear that "mile long yard sale" was a misnomer. It was more like ten miles and it was breathtaking to consider so many people hauling so much junk around the country hoping to make a few bucks by selling a few pieces of it, most likely to someone else who would then carry it to the next yard sale and try to make yet another dollar or two from the same stuff. I doubt that even one percent of it ended up being repurposed in someone's home. But who knows? Maybe some lucky shopper did come away with a find that day.

The yard sales eventually petered out, and just past Mount Juliet the Nashville skyline came into view. Albie and I spent the afternoon walking around the Vanderbilt University campus, justly renowned as one of the nation's prettiest, soaking up the spring sunshine and accepting the compliments and greetings of dozens of college students, many missing their dogs at home, who stopped to say hello to Albie. I harbored no illusion I was of the slightest interest to any of them.

Again, I wondered what Albie was making of it all. I was starting to obsess about whether he was content being on this trip. He had thus far been an unfailingly good sport, climbing in and out of the back seat many times a day, sleeping in a strange room every night and allowing many strangers to pet him or shake his paw. Did he miss Salina and Jamba and Judy? Was he capable of *missing* others as we experience it? Did he wonder if we'd ever be home again? Or was it enough just to be wherever I was? How, if at all, did he formulate thoughts that resembled those I projected onto him? He seemed happy and all I could do was to give him lots of love and affection and rub his belly to his heart's content.

When we eventually did come home, Judy told me something she had kept from me during the trip because she didn't want me to feel badly—that Salina had been morose since we left. Normally energetic and bouncy, she missed Albie (not so sure about me), with whom she roughhoused every day. She looked for him, and her mood drooped. He didn't show it, but maybe Albie missed her, too.

It struck me as slightly ironic that the room we had booked for just one night near Nashville was at a hotel called Extended Stay America. We were in Franklin, Tennessee, a short drive from the northern terminus of the Natchez Trace Parkway.

My fascination with this road began when I read about it in a cycling magazine a few years back. The name, the Natchez *Trace*, was so evocative.

A *trace*. One of the definitions is "an indication of the existence or passing of something." A meteor leaves a trace of light in the night sky. We hope in our lives to leave a trace behind when we exit, something that will mark our brief existence on the planet. Our footprints leave a trace on the trail. Thus, did ancient peoples, Native Americans, and later European and American settlers and traders, wear a pathway through the dense forests of the southland from Natchez, Mississippi, to Nashville that came to be known as the Natchez Trace. By 1809, the Trace was so well-worn it was navigable by wagon. Sections of the historic Natchez Trace still exist; others have evolved into country roads. The Natchez Trace Parkway "commemorates" and hews closely to the historic footpath, but it is not the evolution of it. Construction began in the 1930s and the final segment, the one that allows the modern-day motorist to drive its four hundred and forty-four miles all the way from Nashville to Natchez, was completed in 2005. I had high hopes for this part of our trip, and the Natchez Trace did not disappoint, at least not on the first day. The second was another story.

SIX

Tupelo Honey

E ven though the weather improved the farther south we got, we had been climbing high mountains and descending into valleys so the weather on any given day was highly variable. But the morning we started down the Natchez Trace Parkway promised nothing but sunshine and warmth at the lower elevation. The terrain is gentler, the road flatter and straighter, which, along with the weather, made driving the Natchez Trace more relaxing than the winding, sometimes harrowing, mountain roads we'd navigated through Virginia and North Carolina.

Hawks soared overhead, and quail darted over the grassy areas that bordered the roadway. The white and occasional pink flowers of the dogwoods were strewn throughout the forests like tinsel, as if fairies and gnomes had spent the previous day decorating for our arrival. The roadway itself was paved perfection. Its gentle curves and rises allowed us to sit back, relax, and absorb the magnificence of the day. Dozens of cyclists shared the road, and as a cyclist myself I felt a little jealous. This was a magnificent parkway to drive in a convertible; it looked like heaven for cycling. No "no bicycle" signs here; the parkway welcomes them.

As I often did, I reached my right hand back through the gap in the front seats and took hold of Albie's paw. He seemed to be smiling, and the sun illuminated his gold- and wheat-colored fur.

"You're a good guy, Albie," I said. I often spoke to him this way throughout the day—telling him we'd be stopping soon, that we'd have a walk, that he was my buddy, and such. Dogs can be such perfect companions. As I wrote in my last book, *Rescued*, relationships are so much easier when only one of you can talk. And Albie *never* complained about my driving, not even on the Tail of the Dragon.

After about an hour down the parkway we stopped at Grinder's Stand. The old house, which belonged to a family named Grinder and served as an informal inn for travelers on the old Natchez Trace, no longer exists. But a short distance from the site of the old inn is a grave and a monument dedicated to the memory of Meriwether Lewis.

On October 11, 1809, three years after Lewis and William Clark had returned from perhaps the most epic journey ever taken on the North American continent, Lewis, just thirty-five years old, died here. He was serving as governor of the Upper Louisiana Territory by appointment of President Jefferson, and was en route, by foot, from Louisiana to Washington and Philadelphia to attend to financial matters and the publication of his account of the great expedition.

How Lewis met his demise has been the subject of considerable debate, something I discussed with the park ranger on duty,

Derek Peck. Was it murder or suicide? The overwhelming consensus among historians is that Lewis died of two self-inflicted gunshot wounds, one to the head that left his brain exposed, and another to the chest. Those who subscribe to the murder theory argue that Lewis had no money on his person when he died, suggesting he was killed during a robbery. The most compelling evidence for the suicide theory is that Lewis survived both gunshot wounds for several hours during which he spoke, at times with clarity, to members of the Grinder family. He never mentioned an assailant which he almost surely would have had he been attacked, and he had appeared to Mrs. Grinder to be in a melancholic state earlier in the evening. Some historians have theorized that he was suffering from malaria, others syphilis—for which he may have been treating himself with mercury—and still others pin his desperate act on alcoholism. Perhaps it was a combination of many of these ailments, both physical and emotional. Those who have made extraordinary journeys often find themselves struggling to adapt to a more mundane life where few people are capable of understanding their experience. Astronaut Buzz Aldrin famously suffered from depression and alcoholism after his lunar mission.

Regardless, for me (Albie cared not), standing where Meriwether Lewis once stood, albeit in his darkest hour, and is now buried, was a way of paying tribute to America's first great road tripper. After Lewis's death, Jefferson wrote of Lewis's "courage undaunted," and surely anyone familiar with his and Clark's epic journey would agree.[*]

---

[*] A must-read for every American who wants to understand the history of this country is *Undaunted Courage: Meriwether Lewis, Thomas Jefferson and the Opening of the American West* by Stephen Ambrose (Simon & Schuster, 1997).

❖

A few miles north of the Alabama border we pulled off the
parkway into a rest area near a stream where Albie could have a
drink and lay down in the shallow water. I've always suspected
he ended up a stray because someone had hopes he'd be a good
hunting dog. But Albie does not and *will not* swim, and a hunter
in Louisiana would have had little use for a hunting dog that
won't swim out to retrieve felled water fowl. But he does enjoy
lying down in streams.

About a dozen cyclists on a tour had also stopped at the same
spot. Most were in their sixties and seventies; the oldest was
eighty-three. One, a fellow from Ocean City, New Jersey, asked
about our trip. When I explained we'd been inspired by *Travels
with Charley* he told me he'd made a long road trip, though
without a dog, a few years ago: three months and forty-five
states, "just to see all the places I'd never seen." It was becoming
a familiar refrain among people we were meeting.

"Did you start in Sag Harbor?" he asked me, showing familiarity with Steinbeck, for Steinbeck and Charley began their
trip in Sag Harbor, New York, where they made their home
at the time. It was always fun to meet people who shared an
enthusiasm for Steinbeck.

"No, we started near Boston," I replied.

"Are you going to Salinas?" he asked, referring to Steinbeck's
hometown.

"Yes, we're going to visit the Steinbeck Center."

"*Rocinante* is there, you know."

"Yes, I know!" He certainly knew his stuff.

Another cyclist, a woman from Chicago, came over to meet
Albie. She was missing her dog at home and asked if she could

walk him back to the stream for another dip. But as soon as she took the leash Albie looked at me plaintively and started to pull gently in my direction. His attachment to me, always strong, was especially so now that he hadn't seen another familiar face for a week. The three of us walked back to the stream together.

As we approached the Alabama state line both sides of the parkway were lined with wildflowers—yellows, whites, and purples—and more blooming dogwoods. The air smelled faintly of vanilla. It was near noon, sunny, and seventy-five degrees. We had really hit our stride; the road trip I had imagined was now in full bloom, too. The weather, the road, Albie—everything was just right.

Only thirty-two of the Natchez Trace Parkway's four hundred and forty-four miles are in Alabama so we were soon in Mississippi. My iPhone was set to play more than one thousand songs at random. Thirty miles from Tupelo, Van Morrison's "Tupelo Honey" came on. What were the chances?

In downtown Tupelo we turned off Front Street onto Main and parked in the very first open space, directly in front of the Tupelo Hardware Company. There was a historical marker on the sidewalk in front of the store. In 1946, it said, when he was eleven years old, Elvis Presley's mother brought him to this store to buy him a bicycle. He had no interest in a bicycle, but a .22 rifle caught his eye. His mother didn't want him to have a gun, so they compromised and a salesman by the improbable name of Forest L. Bobo sold them a guitar for $7.90 and the rest, as they say, is history. There was a life-size cardboard cutout of Elvis in the window and Albie obliged me as I snapped a photo of him with the King.

It was late in the afternoon, a Saturday, and Main Street was surprisingly quiet except for what I would soon come to think of as the soundtrack of the South: cars, pick-up trucks, and motorcycles modified to make the most ear-splitting racket possible. The peace and tranquility of the afternoon was repeatedly interrupted by the roar of engines and exhaust systems. It drove me to distraction, but surprisingly Albie didn't seem to notice. Like many dogs he's fearful of loud noises, such as thunder and fireworks, but for reasons I can't explain the din from the passing vehicles didn't bother him one bit.

We found a coffee shop called Crave a block off Main Street, across from the Lee County Courthouse. Though I often felt uncomfortable in the small southern towns we passed through, here the preconceptions that led to such feelings collided with another stereotype that actually happens to be true: that of southern hospitality. I ordered my usual mocha latte and asked if they could also put some whipped cream in a cup for Albie (often referred to as a "puppacinno"), which I offered to pay for. Of course they would give Albie some whipped cream and of course they wouldn't accept payment. We took a table outside and when the server came out Albie had a big cup of whipped cream on which they had sprinkled a few slices of crumbled up bacon.

As we sat, a group of about half a dozen women came out of the building next door, all dressed for an occasion, a baby shower as it turned out. With them was an adorable two-year-old named Addison wearing a pair of oversized sunglasses. She was naturally attracted to Albie. Still adapting to Albie's new, more docile road personality, I tensed up hoping he wouldn't be spooked. He was happy to have Addison pat him on the head, a big relief since I didn't want to have to make apologies for him scaring a cute little girl and making her cry. Albie was really doing me proud. I expect him to shed, he is mostly Lab after all, but I was beyond pleased that here on the road he had shed not just fur, but the more ornery side of his personality, the one that in recent years had made him something of a wildcard when it came to interactions with strangers.

When we'd finished the coffee, whipped cream, and bacon, Albie and I ambled across the street to wander the grounds around the courthouse. One marker commemorated radio station WELO's broadcast of weekly jamborees from this spot, begun in 1946, and hosted by the hillbilly singer Carvel Lee Ausborn, better known as Mississippi Slim. Slim later arranged for a young Elvis Presley, who aspired to be as famous as Slim and to have his own radio show someday, to perform at one of the jamborees, one of Elvis's first public appearances.

Just a few feet away was a granite slab about five feet tall in the shape of the state of Mississippi. Dedicated in 2009, it depicted eight people—some black, some white, some male, some female—holding hands. The inscription read:

> This monument is dedicated to honor all the Lee County citizens who worked, served and participated in the 1950's, 60's & 70's movement to achieve civil & human rights. They placed their lives, families and livelihoods in jeopardy to fight for justice and equality. Their names are too numerous to list here, but their legacies live on.

I wondered: was the decision to establish this memorial controversial? How long did it take to get the powers that be in Lee County, named for the Confederate general, to honor those engaged in the great civil rights struggle? Who backed it? Who opposed it? People in town would surely know so I started asking.

A few yards away two young black women were taking pictures of a young girl—her elementary school graduation pictures I learned—under a huge magnolia tree.

"Hi. Are you from Tupelo?" I asked.

"Yes," one of them answered.

"Do you know if there was any controversy about that monument?" I asked, pointing to it.

"What monument?" the other answered.

"The one at the corner there."

"I don't know, I've never looked at it."

"It's dedicated to people from here who gave their lives to the civil rights movement."

It was clear they were not interested in my questions and were uncomfortable being asked. I tried to put them at ease by saying I was glad to see a monument to the civil rights movement here.

"Well," said one of the women, "I haven't read it, so I don't know." The conversation was over as far as they were concerned. I wished them a good day and they perfunctorily wished me the same.

I wondered if these were just not conversations blacks and whites have here, or whether they truly had no idea that the monument was there and what it commemorated. Or maybe they just wanted to go about the business at hand, capturing a good graduation picture, without a meddlesome outsider pestering them with questions.

We continued around the courthouse grounds past a modest monument dedicated to the Women's Christian Temperance Union* and another to the veterans of Vietnam, Korea, the two World Wars, and Iraq. On the opposite corner, and out of sight

---

* The WCTU was founded in 1874 to protest against the consumption of alcohol, but it evolved into an advocacy organization on behalf of labor laws, prison reform, and women's suffrage. The monument in Tupelo commemorates statewide prohibition which went into effect on January 1, 1908.

from where the civil rights monument stood, was the largest monument on the courthouse grounds. More than twenty feet tall, a statue of a Confederate soldier stood atop a large pedestal. Unveiled in 1906,* the monument bore several inscriptions:

> Erected in honor of
> and to the memory of
> Confederate soldiers
> by their
> comrades, their sons and daughters.
> The love, gratitude,
> and memory of the
> people of the South
> shall gild their
> fame in one eternal
> sunshine.
>
> Those who die
> for a right
> principle, do
> not die in vain.
>
> The loyal and true,
> their faith sealed
> with their most precious blood.

---

* The vast majority of Southern monuments to the Confederacy were erected decades after the Civil War, during the Jim Crow segregation era of the 1890s to the 1950s, as a symbolic protest of the supremacy of the federal government in matters of civil rights. Many have argued they were intended, among other things, to intimidate local black populations.

Within yards of each other, here were monuments to those who fought and died to preserve slavery and those who, a century later, did the same to erase the lingering stain of racial injustice, one step in a long march that began with the Civil War and continues to this day. The jarring juxtaposition of these two monuments, on opposite corners of the same small courthouse grounds but out of sight of one another, seemed to epitomize the complicated legacy of race relations in the South and of the Civil War itself.

We checked into our hotel, and around 6:30 P.M. headed back to downtown Tupelo. I'd checked *Yelp* for some restaurant ideas and had decided, for no particular reason, on a sandwich and pizza place called Vanelli's Bistro on Main Street, just a couple of blocks from where we'd parked in front of Tupelo Hardware earlier in the day. The town was more alive than it had been in the afternoon; it was a Saturday evening, after all.

In front of Vanelli's two men were sitting on a bench just to the left of the entrance: a young black man and an older white man who was noodling around on a guitar. The guitar player was wearing a baseball cap, jeans rolled up into cuffs above his moccasins, and a large, baggy open sweater over a checkered shirt. He had round, black-framed glasses which offset snow-white hair that fell well beneath his shoulders and an equally long white beard and moustache. He looked like Santa's little brother. He was all of about five feet five inches tall and as we approached he gave me a hearty greeting. His friend was showing him a few chords. I introduced myself and Albie, and he introduced himself as "Voz." His friend was Jason.

I assumed they were just hanging out in front of the restaurant because there was a bench to sit on. Then Voz told me he owned the place. He goes by Voz Vanelli, but his real name is Vasily Kapenakas, and over the next three hours we became well acquainted.

Voz defied every stereotype of the South you can imagine, except for his unremitting hospitality. Albie and I even had to decline his invitation to spend the night at his house on Lake Elvis Presley (yes, Lake Elvis Presley), partly because we had already unpacked all our things at the hotel (which I would have undone for the opportunity to accept Voz's invitation), but mainly because we weren't sure how Albie would take to Voz's cats. (Well, Voz wasn't sure, but I was confident that given the opportunity Albie would have disemboweled them.)

Born and raised in Detroit, Voz attended Eastern Michigan University. His father, Demetrios, was born in Greece and moved to Tupelo from Detroit in the early 1970s. When Voz graduated from college in 1975 he came down with the intention of going to law school or getting a graduate degree in English. Instead he went to work in his father's restaurant business. Demetrios didn't think people would buy pizza from a Greek so he named his place Vanelli's. In 1991, Demetrios and his two sons, Voz and his brother, built a larger restaurant that was destroyed by a tornado in 2014. The current restaurant is the third incarnation of Vanelli's in Tupelo. Demetrios had an American dream and he made it come true.

Voz told me he's an anomaly in Tupelo, a confirmed progressive in a deeply conservative town. But he's also, for reasons that became obvious, widely beloved. As we chatted, there wasn't a person who walked by who didn't get the full Voz treatment. He had a good word for everyone, friend and stranger alike, black and white, young and old. He organized families to get together for photos he'd take with their smartphones, he hugged the women and put his arms around the men. He told little children to go inside and tell the staff Voz told them they could have a soda, or he would produce a Tootsie Pop from the pocket of his oversized sweater. It was hard to tell who knew him and who didn't; he was buoyant and chipper and quick-witted. He seemed to love everyone and vice versa. He was the star of his own sidewalk show, the maître d' of Main Street, the *tummler* of Tupelo.* He improvised riffs and songs on his guitar, including one he stood up to perform about my cross-country trip with Albie. Cops came by and he bantered with them, too, and offered them a soft drink. He could have been one of Ken Kesey's Merry Pranksters—small of stature, big of heart, and a twinkle in his eye. His philosophy is that if you give to people generously, they will do the same. All this time Albie was his best self, making friends with the passersby who stopped to chat with Voz.

Voz asked me what I wanted to eat and had one of the staff bring dinner out in a takeaway container, so I could eat outside on the bench with him.

I asked Jason and Voz about the civil rights monument I'd seen earlier in the day and neither of them was familiar with it. Then I asked Jason, a musician and audio engineer, if everyone seemed to get along as well as he and Voz do.

"Black and white coexist here," he said. "Especially younger people. They don't carry the same baggage as the older folks."

---

* *Tummler* is a word of Yiddish origin that means "to stir," but it is the term used to refer to an employee, usually male, of a Borscht Belt resort (the resorts in New York's Catskill Mountains that are generally patronized by Jews) charged with the duty of entertaining guests throughout the day by providing any number of services from comedian to master of ceremonies.

As I was finishing up my dinner a fellow named Dan Widdington joined us, and Voz quickly filled him in on Albie and me and our trip. Dan took a seat next to me. He was dressed in rugged work clothes and an Ole Miss baseball cap with a camouflage motif. Dan is a long-distance trucker with a full beard and a very thick southern accent, and I struggled, as I had the day before with the Richard Petty look-alike we met in Sparta, Tennessee, to understand him. Dan was born and raised in Tupelo.

"Tupelo was nothing until Elvis died," he told me. "Then people started showing up."

For close to an hour Dan regaled me with Elvis stories. He's fifty-seven, a good twenty-five years younger than Elvis would have been, but he has many memories of the times when he and groups of local kids of all ages would gather on the local playing fields for pickup games of baseball and football.

"Almost every year a fancy car would pull up, and Elvis would step out from behind the wheel wearing jeans and a white shirt," Dan told me. "He'd ask each kid to introduce himself and then join the pickup game. He'd drive himself down from Memphis and come home just to play ball with the local kids." Dan surmised it was a welcome break from the pressures of stardom and the controlling personality of Elvis's manager/Svengali, Colonel Parker.

"One year he came back to give the mayor heck for not doing something with money he had given the town," said Dan. "It was in all the local papers. He was always giving money to the town." Dan also had a theory about why Elvis started touring again in 1965.

"After he was in the service he had a contract to make thirty movies and was doing studio albums and the Beatles passed him," Dan told me. "That's why he started doing live shows again."

How much of what Dan had to say about Elvis—and it was about a good hour's worth—was accurate, I don't know, but it was sure fun listening to him. Like a lot of people, Dan thinks his hometown is the best place in the world.

"I've been lots of places, even used to drive my truck to Boston a lot, and the people here are real good people." He nodded toward Voz, who was taking yet another family portrait with a smartphone. "OK, say 'world peace!' Peace, love, pizza!" Voz said to get everyone smiling for the picture.

"Now there's a good man," Dan said. The truck driver and the hippie; an odd couple. Dan first met Voz when Dan was a teenager and used to frequent the original Vanelli's.

"I could retire," Dan then added, apropos of nothing, "but I know too many people who retire and die within a year because they have nothing to do and no purpose."

As the evening wore on Voz shared more of his story, too. He was widowed in 2012 and it continues to be a source of great sorrow. He has a daughter in her twenties who works in the restaurant; we met her briefly after they'd closed, and she was headed home. His daughter was the result of what he described as "a three-day adventure" he'd had with another woman. His brother, who was in the restaurant business with him for a while, is serving time in federal prison and has three years left on his sentence. I didn't ask why his brother was serving time, and Voz didn't volunteer that information, but he calls his brother several times a week and sends him money.

After the restaurant closed and the streets had emptied, Voz and Albie and I were still together, and he invited us to walk with him over to his office near the courthouse. In addition to the restaurant, Voz creates short animated videos and he wanted to show me some.

As we walked, his demeanor changed noticeably. All evening he'd been positively buoyant as he played the host with the most on Main Street. With no audience to play to, he was quieter and more subdued. He obviously thrives on the bonhomie he creates on the street, and I surmised that for this 65-year-old widower the quieter hours when he's alone are harder. We watched some of the videos he created, and he told me he needed to learn more about that civil rights monument just yards from his office. As a parting gift, he gave me a T-shirt with the Vanelli's logo on it. I think we were both a little sorry Albie and I weren't spending the night out at Lake Elvis Presley.

Reflecting on the evening we'd spent with Voz, I thought, *This is why we travel.* We travel for the chance encounters that enrich us in small ways. I could have picked another place to eat, one that served me a meal and nothing more, or picked up something at a grocery store. Instead, serendipity played its hand and we met one of the unforgettable characters of our journey across America. How many other characters had we passed by or just missed by a minute or two or a mile or two?

The whole evening also had me rethinking the sense of unease I'd had while driving through small towns in the South. Maybe I had it all wrong, though I was still deeply troubled whenever I saw the Stars and Bars. Everyone we'd met—and Voz introduced me to a lot of people that night—was friendly, polite, and warm. The anger and vitriol that spill out on social media and in our politics seemed out of sync with what I was experiencing on a person to person level. You'd never know the country was busy tearing itself apart.

A couple of days after we left Tupelo, Voz e-mailed me, an e-mail that seemed to capture the spirit of the independent, free-thinking man we'd just met:

[W]hat I've been witness to in my 65 years is an endless cycle of misguided individuals and groups whose moral hypocrisies are masked in the guise of "patriotism" or "good intension-ism" whose real intent has been to propagate ideologies crafted upon manipulation and commercialism whose resulting effect has been the proliferation of poverty, ignorance and war.

So, I've come to recognize the only purposeful change I or any have control over is within "our/my own being." The future, our futures, are tales yet to unfold; "crafted in the moment." Moments; precious to all, in every instance we've the privilege to exist in. To share good counsel, to give kindness, to encourage, to bring joy is something purposeful all are capable to do.

Thank you for the considerate individual you are. Searching, Seeking, Exploring. I wish that Albie and You will find the America you are hoping to find.

It was signed, "Peace / vOz."*

Rain fell heavily as we got back to the Natchez Trace Parkway on the outskirts of Tupelo the next morning. It was a Sunday and I turned on the radio for the first time since we'd left home. My self-imposed news blackout had been rather enjoyable. On the very first station we tuned to, a female host, an evangelical Christian, was railing against other evangelicals who were

---

* Voz and I have stayed in touch. A couple of weeks after we returned home, he e-mailed me a play he had written. He's a man of many talents.

having their doubts about Trump, and against "Democrats and liberals" who were ruining the country.

"He won the election," she crowed. "Get over it!"

With no apparent sense of irony, she went on screeching about the "intolerance" conservative evangelicals faced from some churches as those churches moved toward liberalism. "If you don't believe the Bible is the inerrant word of God," she said, "you cannot be a Christian! You cannot be a Christian!"

I turned to the next station. The program host was singing the joys of sharing your faith every day with others.

"It's the most fun you'll ever have!" he exclaimed. "I know a famous tennis champion. Now that he's found God he's sharing his faith every day and he says that even the high of winning a championship doesn't compare to it!"

I switched stations again. Another host was telling his listeners how to befriend Muslims in their communities. Because they tend to be isolated in American communities Muslims are very open to people who approach them in friendship, he explained. But the whole point was to earn their friendship and their trust so you could turn them away from the darkness of Islam and "lead them to the Lord Jesus Christ." Friendship was just a ruse for proselytizing.

Next up was American Family Radio out of Chattanooga. I listened for as long as I could take it, which is to say about five minutes.

"What pain would you suffer for his forgiveness?"

"There's nothing free about salvation."

Family. Freedom. Faith. Heaven. Hell. Light. Darkness. Forgiveness. Grace. Kingdom. Sin. Jesus is the only way. Come to Christ or die without hope.

I understood the words but failed to grasp the message because I don't speak the language. Faith, it seems, allows for no dissent and no deviation from someone else's idea of absolute truth with a capital "T." If what they are pushing was so wonderful, why does it need such a hard sell? Under all the nice-sounding words lurked an intolerance of anyone who is not "a believer." Jews, Muslims, Sikhs, Buddhists, Hindus, atheists, and agnostics are all on the outside looking in. "Lord have mercy on their souls." It was all very oppressive.

Though it was now pouring rain, we were making good time. In the first hour, no more than a dozen oncoming cars passed us on the parkway. The terrain had gradually changed from modest rolling hills to flat.

Then, about forty miles north of Jackson, we came to a screeching halt. A huge tree lay across the parkway. It was probably sixty feet tall (or long now), with a trunk many feet in diameter. The ground was so sodden, the tree had simply lost its footing and crashed down across the roadway. And it had fallen recently because there wasn't a single car around and no emergency crews were on the scene. Who knows? Had we left Tupelo a minute earlier we might have been *underneath* that tree instead of looking at it.

The roadway was completely blocked and there was no way around. Exits and entrances to the parkway are few and far between, but fortunately there was an exit a half mile behind us, so we turned around and found our way back onto the Trace a couple of miles farther south.

Trees were down everywhere alongside the roadway, enormous trees no longer able to maintain their grip in the wet earth. It made for nerve-wracking driving. As we drove through densely forested areas where large trees loomed above the roadway, I found myself looking up as much as ahead, preparing to dodge the next one to come crashing down. The day before had been a carefree, top-down drive. Today the weather had turned the Trace into a nightmare. Maybe it *was* time to accept Christ as my savior.

We were smack-dab in the middle of Mississippi and I started to wonder what I might be missing by staying on the parkway, aside from falling trees. After all, it didn't pass through any downtowns; it was a scenic drive through the countryside. So, we pulled off to see the tiny town of Ethel, population five hundred. The streets were deserted on this Sunday morning, but within a couple of minutes I'd seen enough Confederate flags on garages and trucks and cars to make me feel it would be safer for this liberal in his little BMW convertible with Massachusetts tags to be back on the parkway, even if trees were toppling over with unnerving frequency.

For more than three hundred miles the Trace had been our friend, but now it was tormenting me. The rains were torrential, the visibility poor. Every tree was a threat. I searched in vain for a safe place to pull over (it was also time to let Albie do his business) but found none. Albie, oblivious to the danger all around us, slept peacefully in the back seat. Sometimes it would be nice to be a dog. I was glad I'd affixed my emergency contact information to my driver's license. It seemed a little neurotic at the time, but now it seemed downright sensible. How will the Mississippi State police tell Judy we died? That we hydroplaned and careered off the road? Or that a tree had flattened the convertible top and us with it? That an oncoming vehicle struck us head-on trying to avoid a falling a tree?

As we passed the enormous Ross Barnett Reservoir the rain let up a little and there were a few spots where the trees no longer hugged the roadway, so I was able to take a breath. Alas, we were not yet out of the woods, literally or figuratively. About sixty miles north of Natchez a group of cyclists was stopped by another huge tree that had fallen across the parkway. My heart jumped. I feared one or more of them had been caught as the tree fell. The rain had stopped, and I rolled my window down. The cyclists, one of them told us, had just come upon the scene; no one was hurt. Through the foliage I could see that an emergency crew had approached from the south. Another of the cyclists said they'd been told it would take at least an hour to clear the tree and open the roadway.

I couldn't recall, probably because the rain was so heavy and I couldn't see, where the last exit off the parkway was. The map on my phone was no help. We turned around and headed back north to look for a way off. Ten miles back up the road and we still hadn't reached an exit, so we turned around yet again and drove back to the fallen tree to wait for the parkway to reopen. By the time we got there, a line of about twenty southbound cars had formed. As we waited, a National Park ranger police car pulled up and a man got out. (The Natchez Trace Parkway is part of the National Park System.) I stepped out of the car to talk to the ranger. This was the fourth tree to topple across the parkway that morning that he was aware of, he told me. The combination of the water-saturated ground and the weight of all the rain in the tree canopies, which were fully leafed-out, was too much.

"If you want to get to Natchez anytime soon," he said, "I'd get off at the next exit, head north to Vicksburg on 27 and then down to Natchez on Route 61."

One tree down is a warning. Two are a sign. As much as I wanted to lay claim to having driven the entire Natchez Trace

Parkway, once the road reopened a few minutes later we took his advice and exited the parkway and headed northwest on Highway 27 about twenty miles to Vicksburg.

Approaching Vicksburg, we had our first glimpse of the mighty Mississippi River. More than 2,300 miles long, it has profoundly impacted the history of the nation and delineates east from west.* Reaching the Mississippi felt like a milestone of sorts. We were on the edge of the rest of the continent, looking out at the main artery of one of the greatest natural transportation systems anywhere in the world. Some five hundred million tons of goods pass through the Port of South Louisiana at the river's southern terminus every year and the Mississippi River Basin, which stretches from Montana to western Pennsylvania and New Mexico to North Carolina, produces more than ninety percent of the nation's agricultural exports. Without the Mississippi, the United States would be a very different country.

The rain had stopped but the sky was still leaden and the air damp as we walked around a nearly deserted downtown Vicksburg. Perhaps it was because I was tired from the stress of the morning's drive, or maybe because it was a Sunday and the weather gloomy, but the town, even with its rich Civil War history, seemed forlorn. With all the delays caused by the heavy rain and the felled trees it was already late in the afternoon and we still had a ninety-minute drive down Highway 61 to get to Natchez where we were spending the night. We didn't linger long in Vicksburg.

---

* The great arch on the riverfront in St. Louis is called the Gateway Arch because it is the gateway to the West.

Natchez was prettier and seemed more prosperous than Vicksburg, and there were beautiful views of the river from a park across from our hotel. After we'd had a walk, we drove down to a landing along the river where a cluster of restaurants and bars hugged the river bank. It had turned into a clear, sun-drenched evening. Albie and I enjoyed a takeout salad from one of the restaurants (I shared the chicken strips in the salad with him; he's not a big fan of lettuce) and watched the barges making their way along the river. In the background was a bridge connecting Natchez to Vidalia, Louisiana, and as the sun dipped farther toward the horizon the whole scene was infused with a rich, golden light. At river level you can use your imagination and take the river south to New Orleans, where we were headed, or north up past Memphis, St. Louis, and Minneapolis, or board a raft with Huck Finn and Tom Sawyer.

My mind was on New Orleans. We were north, but about seventy miles west, of the city. In the morning we'd get back on Highway 61 and travel southeast to the Big Easy, a city I first visited when my older son, Dan, went off to college at Tulane in 2009 and where he lives today. We'd been driving every day now for more than a week. In New Orleans we'd slow it down, stay for three nights, and breathe the jasmine-scented air.

PART TWO

To There . . .

SEVEN

Do You Know What It Means to Miss New Orleans?

I first fell in love with New Orleans while walking along the waterfront in Portland, Maine, during the summer of 2005. From somewhere in the distance, the strains of live music floated on the breeze and I followed my ears until I rounded the corner of a cobblestone street. There, a large crowd was listening to three black musicians, a solid woman on clarinet and vocals and two men, one on tuba and one playing rhythm guitar. The woman's voice rivaled that of great jazz singers, such as Ella Fitzgerald and Sarah Vaughn. And the sound she coaxed out of her clarinet was ethereal, like nothing I'd ever heard before.

When they took a break I approached the woman, clearly the star of the show, and bought one of the CDs she had for sale. She told me she was from New Orleans and was spending part of the summer busking in small New England cities from Burlington, Vermont, to Portland and would soon be heading home. Her name was Doreen Ketchens, and the tuba player was her husband, Lawrence.

A few weeks later Hurricane Katrina devastated New Orleans. I'd never set foot in the city. As desperate, heartbreaking scenes unfolded on TV, I thought of Doreen and Lawrence and wondered how they had fared in the storm. When disasters like this happen, I try and help in my own modest way locally rather than giving to a large relief organization with high overhead. Doreen was the only person I knew (and barely at that) who lived in New Orleans. The small print on the CD I'd purchased from her a few weeks before had an e-mail address, so I wrote her, reminded her that we'd met in Portland a few weeks before, and asked if she was OK. To my surprise and relief, a reply came a few days later. Their house was damaged, Doreen wrote, but they were OK. I asked for her mailing address and sent a small check to help with the repairs.

Four years passed. In 2009, our son Dan was accepted at Tulane University and Judy and I were planning to take him down for an admitted students' day. I thought of Doreen and e-mailed her again, reminded her that we'd met in Portland a few years before, and told her we'd be visiting New Orleans.

"We play regularly at the corner of St. Peter and Royal Streets in the French Quarter," she wrote me. So, on my first-ever trip to New Orleans we found Doreen and Lawrence and became reacquainted. Dan attended Tulane, and for the next four years, whenever we visited, which was often, we made a point of finding Doreen at the corner of St. Peter and Royal.

Dan graduated, moved back to Boston for four years, and earned his MBA at Boston College. In 2017, he returned to live in the city that he, and we, had come to love during his college years. When we made our first visit after his return, during Christmas week of 2017, we again beat a path to the corner of St. Peter and Royal and there was Doreen, bundled up on a cold day, belting out songs and drawing a big, appreciative crowd. Some things never change.

As always, I reintroduced myself as "Peter from Boston," to help her remember because she meets a lot of people. When I dropped a twenty-dollar bill in her white plastic bucket, she insisted on giving me a copy of her new CD. She adamantly refused more money. "You have to learn how to receive," she said, scolding me gently.

Doreen's love of music is rooted in her Tremé childhood. The Tremé, as it's called—always *the* Tremé—is the cultural heart of New Orleans's black community. Jazz, the blues, gospel, soul, rock and roll, and even rap all have their own roots in this neighborhood just north of the French Quarter.

Enslaved people in New Orleans enjoyed an unusual "luxury": Sundays off to attend church. After church they gathered in Congo Square in the Tremé where they danced, sang, and played music. The enslaved themselves hailed from many different places throughout Africa and the Caribbean. In Congo Square they swapped, shared, and blended their musical traditions with Creoles and free people of color, and new musical forms were born.

So many musical greats have come out of New Orleans it's hard to keep track: Louis Armstrong, Wynton Marsalis, Mahalia Jackson, Fats Domino, Dr. John (Malcolm Rebennack), and the Neville Brothers, just to name just a few. Though little-known outside New Orleans, Doreen, also known as Lady Louis (for a style that reflects Armstrong's) and Queen Clarinet of the

Crescent City,* is well-known within it. She belongs in that remarkable pantheon of New Orleans's musical greats, and she is one of the many unique characters that make New Orleans such an effervescent joy.

A few years back, Doreen told me there were three funeral homes on the street where she grew up and since traditional New Orleans "jazz" funerals feature so-called "second lines," lively musical parades that follow the funeral procession, second line music became part of the soundtrack of her early years. Her parents owned a sweet shop with a jukebox and she frequently sang along. She discovered the clarinet in fifth grade when she impulsively joined the school band to escape a pop quiz in history class. By the time she got to select an instrument all the flutes she admired were taken, so she settled for the clarinet and discovered she had a natural talent for it. "It's by the grace of God that I stumbled on the clarinet," she once wrote me.

Living in a home that was slowly rebuilt after Hurricane Katrina, Doreen is emblematic of the grit and determination of the New Orleanians who refused to let the music, and the city, die.

So, over the years I came to love New Orleans—the spirit, the people, the food, the music, the architecture, the gardens, and the charming, boisterous disorderliness of it all. It isn't just a city I look forward to revisiting, it's a city I *yearn* to return to over and over and over again. I do know what it means, as the song goes, to miss New Orleans.

---

* Better known as the Big Easy, New Orleans is also called the Crescent City because of the way the Mississippi River arcs around the city.

Since Dan was now making his life there, I was excited the morning Albie and I woke up in Natchez because later that day we would arrive in the Big Easy, take a three-night break from the road, and wander the streets of the city our family had come to love. Though we'd only been on the road a week, I was also looking forward to being in what had become, over the years, familiar territory, a bit of home away from home. I knew where to get my coffee (French Truck on Dryades or Rue de la Course on Carrollton), who had the best almond croissant (La Boulangerie on Magazine), and where to take a beautiful walk (the quiet streets of the Garden District or the loop path in Audubon Park).

It was a picture-perfect day in the southland as we rejoined Highway 61 in Natchez, the road we'd taken from Vicksburg and would follow all the way into New Orleans.[*] The New Orleans playlist on the car stereo was getting me in the mood.

As we drove from Mississippi into Louisiana, it occurred to me that other than barking at a Golden Retriever puppy we'd passed on a walking path in Maryville, Tennessee, Albie hadn't barked at all since we'd left home. He didn't bark when a loud group of partiers gathered in the hallway outside our hotel room in Tupelo at 2:00 A.M., and he hadn't barked at any of the other dogs we'd passed on our many walks. At home he barks at everyone who approaches the house and, to my chagrin, at many dogs we pass while walking. He barks at Salina

---

[*] This is the highway that inspired Bob Dylan's sixth studio album, *Highway 61 Revisited*. The southern portion of the highway passes through country that gave rise to many of the nation's most influential blues musicians. The great blues singer Bessie Smith was killed in a car accident on this highway in Clarksdale, Mississippi, in 1937.

in the morning when it's time for breakfast, or when he feels she's getting too much attention at his expense. But he'd been uncharacteristically quiet all week. Was it because he no longer had territory to defend? No one to compete with for my attention and affection? There was no way to know but I appreciated the quiet and the more mellow demeanor he had brought with him on the road. I hoped it would last.

Maybe it's because he was our first dog, or because there's something especially soulful and vulnerable about him, or because he had the hardest life of our three rescues before finding a home with us, but I have a little something extra in my tank for Albie. Don't get me wrong; I love them all dearly, but Albie pushes my buttons, all the good ones, every time. I never imagined taking this trip with either of the other two. It was always going to be Albie and me.

A few years ago, while in Louisiana working on my book *Rescue Road*, I had a free weekend and drove from Alexandria to St. Francisville, a small town in the heart of Audubon country I'd read about in the travel section of the *New York Times*. John James Audubon, the great naturalist and painter who created the legendary and lavishly illustrated book *The Birds of America* in the early 1800s, did most of his work and extraordinary painting while living in this part of Louisiana, south of the Mississippi border and about twenty-five miles north of Baton Rouge.

St. Francisville is a small Mississippi River town of well-tended houses and gardens, and many galleries and boutiques. It's a lovely place to take a stroll—some say it's the state's most beautiful town—so about an hour after leaving Natchez we stopped there.

There are parts of Louisiana, St. Francisville being one of them, that drip with Old World atmosphere. Even the street names are evocative. We parked at the corner of Royal and Prosperity Streets and wandered into the large burial ground surrounding the Grace Episcopal Church.* Spanish moss hung from the massive live oaks and a black man in green work clothes and a hat draped with mosquito netting, the caretaker I presumed, poked gently at the ground with a rake. He saw us but did not acknowledge us. Elaborate wrought iron fencing enclosed the cemetery, and the sound of a thousand crickets filled the languid, humid air. And the smell: moist, fecund, and fragrant. Many of the lichen-tinged headstones dated to the early 1800s. The scene before us was both mysterious and inviting, and unmistakably Louisiana.

To say Highway 61 between St. Francisville and New Orleans isn't scenic would be a spectacular understatement, and it was particularly dreadful as we made our way through Baton Rouge. The seemingly endless stretch of horrifyingly ugly streetscape was littered with every conceivable blight of our consumer culture: mile after mile of fast-food restaurants, chain stores, tire and auto parts stores, all plunked down with absolutely no regard for aesthetics. We've all seen these stretches of highway; they're a common feature of the American landscape that has grown like kudzu to accommodate the consumer needs of a country whose population has nearly doubled since Steinbeck's travels with Charley.

---

* Many street names in New Orleans are also part of that city's charm. For example, there are streets named Constance, Desire, Felicity, Harmony, and Annunciation.

As we drove this nightmarish stretch of highway, hitting stop-lights every quarter mile or so, I became preoccupied with the fate of a man named Gordon McKernan. Nearly every mile or two for many dozens of miles there was a huge billboard with a picture of a nice-looking middle-aged man and his name, Gordon McKernan, in big letters. The billboards were very simple. One said: "Gordon McKernan. Injured?" At the bottom was a phone number. Nothing else. Just the name, the phone number, and a question. "Gordon McKernan. Car Wreck?" "Gordon McKernan. Big Truck Accident?"

Apparently, something terrible had happened to Gordon McKernan, but no one seemed to know what. By the time we pulled into the parking lot of the Household of Faith in Gonzales, fifty miles north of New Orleans, so I could make some notes, there'd been dozens of billboards pleading for information about the fate of poor Gordon McKernan. How long had he been missing? Why didn't anyone know what had happened to him? His family must have been beside themselves. At least every motorist in this part of Louisiana, bombarded with these billboards, knew who to look for.

As we approached the New Orleans airport there was another billboard with a large picture of another fellow with a huge smile named Mike Branden. "Have a wreck? Need a check?" Mike was holding a facsimile of huge check about three times the size of his head that said "check" on it, just so it was clear he wasn't waving around a meaningless piece of paper. Mike was identified as "attorney at law." Wow, I thought, if Gordon McKernan ever surfaces he needs to connect with Mike!

As all of this was tumbling around in my head I realized that after more than a week of driving, a little break from the road was sorely needed. I was constructing elaborate fantasies based on billboards to keep myself occupied. A few days in New Orleans would be just what the doctor, or a personal injury lawyer, would have ordered.

Laissez le bon temps rouler! Let the good times roll! No city in America celebrates life, and living in the moment, more lavishly, more spontaneously, and more regularly, than New Orleans. Why? One reason is that the specter of death is never far away.

Half the city is below sea level. There are places in New Orleans where you can watch large freighters on the other side of the levee making their way along the lower Mississippi and the ship's hull is *above* you. Surrounded on three sides by the Mississippi and one by Lake Pontchartrain, which is actually an ocean bay, New Orleans lives life ever on the edge of catastrophe. Those chickens came home to roost in 2005 when the levees broke, and the water came pouring in. That sense of vulnerability makes life worth celebrating every day because any day could be your last.

The fragile line between life and death is also the ethos of the second line parade, the parades Doreen Ketchens watched as a child. Musicians and dancers, and anyone else who feels like joining in, follow the hearse and the mourners in a jazz funeral. There but for the grace of God, that could be me riding in the hearse to my heavenly reward, so why not dance in the streets today? And because the water table is so high, people aren't buried in the ground in New Orleans, but in crypts above

---

* Neither the river nor the lake overflowed their banks: it was the failure of key levees that caused New Orleans to flood. *The Great Deluge: Hurricane Katrina, New Orleans and the Mississippi Gulf Coast* by the great historian David Brinkley (Harper Perennial, 2007) is an extraordinary account of Katrina.

it. This makes the cemeteries more visible, a constant reminder of life's impermanence.

There's a certain sense of . . . well, not quite chaos . . . but joyous disorderliness about New Orleans, and I'm not talking about the public drunkenness on display every day on Bourbon Street. Streets are routinely closed without notice for a couple of hours when a local community parade breaks out. Police officers can sometimes be seen partying while on duty during one of the countless festivals that dot the New Orleans calendar, *Mardi Gras*, of course, being the most famous. It's been said that you shouldn't think of New Orleans as the worst organized city in the United States, but as the best organized city in the Caribbean.

Few cities are as atmospheric as New Orleans, or as exotic, the result of a mixture of French, Spanish, and Caribbean influences. The iconic streetcars that ply St. Charles Avenue under live oaks draped in Spanish moss, the ever-present sound of music, mostly jazz, riding gently on the breeze, the smell of jasmine and honeysuckle wafting in the air—New Orleans has a soundtrack and a fragrance all its own, and it's all very intoxicating.

We arrived early in the afternoon and went directly to Audubon Park, across St. Charles Avenue from Tulane University, to take a good, long walk on the oval path that winds through the park and under the oaks. As soon as we got out of the car, Albie broke his self-imposed silence of the past several days by giving a little pug what for. In fairness, the pug barked at him first. A few minutes later he barked at some ducks in a pond, but in fairness they quacked at him first, too. This was the Albie I knew at home.

Danny met us after we'd checked into our hotel on St. Charles Avenue. We took Albie to get a po'boy at the Bayou Beer Garden and later to the pottery studio where Danny takes classes. Albie charmed everyone there; he was on his best behavior once more and endeared himself to all the potters by offering up his paw and not breaking any of their work.

Judy and I had last been in New Orleans just a few months earlier, around Christmas, but now the spring had brought forth the honeysuckle and the magnolias and I learned all over again why I yearn for New Orleans. As we drove down St. Charles Avenue Danny looked around as a streetcar passed, its bell clanging. "It never gets old," he said. No, it most definitely does not.

New Orleans was the last place Steinbeck wrote about in any depth in *Travels with Charley,* and he left the city deeply troubled by what he'd seen there. He watched in horror as a small group of white women, known as "the Cheerleaders," arrived at a local school at the beginning and end of each school day to harass and heap verbal abuse on "tiny Negro children" attending a predominantly white school. It was, he wrote, "cruel and obscene." The Cheerleaders attracted the attention of local television news, which was in its infancy back then. Thus amplified, the entire spectacle attracted a mob that egged the Cheerleaders on to new heights, or lows. The frenzy fed on itself.

Growing up in Salinas, Steinbeck wrote, he had known only one black family, the Coopers, who were widely respected in the community. By the time he was an adult he was "perhaps too far grown to reform the inflexible habits of childhood. . . . Thus it remains that I am basically unfitted to take sides in the racial conflict."

---

* Remember that Steinbeck was near the end of his trip when he reached New Orleans; we were toward the beginning of ours.

"Beyond my failings as a racist," he wrote of witnessing the Cheerleaders, "I knew I was not wanted in the South. When people are engaged in something they are not proud of, they do not welcome witnesses."*

"But there was something far worse here than dirt," he continued, "a kind of frightening witches' Sabbath. Here was no spontaneous cry of anger, of insane rage. Perhaps that is what made me sick with weary nausea. . . . Theirs was the demented cruelty of egocentric children, and somehow this made their insensate beastliness much more heartbreaking. . . . It would be difficult to explain to a dog the good and moral purpose of a thousand humans gathered to curse one tiny human."

"[I] knew something was wrong and distorted and out of drawing," he wrote. "I knew New Orleans, I have over the years had many friends there, thoughtful, gentle people, with a tradition of kindness and courtesy."

Steinbeck lamented that the Cheerleaders were now misrepresenting New Orleans to the world. His disgust at what he witnessed, plus a racist earful he got from a hitchhiker near Jackson, Mississippi (and whom he evicted from *Rocinante* shortly thereafter), about "niggers," "nigger lovers," and "commies," seemed to drain his spirit and spell the end of his journey. He made a beeline for home, barely able to recall anything about the trip from that point on.

When I sat down with 79-year-old JoAnn Clevenger in the dining room of her famed restaurant, Upperline, on our second

---

* Steinbeck's reference to his "failings as a racist" is ambiguous. I don't think he was confessing that being a racist was one of his failings. Rather, he was saying that since he failed to be a racist he was not welcome in the South.

day in New Orleans, she remembered the Cheerleaders clearly. She was about 20 then and had only been in New Orleans for a few years.

"That period in New Orleans was short-lived," she told me. "Television amplified what they were doing, and it became drama for the sake of drama. TV kept it going and blew it into a bigger thing."

JoAnn, like Albie, hails originally from Alexandria, Louisiana, and came to New Orleans when she was seventeen. Her demeanor ranges from bemused to perpetually delighted—by people, by New Orleans, by life, and by her work. She called to mind Ruth Gordon's title character in the 1971 film *Harold and Maude*.

She was attired in her trademark black-and-red dress (she has many); her hair, as always, was swept up in a stylish bun. She looks at the world through round, horn-rimmed glasses and her Bohemian spirit is evident in her conversation and the eclectic art collection that adorns the walls, mostly paintings that capture the diversity and exuberant spirit of her adopted city. JoAnn epitomizes the city itself—indomitable, spirited, resilient, full of life, and utterly original.

When she was a teenager her mother fell ill. Physicians at Tulane Medical School, which has long had one of the nation's preeminent tropical medicine departments, diagnosed her with a rare tropical illness that required long-term hospitalization. JoAnn moved into her mother's hospital room to care for her at night and took the streetcar to high school during the day. At a downtown cafeteria she had her first epiphany about food.

"That's where I first saw shrimp remoulade served over iceberg lettuce," JoAnn told me as if remembering for the first time. "I never knew you could eat shrimp that weren't fried!"

Despite living in a hospital room and caring for her mother, JoAnn was a National Merit finalist and won a scholarship to Tulane, where she began studying electrical engineering before switching to the business school. But her mother died her freshman year and she dropped out to take a job as an assistant medical librarian. Before long she succumbed to what she calls "Big Easy Syndrome."

"Big Easy Syndrome allowed me to flourish with no money and no education," she told me. "It lets people's creativity bubble up. Everyone has creative potential but for so many, survival takes precedence. But in New Orleans, with its ease of spirit, people have time for creativity whether its music, art, or food."

"What is the source of creativity in New Orleans?" she asked rhetorically. Then she reinforced what I and many others have observed about the city's zest for life. "It's death. Cemeteries are everywhere here, and they are visible because they are aboveground. You can't avoid mortality here, so live today! Life isn't a dress rehearsal, so reinvent yourself a little bit at a time every day."

JoAnn has reinvented herself many times over in the years since high school. She sold cut flowers and successfully organized flower sellers who the licensed florists were trying to drive out of business. As a young mother she worked as a cocktail waitress on the overnight shift at King's Room on Iberville Street in the French Quarter. She'd come home, get her children off to school, and return to King's to do the payroll and the banking and order supplies, experience that would serve her well years later when she opened Upperline. She had a costume shop and designed and made costumes for the musical *One Mo' Time* which was performed around the world. In the late 1960s, she opened a music club on Bourbon Street named Andy's. Many famous performers came just to hang out and occasionally do a number or two, including Joni Mitchell, Phil Ochs, Richie Havens, and The Band. She opened a bar called The Abbey, still around, though she sold it decades ago.

"The most wonderful part of life in New Orleans is that people who are very different from one another all rub shoulders here," she said. "It makes us more complex and more joyful. We have all these divisions of wealth, race, religion, gay, straight, but still we all rub shoulders." Though New Orleans has had its share of racial strife (witness the Cheerleaders that so appalled Steinbeck) and Jim Crow laws, it has generally been more harmonious and less racially explosive than many other cities, perhaps because of its pervasive, easygoing, laissez-faire ethos.

"The businessmen, the maids, and the gardeners all rode the same streetcar together," JoAnn told me, "and black and white neighborhoods are typically just a few blocks from each other." She believes familiarity, far from breeding contempt, breeds tolerance and acceptance. To illustrate she told me a story.

Several years ago, she had a party of proper "country club types" in Upperline—the husband was wearing a plaid sports jacket, she recalled—and she sat a couple at the table next to them—"punk types." The man was sporting a Mohawk haircut. When the plaid-jacketed gentleman discreetly complained, JoAnn said, "Just wait. See what happens." (JoAnn is ever present in the dining room; she is your hostess and attends to everyone and makes introductions when she senses it's appropriate.)

"The punk couple were perfect guests," she told me. "As the gentleman was leaving he said to me, 'I learned something this evening about not judging people by the way they look,' and he thanked me!" She pulled herself upright in her chair and an impish, delighted smile flashed across her face.

She opened Upperline in 1983, without enough money to meet the first week's payroll. At the time, her Uptown neighbors wanted her to have a formal dress code, thinking it would ensure a better class of clientele. JoAnn refused. She wanted everyone to know they were welcome at Upperline. To send that message, JoAnn also broke with what had, intentionally or not, become an unwritten rule at New Orleans restaurants—that waitstaff was either all black or all white. She always wanted to have black and white employees working at the "front of house," as they say in the business. "It sets a tone of acceptance," she told me. "So, Upperline has in its own way been a social experiment. Our waitstaff is black and white, gay and straight. I wish we had more women, though."

JoAnn also believes in cultivating and bettering the lives of her employees and takes joy in the fact that Upperline has been part of their life journeys, wherever they lead. The bartender, Gerard Crosby, is African American and started working at Upperline twenty-four years ago as a dishwasher when he had just turned seventeen and was still in high school. Now she trusts him to run the place when she's not there. One of the head chefs, Kenny, became a Catholic priest. In its nearly forty years, there have only been five head chefs at Upperline, astonishingly low turnover in a business known for it. JoAnn keeps at least one item developed by each of them on the menu at all times, her way of honoring their contributions to her success. She has twice been a James Beard Award finalist, and Upperline was named New Orleans's best restaurant in 2017 by the *New Orleans Times-Picayune*.

Toward the end of our conversation JoAnn showed me a framed menu from October 19, 2005, the day Upperline reopened about two months after Hurricane Katrina. Every such reopening marked another tiny step back toward normalcy for the devastated city.

"We had only four people working that day," she told me. "My son came in from St. Louis and my husband, who was in London, came back to help. We had to scrape the goo off the floors. But having the restaurant open with white table linens gave people a sense of hope that the past could be re-created and maybe even be made better. One customer remarked that this must have been what it was like in London after the Blitz, when a little civility gave people hope and courage. It's like spring following winter. Renewal.

"There have been a lot of positive changes that came after Katrina," she went on. "Maybe not enough to make up for the negative, but many young professionals came to be a part of New Orleans's rebirth. So many people feel they can't change the world, but after Katrina there was the promise that you could make a difference. Just the idea that you might be able to change things is uplifting."

JoAnn pointed out that the word "restaurant" comes from the French verb *restaurer*, which means "to restore or refresh." For JoAnn that means both creating an atmosphere that will refresh her customers at the end of a long day and doing what she can to restore and refresh the world.

"Restaurants were originally more than just a place to find a meal," she has written, "they existed to soothe and bolster the weary soul with comfort and indulgence. My goal with the Upperline is to be just that, a haven for our guests: to help restore their serenity with great Louisiana food and wine, and of course hospitality."

"New Orleans has that *joie de vivre*," she said as our conversation started to wind own. She practically bounced out of her chair. "It's the clang of the streetcar, the foghorns of the tug-boats on the river, and the sound of the trains rumbling down Tchoupitoulos Street; the smell of olive trees in winter, jasmine in spring, and the coffee roasters all year!" She seemed not so much to be describing these things but *experiencing* them as she spoke.

Before we wrapped up I told JoAnn the story, in brief, of my great-grandaunt Annie, the 'round the world cyclist of the 1890s. They seemed to be kindred spirits—enterprising, larger-than-life women, women ahead of their times, who reinvented themselves and lived lives undaunted by the obstacles that prevent so many from realizing their dreams. JoAnn was utterly capti-vated by the idea of a woman in the 1890s gallivanting around the world on a bicycle, so I promised to have Danny deliver a copy of my book about Annie to her. The fitness center Danny manages and co-owns in Uptown New Orleans is immediately around the corner from Upperline, and he and JoAnn had been working together with the city to resolve some parking issues. That's why Danny was able to arrange our meeting. JoAnn had become quite fond of him and appreciative of his efforts. They see each other all the time now.

The next evening Danny and I had dinner at Upperline while friends of his, Quinn and Danielle, watched Albie, one of the few times we were apart, even for a moment, during our six-week trip. Having dinner at Upperline allowed me to watch JoAnn work her magic as she presided with grace and charm and gentle good humor over her dining room.

After dinner we met up with Quinn and Danielle and Albie at the Creole Creamery, my favorite New Orleans spot for ice cream, just a hundred yards or so from Upperline. Then we walked over to introduce Albie to JoAnn, a fellow good soul from Alexandria, Louisiana. Again, JoAnn's perpetual delight was very much in evidence and she gave Albie, as she had me the day before, her undivided attention. She's *very* present when she talks to you.

I suspect everyone who meets JoAnn comes away with a similar feeling: I could have talked to her for hours on end and felt fortunate to have spent time in her presence. She has poured herself into New Orleans and New Orleans has poured itself into her. Like Doreen Ketchens, she's a New Orleans original.

And like an evening at Upperline, our three-night layover in New Orleans was restorative and gave me renewed energy and enthusiasm for what lay down the road. We did laundry and had the car washed and vacuumed so we could start, as JoAnn might say, refreshed. But mostly, we just walked the streets of the Uptown and Garden District neighborhoods and met many of the people—friends, neighbors, members of the gym he runs—who populate Danny's world in the city.

With so much walking, by the end of the day Albie was pretty tuckered out. The arthritis in his front legs has gradually worsened over the past year or so, and though he is still capable of giving a squirrel a good chase, he was a little stiffer than he had been just a few months earlier. Back at our hotel that last night in New Orleans, I stroked his head and his face, showered him with little kisses and whispered sweet nothings in his ear.

"You're the best guy, Albie," I said. "Thanks for coming with me."

There is something especially poignant about loving a rescue dog, a dog once lost, abandoned, abused, or neglected and now found. They put their complete faith and trust in you, and you need to be worthy of it.

Perhaps our last night in New Orleans was especially tender because our next stop, just a couple of hours to the northwest, was going to be Alexandria, where Albie had survived five months in a high-kill shelter until he came to live with us in Massachusetts. Tomorrow we would have our much-anticipated reunion with Krista Lombardo and Keri Toth, the two women most responsible for saving Albie's life. Krista is the volunteer at the shelter who took a shine to Albie and kept buying him time until Keri, then a volunteer with Labs4rescue, could find him a home, *our home*, as it turned out.

Because Krista still volunteers at the shelter and it was her day to be there, we agreed to meet on the grounds outside, but I was wary. Would Albie remember the place, especially the distinctive smells of the shelter, and think I'd brought him there to return him? (When in doubt, I almost always go directly to the worst possible scenario, whatever the issue.) What would it be like for *me* to be back at this shelter, which I had visited a couple of years after we adopted Albie while working on *Rescue Road*? It had been deeply upsetting to see so many dogs like Albie confined in Spartan cages, especially knowing that most of them would be dead within a week. Imagining Albie there with death all around him and little to do but lie on a concrete floor day after day had been almost too much to bear. Now, we were less than twenty-four hours away from returning to this place *together*.

But I wanted Krista and Keri to see Albie again and to thank them, as I had before, for all they had done to make Albie's life with us, and the journey we were on, possible, and meeting at the shelter was the most convenient place for them. Rescue work is tough, physically and emotionally. People like Krista and Keri see a lot of suffering and death, and for every dog whose story has a happy ending, there are countless others whose stories end badly. There are millions of dogs like Albie, especially in the South where the overpopulation problem is most acute, and those that luck out and find their way into an adoption program mostly find homes up North. So, Krista and Keri, two people who have cared for and saved thousands of dogs, rarely, if ever, see those dogs again. Reuniting them with Albie, even if just for an hour, was something I'd been determined to do since the idea for this trip first popped into my head. So, our last night in New Orleans, anticipating the next day's reunion, was especially bittersweet.

Before getting back on the road the next morning we stopped at French Truck Coffee on Dryades Street. French Truck is one of those hip, funky java saloons where they sling gourmet coffee, pastries, and other sundries and is frequented by millennials with earbuds in, laptops up, and seemingly endless free time on their hands. I love these places, and I'm usually the oldest person in them by about thirty years.

Dogs aren't allowed inside and since it was raining the patio wasn't an option. Albie waited for me in the car. Standing in line I looked behind me and saw the distinctive, familiar face of a man I'd never met. Mitch Landrieu was in the final weeks of his second and, by law, last term as mayor of New Orleans and there he was, waiting in line like everyone else and chatting easily with other customers.

After the violence in Charlottesville in August 2017 that led to soul-searching in many southern cities and towns, Landrieu gave a powerful, deeply thoughtful and historically literate speech explaining why he had decided to order the removal of the city's Confederate monuments. It was a controversial decision, but Landrieu's speech, which I'd watched, led to speculation that he might make a viable presidential candidate, a southern moderate who could have wide appeal.

He seemed utterly approachable, so I introduced myself. He had none of the false, glad-handing, made-for-TV polish so many politicians exude. He seemed like a regular guy—affable, genuine, and unassuming. I told him my son had gone to Tulane and settled in the city and about my trip with Albie.

"Cool!" said the Mayor. "I'd love to do that myself someday. Get a little Mississippi red clay under my feet!"

He seemed delighted by our adventure and asked me several questions about it.

"Are you married?"

I said I was.

"And your wife is OK with you being away for six weeks?"

As I did to many people along the way, I told him, "My wife has been suspiciously supportive of the trip," and he laughed.

I told him every morning when I woke up and surveyed the damage the current president was doing to the country I was deeply dismayed.

"You *should* be dismayed," he said, nodding in agreement.

"So, are you going to run for president?"

"Oh, I don't think so," he said shaking his head slightly and smiling. "But there will be a lot of good candidates who will, and there are a lot of ways to change the country."

I didn't expect him to announce his political plans to a stranger in a coffee shop, but we'll see.

At last, it was time to head up to Alexandria for our reunion with Krista and Keri. To get there we would be deviating from Steinbeck's route. Steinbeck, as he made his way *east* toward the end of his trip, traveled from Amarillo down through Austin and Beaumont, Texas (east of Houston), and then across southern Louisiana to New Orleans. Our route, on the *westbound* portion of *our* journey, would take us from New Orleans up through Alexandria and Natchitoches (pronounced "knack-uh-dish") in central and northwest Louisiana, respectively, to Paris, Texas, and then to Okemah, Oklahoma, before rejoining Steinbeck's trail in Amarillo.

The reunion with Krista and Keri was one reason for this deviation, but there was another, which was also quite important to me. I didn't have a long list of "must-dos" for this trip, but one was to visit Okemah, the birthplace and hometown of one of my lifelong heroes, the folksinger, songwriter, and social activist Woody Guthrie. And if one were traveling to Okemah from New Orleans, Alexandria was right on the way. It all made sense. And so, there we were, on the road again, with The Big Easy disappearing in the rearview mirror

EIGHT

Every Dog Will Have His Day*

Albie's is the story of countless dogs across large swaths of the southern United States. Hundreds of thousands of dogs enter shelters in the United States every year, and while the "kill" rate has been dropping nationally as rescue awareness has increased, at some shelters it remains horrifyingly high.

The Alexandria shelter, where we were now headed for our reunion with Krista and Keri, serves a human community of about 155,000 people. When we adopted Albie in 2012, the kill rate there was close to ninety percent. In 2013, for example, 3,499 dogs came into the shelter and 3,041 were "put down" (eighty-seven percent). By comparison, that same year, public shelters in the entire state of New Jersey, with a population of

---

* This familiar saying is also the title of a song by Procol Harum from the 2003 album, *The Well's on Fire*.

nine *million* people, impounded 33,538 dogs and put down 4,509 (thirteen percent). Fifty-seven times as many people though only ten times as many dogs impounded as in one small Louisiana parish, and a vastly lower kill rate.

Keri, a prolific dog rescuer, routinely pulls litters of puppies alive from Dumpsters in central Louisiana, disposed of by people who don't spay or neuter their dogs and simply throw unwanted puppies away. Houston, where I spent time while doing research for *Rescue Road*, has a stray dog population in the hundreds of thousands, according to city officials. Dogs, many malnourished and sick, wander the streets struggling to survive. It really is *that* bad.

Take a walk in New England or other parts of the Northeast and ask every dog owner you pass where their dog came from, and you will be amazed at how many will say, "Oh, he's a rescue from Tennessee," or Texas, Arkansas, Mississippi, Louisiana, or another southern state. Do the same down South and you will never hear, "Oh, she's a rescue from Vermont," or Massachusetts or Connecticut. That isn't to say there aren't stray dogs, or abandoned and abused dogs, everywhere, but in the United States the problem is heavily concentrated in the South. Why?

The answer is complicated. People often say the root of the problem is that spaying and neutering are not as common in the South. While true, it begs the question: why not? The problem has social, economic, and political dimensions. But as I traveled parts of the South—including central Louisiana and southeast Texas—to write *Rescue Road*, I concluded the problem is primarily a cultural one. This is a generalization, but a fair one: many people in the South simply don't value dogs, or live with them, as most people in other parts of the country do. Many dogs are obtained to serve a purpose—for protection or to hunt, for example—not to be companions. The notion that a dog should live *in* the house as opposed to outside is foreign to many, let alone sleep in the bed or sit with the family at dinnertime. It's a way of living with dogs that has persisted for generations and is hard to change. Many a Southerner told me, "this is the South and change comes very slowly here." The prevailing attitude toward dogs in parts of the South is captured in a phrase you often hear, "It's *just* a dog." *Just* a dog. I hasten to point out that most of the heroes of the canine rescue movement, those such as Keri Toth who work tirelessly and at great emotional and financial expense to save lives, are also Southerners. But there is no ducking the reality that the canine overpopulation problem is concentrated in the South.

So, my head this morning on our way to Alexandria was filled with thoughts of Albie, at the moment lying with his paws outstretched in the back seat with his head set down between them, and how he had to beat the longest imaginable odds to find his home with us, and gratitude to Krista and Keri and the countless other people, many whose names I will never know, who extended their hearts and hands to save Albie's life and help deliver him to us.*

---

* Some of them I do know. Cathy Mahle and Harvey Wiener of Labs4rescue, the rescue organization through which we adopted Albie; Greg (Cathy's brother) and Adella Mahle of Rescue Road Trips, which provided transportation; and the many "angels" who meet Greg's truck along the way every other week to help walk and care for the dogs. Greg was the central figure in *Rescue Road*. Every other week he leaves home in Ohio in a big rig to drive 4,500 miles to Texas and the Gulf Coast to pick up approximately eighty dogs saved by people such as Keri and deliver them to their "forever" families in the Northeast. In early July 2012, Albie was one of those lucky dogs on Greg's truck.

As we made our way across Interstate 10 and then north on Interstate 49 it quickly became clear that the mystery of Gordon McKernan had not been solved during our three days in New Orleans. And Gordon's fate, which I assumed was of interest only to people around Baton Rouge, seemed to be a statewide matter because the billboards continued every few miles all the way to Alexandria. In fact, they took on a new dimension, literally. As we got into central Louisiana, some of the billboards were three-dimensional, with a re-creation of the hood of a large semi protruding a few feet straight out. And there atop the hood, legs spread wide and facing forward with his arms pinned up against the truck windshield, was a 3-D replica of Gordon McKernan, bigger than life. It was terrifying. Maybe Gordon had been squashed like so many bugs on the windshield of a huge truck rumbling down a highway somewhere in Louisiana. Or, worse yet, maybe he was still hanging on for dear life. Near the Alexandria Airport was yet another billboard exactly like many of the others we'd seen with Gordon's name and picture and the words "Car Wreck?" on it. But on this one, inexplicably, Gordon was wearing dark-framed glasses, and an elaborate Western-style black handlebar moustache, both of which appeared to have been painted by an athletic graffiti artist. What was the message here? That Gordon might be alive but wearing a disguise? That he'd gone to ground? Who knew?*

---

* After we returned home I Googled Gordon McKernan and learned that his ubiquitous billboards are the source of a lot of talk and jokes in Louisiana. One local media outlet in Lafayette, WHOT Radio, ran a short piece on its website asking whether the glasses and moustache, which were popping up on McKernan's billboards all around the state, were the work of vandals or just clever marketing, a way to get people talking about them. The writer concluded it was the latter.

The mystery of Gordon McKernan was, on this morning, more than a way to occupy myself while passing time behind the wheel. It was a distraction from my concern about bringing Albie back to the shelter where he'd languished for five months. I started to wish I'd pressed harder for a different meeting place, but I wanted to make it as easy as possible for Krista and Keri and it was the logical spot.

There is nothing especially foreboding about the shelter from the outside. But knowing what goes on inside still unnerves me. When I walked past the kennels here just a few years ago, I saw many dogs who looked like Albie, dogs in chain-linked enclosures with soiled concrete floors and nothing to occupy their time, dogs that were desperate for a minute of my attention and strained to push their noses through the kennel bars so I could touch them. Most were never going to get out. I wanted to take them all home.

Keri and I pulled into the parking lot at the same time. We'd met several times since we adopted Albie. I'd spent a couple of days shadowing her as she went about her rescue work while researching *Rescue Road*, and she often travels from Louisiana to Rhode Island with a passel of dogs bound for adoption events in the state, and we'd met there, too. I'd also met Krista once before. Would Albie remember them and, if so, how would we know?

We quickly found Krista and she and Keri gave Albie lots of hugs and kisses. Watching Albie reunited with his saviors was one of the most emotional moments of the entire trip. Nothing betrayed his previous knowledge of them, however. He was happy for the attention, but there was none of the uncontrolled excitement you see on so many YouTube videos where a soldier, for example, is reunited with his dog after a two-year deployment. And he didn't seem to remember the *place*, either.

We took Albie to the small yard, which is enclosed by a chain-link fence, where Krista took his adoption photos (in which he was wearing a little green kerchief) and a short, thirty-second video that had us falling in love long before Albie ever walked through our front door. A couple of times a week, Krista would bring Albie here to play fetch and give him a break from his cage during the five months she kept getting him a reprieve from the death chamber.

Albie rolled over on his back and squirmed energetically on the grass, something he loves to do.

"His face is whiter, but he still has his playfulness," observed Keri. I told them about Albie's life at home, how he roughhouses with Salina, and about our life with three dogs now. (Keri played a role in our adoption of all three.) Then he found a stick to chew on and settled under a concrete table in the enclosure where it was shady.

As we were getting ready to leave and stood chatting in the parking area, Henry Wembley, the longtime shelter director, wandered over to join us. We had circled each other warily while I was writing *Rescue Road*. He grudgingly agreed to let me tour the shelter back then with Dr. Sara Kelley, another rescuer I spent time with when I was in the area, but he insisted she not take me to the death chamber.* Later, when I'd returned home and was writing, he reluctantly returned a message I'd left for him—I wanted to interview him for the book. But I

---

* "Euthanized" is the word typically used, but it sugarcoats the reality. Some dogs, to be sure, are euthanized either because they are sick or in pain or dangerously aggressive. But many more are killed simply because the shelters are overcapacity and more dogs come pouring in every day.

missed his call and was never able to get him to return my calls again. I had some less than flattering things to say about the shelter in *Rescue Road*, but on this day Henry Wembley seemed to have no idea who I was—at least he gave no indication that he remembered meeting me before—which was just as well. He simply expressed his pleasure that things had worked out so well for Albie.

To my surprise, he then invited us inside the shelter. I demurred. Just being outside was close enough. I didn't think I could bear the sight of dozens of caged dogs, forlorn and waiting, against all odds, for someone to step up and save them from extinction. It was hard enough when I was here a few years ago to imagine Albie in this place; there was no way I wanted to go back inside with him by my side. When you walk through a shelter the dogs typically become overexcited and the noise from all the barking can be deafening. Shelters are inherently stressful places for dogs, and I saw no point in putting Albie back in that environment, even for a minute. Any one of the hundred and fifty days or so that Albie spent in this shelter could easily have been his last. I'd seen enough last time around.

Shortly before we left, a familiar scene unfolded, one I'd seen at several shelters in the South before. A woman in a large black pick-up truck pulled up and surrendered two dogs to the shelter staff right there in the parking lot. Dogs surrendered by their owners often have a shorter lease on life than the strays picked up by animal control. They're not lost, and shelter staff know that no one is going to come looking for them. But, still, those may be the lucky ones. Many are simply let go to fend for themselves, abandoned on remote roads, or even shot.

The heartbreak people like Keri and Krista experience every day is what makes rescue work so difficult and hard to sustain. For every dog like Albie with a happy ending, there are countless others whose stories end with a heart stick* or in a gas chamber.

We stayed with Krista and Keri for about an hour and a half and then it was time to say goodbye. I'm so grateful to them for what they do in general, but eternally grateful for what they did for the sweet soul who obligingly climbed once again into the back seat.

Natchitoches is the oldest city in Louisiana and just fifty miles north of Alexandria. I was looking forward to returning there. It's a lovely town astride the Cane River. The heart of historic downtown is Front Street, which parallels the river and sits about twenty-five feet above it. The commercial buildings on Front Street look across the brick-paved street to the river; the views are unobstructed, for there are no buildings on the river side of the street. Most of the second stories have balconies lined with elaborate railings of wrought iron, giving it the look of a mini-French Quarter in New Orleans. The river bank has been turned into a beautifully planted park, with flower baskets hanging from the lamp posts.

I had traveled to Natchitoches while working on *Rescue Road* to meet the young man, CJ Nash, whose dog, Mia, had given birth to a litter of puppies, one of which, Salina, we adopted in 2014. Mia, like many southern dogs, lives outdoors and isn't spayed. The Nashes live about fifteen miles outside of

---

* A heart stick is an intra-cardiac lethal injection. A needle and syringe containing sodium pentobarbital is pounded through the chest wall into the dog's heart.

Natchitoches in a very remote, rural area. When the puppies were born, CJ's father told him to take them to the local pound, but CJ knew that was likely a death sentence. So, he reached out to a friend's mother, Rae McManus, who was involved in humane work and she, in turn, contacted Keri Toth. Thanks to them the puppies were saved and adopted.

Rarely can an adopter trace their dog's history with such specificity, and CJ would later become an unofficial part of our family, spending a summer in Boston with us, and we are in touch to this day. I had hoped CJ might be home from college while we were in Natchitoches, but he was otherwise committed so we missed each other.

After checking into our hotel, Albie and I headed into town to enjoy the evening by the river. A Cajun band was warming up in the bandstand on the riverfront; one of the sororities at Northwestern State University, located in town, was having an event.

We settled on an Italian restaurant with a patio overlooking the water for dinner. Since it was early we had the patio to ourselves. The evening was perfect, about seventy degrees with a gentle breeze and a cloudless sky. Our servers were two students from Northwestern State, a young woman and a young man she was training. We learned the young man was from Paris, Texas, tomorrow's destination. Knowing nothing about Paris I asked him what we should see and where we should eat.

"The best restaurant in Paris is a Mexican place," he said. "Dos Marias."

As to what we should see, there was a long pause, one that seemed prompted not by his inability to choose just one of Paris's many worthy attractions, but an inability to summon any at all. Finally, he said, "There's a replica of the Eiffel Tower . . . with a red cowboy hat on top."

❖

As the evening deepened the entire town took on a golden glow. We walked some of the residential streets with their charming houses and well-tended gardens and eventually wandered back to Front Street. As always, Albie made a few friends along the way, people who just wanted to give him a pat on the head or shake his paw. Perhaps because we had just been at the shelter a few hours before, my love and appreciation for him seemed to swell as I watched strangers fawn over him. It had been our mission for the past six years to turn his up-side-down world right-side-up and we had succeeded. As we walked back toward the river, I felt an intense sense of well-being, appreciating, not for the first time, just how precious he is.

By now the sorority party was in full swing, which meant the peace and quiet of the evening along the river was shattered. Separate from the party, loudspeakers affixed to the lamp posts all along Front Street were broadcasting rock music from a local radio station. Between the Cajun band and the competing radio music the din was pretty much intolerable. On my previous visit to Natchitoches I hadn't noticed the loudspeakers, but it was clear they were a permanent fixture. Why anyone would want to give a peaceful, quiet, and charming downtown the feel of a shopping mall I have no idea, but Natchitoches would not be the last town in this part of the country where we'd encounter this situation.

Forced from downtown by the noise, we drove to a local supermarket to buy a few things and watched the western sky turn purple, blue, and pink as the sun set. It was too early to go to bed, but there wasn't much else to do so we headed back to the hotel and some loneliness crept back into the journey. I tried calling Judy but got her voice mail, as was often the case. I left a short message about our day—about our reunion with Krista and Keri—and said we were going to bed and would talk tomorrow.

The previous three nights we'd been in New Orleans with Danny, having dinner together or with some of his friends, and meeting others along the way. We'd run into the parents of good friends from home who live in the city and talked an afternoon away with JoAnn Clevenger. We'd reconnected earlier in the day with Krista and Keri, two people both of us had known before. There were familiar faces and familiar places. Now, once again, it was just Albie and me, alone together, and about to head west all the way to California. Barring some odds-defying random encounter, we wouldn't see another soul we knew until we reached the Bay Area, where we planned to stay with Judy's brother, my brother-in-law Andy, and my sister-in-law Ceci for a few days. Until then Albie's would be the only familiar face I'd see.

On that night, feeling a bit lonely, having each other was all we really needed. Here in central Louisiana where you so often hear, "It's *just* a dog," Albie was proving there's nothing *just* about it. Being a dog is a fine thing to be, and maybe the best thing a being *can* be.

NINE

Texas Two-Step

Albie was up early, so we got started earlier than usual.

Natchitoches is such a pretty place, I wanted to go downtown one more time before we left. Having a coffee and sitting by the Cane River before getting back in the car seemed like a grand idea, provided the music had stopped. We were downtown a little before eight but, alas, the only coffee shop in town didn't open until ten, which was rather odd because there was a sign in the shop window that urged, "Start your day with coffee!" Well, I was *trying*.

With no coffee in hand, Albie and I strolled along Front Street for a while, then I took a seat on a bench by the river and watched the morning slip over Natchitoches. When Albie lies down, as he did next to me, he often assumes the position of the stone lions that grace the entrance to the New York City Public Library. His paws extend straight out, his neck is straight, and his head erect. He looks very regal and alert in that position. He remained like that for a few minutes, sighed, and then lay his head gently on the grass. Albie is so handsome; I could look at him all day.

Mercifully, the band that had been playing in the riverfront pavilion the night before had gone home, and the speakers mounted on the lamp posts had gone silent. Chirping birds and the muffled sound of car tires rolling over the brick-paved street up the riverbank behind us were all we could hear.

In a couple of hours we'd be in Texas, and just as I had wondered when North would become South earlier in the trip (and decided it was when we were driving on the Patsy Cline Highway near Front Royal, Virginia), I wondered when the Southeast would become the West. Probably, I thought, when we come to a replica of the Eiffel Tower with a red cowboy hat on top. As it turned out, we didn't have to wait that long.

"Oh, for God's sake," I said out loud. "Seriously?"

I don't make a habit of talking to myself. I'm just self-aware enough to know it makes me seem like I'm losing it. But Albie was asleep in the back seat, so I was, for all practical purposes, talking to myself.

I thought we'd buried Gordon McKernan yesterday. But there were three more of his billboards north of Natchitoches and six or eight or ten around Shreveport—so many I lost count. His face was a constant fixture wherever we went in Louisiana and I was really tired of seeing his mug everywhere. It felt as if Albie and I *and* Gordon had been traveling together since Baton Rouge. Of course, I'd known from the git-go he was a lawyer trolling the entire state of Louisiana for business. Now I was desperately hoping he wasn't a member of the Texas bar, too.

We stopped after a couple of hours in a small town to take a walk. I knew we were in Texas but didn't know where. As we walked along First Street a group of women came out of a shop and admired Albie, so I asked them, "Where are we?"

The woman who answered was tall and thin and, I'd guess, in her late seventies. Her hair was done up in a beehive and she was wearing flared pants the bright yellow color of French's mustard, a white blouse, and a yellow vest to match her pants. She looked like she was about to take the stage at the Grand Ole Opry in 1968.

"Why, this is Hughes Springs, honey!" she said with a twang. Since I was obviously clueless, she added, helpfully, "Texas!"

"And look at *you*! Aren't you just the sweetest thing." Perhaps it goes without saying, but she was talking to Albie.

As in Natchitoches, there were loudspeakers mounted on lamp posts along the street blaring music. Whoever the powers that be are in these towns, and whoever decides what radio station everyone has to listen to as they walk down the street, really ought to reconsider. It's Orwellian. And incredibly annoying. At least they were playing classic rock in Natchitoches. Here in Hughes Springs the only song I recognized was *"All My Ex's Live in Texas"*:

> *All my ex's live in Texas*
> *And Texas is the place I'd dearly love to be*
> *But all my ex's live in Texas*
> *And that's why I hang my hat in Tennessee*

If I had to listen to this music every time I went into town to run an errand, I'd probably live in Tennessee, too, or even Mogadishu.

We walked around a corner and saw a festival of some sort in progress, so we wandered over. There were carnival rides and vendors selling funnel cakes, cotton candy, and corn dogs (they really could have used a kiosk that dispensed Lipitor), and dozens of people selling crafts of one kind or another under portable tarps. One of them, an older woman selling knickknacks, greeted Albie, and I told her we were on a road trip from Boston.

"I didn't think you were from around here," she offered.

"Is it *that* obvious?" I asked.

"You sound like someone I knew from Michigan," she answered. "He played basketball."

I wasn't quite sure how to parry that *nonsequitur*, or what makes people sound like they're from Michigan, but she was kind and was enjoying petting Albie. The fair, she explained, was part of the Texas Wildflower Festival, an annual statewide celebration of the season when Texas's abundant roadside wildflowers bloom, a legacy of Lady Bird Johnson's highway beautification program in the 1960s. As we started to move on she had one more thing to say.

"Welcome to Texas! Drive safely. The truckers will run right over you!"

I had been surprised that the speed limit on the two-lane roads we'd been driving since entering Texas was a very speedy seventy miles per hour, and still there were plenty of trucks blowing right past us.

"If the speed limit is seventy," she added, "they'll be pushing eighty."

Like many parts of Texas, this corner northeast of Dallas is cattle country and between Hughes Springs and Paris we passed several ranches with gated entrances adorned with the name of the hacienda on top. It was all reminiscent of Southfork, the Texas ranch where the dysfunctional Ewing family plotted against one another in the 1980s television melodrama *Dallas*.

As we approached Paris that afternoon I kept scanning the horizon trying to glimpse this Eiffel Tower replica we'd heard about from our waiter in Natchitoches the night before. It was apparently the biggest tourist attraction, maybe the *only* tourist attraction in town. Surely, we would see it rising above the treetops, but all we saw were radio and cell phone towers and none were adorned with a red cowboy hat. Maybe, I thought, it's a ways out of town, or perhaps we're looking in the wrong direction, but we'd find it after checking into our hotel.

After we'd unpacked a few things and Albie had some water and a short walk, I looked up the Eiffel Tower on my iPhone. It was less than a ten-minute drive away so off we went to see the biggest thing in Paris. But even as Google Maps suggested we had arrived at our destination, there was no Eiffel Tower in sight. We were in a big, empty parking lot directly in front of the Paris Civic Center. Where in the world was this thing? Then, off to the side of the Civic Center, I saw it. It wasn't the biggest thing in Paris, after all.

Now, it would have been unrealistic to expect a *full-scale* replica of the Eiffel Tower, but something built a third or a quarter to scale wouldn't have been unreasonable. The real Eiffel Tower, the one in Paris, *France*, stands over one thousand feet tall and it is intricate and graceful and ornate. But there it was, all of seventy feet tall, *including* the hat, according to the website I perused as I stood there trying in vain to ascertain why this was such a big attraction. It looked like a slightly oversized jungle gym, or a regular-sized jungle gym for overachievers, built using a child's Erector set, just black piping assembled into a tower with a big red cowboy hat mounted at a jaunty angle on top. Yes, it was kind of shaped like the real Eiffel Tower, a splayed, arched base under a pointed spire, but all in all it was, to put it mildly, stupendously underwhelming. Albie seemed to think the whole thing was a gigantic fire hydrant.

To my utter astonishment, the website I was studying to get the dimensions of the thing offered this fascinating tidbit: "The average visitor spends one hour here."

Really? *An hour? A full sixty minutes?* This was harder to apprehend than the Lilliputian scale of the tower itself. What could one possibly do here for an hour? You can't climb it or swing from it or even find a nearby café from which to admire it. The red cowboy hat at the top doesn't even rotate or spray water or blink on and off. I can only imagine that for the "average visitor" the last fifty-nine minutes of the interminable hour they loiter here are spent in an embarrassed silence as they try to figure out why they spent any time at all finding the place.

We did *not* spend one hour at the Eiffel Tower; I'd have passed out from boredom. So, about five minutes after we arrived, we hopped back in the car to check out downtown Paris which would, hopefully, redeem our decision to spend an entire afternoon and evening here, hopes that were soon dashed.

There wasn't much happening in town. Actually, there was *nothing* happening in town. Empty and forlorn storefronts lined the streets; the only eatery in sight was a Subway sandwich shop on a corner in the main square. There *was* a lovely fountain in the square, and we took a seat on a nearby bench, but once again we were subjected to the bizarre practice, now firmly fixed in my head as a feature of southern towns, of being forced to listen to a radio station selected by persons unknown being played through loudspeakers mounted on lamp posts. At least the music was good: an all Beatles radio station. But between songs we had to listen to a fast-talking AM deejay prattle on about the weather and the discounts being offered at various car, RV, and motorcycle shops around town. Peace and quiet doesn't seem to be much in fashion in these towns. Once again, as in Tupelo and many other towns we'd passed through in the southland, there was the intolerable ear-splitting sounds of pickup trucks and aging muscle cars either without mufflers or modified to make the maximum racket, and drivers intent on burning as much rubber as humanly possible. This cacophony was quickly becoming the official soundtrack of East Texas, too: cars, pickups, and motorcycles competing to see who could be more disruptive of the civic peace and, once they had passed, the return of music being blared through public loudspeakers. It's a wonder anyone in these towns can hear anything anymore. Then again, maybe that's why they have to keep cranking up the volume, on the motor vehicles and the music; because no one *can* hear anymore. It's a vicious cycle.

What were people trying to say with all this noise? I recalled something Voz Vanelli, the restaurateur and raconteur I met in Tupelo, had told me. We were talking about how one bad review on social media can really hurt a business like his and how business owners can ill-afford to ignore such reviews. The few negative reviews he's had, he told me, were all written by men.

"For many of them," Voz told me, "writing a bad *Yelp* review is as much power as they have in their lives."

Maybe Voz was onto something, something that may explain the gnawing resentments and sense of displacement so manifest in our politics, especially among men in economically strug-gling towns, men who feel powerless, maybe even emasculated by their diminished circumstances. They are drawn to politicians who give voice to their anger, resentment, and grievances, especially someone who is willing, figuratively (or in our current circumstances, almost literally), to say "fuck you" to everyone they think is responsible for their plight. Maybe all this noise coming from their cars, pickups, and motorcycles is a primal scream of sorts that says, "Look at me; *pay attention to me.*"

When we'd had our fill of the Beatles, after Ringo had wrapped up his stirring rendition of "You're Sixteen," we went off in search of an afternoon treat. Among the shuttered and worn-out storefronts we found an open shop with a sandwich board out front that said, "Candy and Ice Cream." Perfect. Ice cream was what we were looking for.

The place was huge, about the size of a small banquet hall, and mostly empty save for a glass case housing some weary-looking pastries. We were the only customers (maybe not just at that moment but for several months or more), and it took a minute for a man, the proprietor I assumed, to make his way to the front from somewhere in back. He seemed indifferent to find customers in his store and greeted us with a distinct lack of enthusiasm.

"Hi," I said, "we'd like some ice cream, please," even though there was no ice cream anywhere in sight.

"Sorry, we don't have ice cream," he replied. Rather than point out that the big sign in front of his shop said, "Ice Cream," which he probably knew, I just thanked him, and we left. It certainly didn't seem like a busy place, and I had a pretty good idea of why his business might not be booming, but it seemed so pathetically sad that even with plenty of time on his hands to make a couple of minor changes he hadn't bothered to get a different sign, one that didn't promise "Ice Cream" to unsuspecting tourists in search of a frozen treat.

As we continued our walk it seemed, though maybe we just missed a lot, that all Paris really had going for it was that it shared a name with a city in France. Everywhere we looked, from the masthead of the local newspaper to the city logo, the word "Paris" was spelled with an image of the Eiffel Tower (the local one with the red cowboy hat on top) where the "A" would normally be. The city's bus system, comprised as best I could tell of a few small shuttle-type buses, was called "Paris Metro," again with the "A" in Paris denoted by the tower with the red cowboy hat. Like the "ice cream" shop, it all seemed kind of sad. Paris, Texas, bears as much resemblance to Paris, France, as I do to the late musician formerly known as Prince. But you go with what you've got and if sharing a name with the French capital is the best thing Paris has going for it then, by all means, they should make the most of it.

Now, we had only one restaurant recommendation for Paris and it came from the same young waiter we'd met the night before in Natchitoches who recommended a visit to the Eiffel Tower. There was ample reason now to question his judgment, but I figured with nothing else to go on we'd give the Mexican restaurant he told us about, the best in Paris he assured us, a shot. I did not write a negative *Yelp* review, but the takeout burrito was the consistency of soup and it sloshed about in the Styrofoam container I'd been given to convey it back to our hotel room.

It would be a fair criticism of my judgments about Paris that we were there for less than twenty-four hours, and that we no doubt just missed whatever it is that makes people proud to be from Paris. But unless the traveler lingers for many days, perhaps even longer, in every place he or she visits, the same critique can be made. The best he can hope for is a glimpse of a place, and some charm us and some do not. Some beckon us to return for more, some make us ready to move on. So far, Paris was squarely in the second group.

By early evening we'd only been in Paris a few hours, but we seemed to have already exhausted its possibilities. I bought Albie a soft serve vanilla ice cream cone at the Dairy Queen next to our hotel on the ring road that circles Paris, but then decided we should give the town one more shot. Surely if we drove around we'd find a nice park or another place to take an evening walk, something, *anything*, that might give us reason to fall, if not in love with Paris, but "in like" with it. Half an hour of driving later and we couldn't find a single place where I even wanted to get out of the car. Maybe it was my irrational fear of dilapidated, vacant buildings and overgrown empty lots. Whatever it was, we called it an early night and headed back to the hotel where I left Judy another voice mail message. She's a hard woman to reach.

In the morning we'd be leaving for Okemah, Oklahoma, and it turned out, happily, to be one of those places that beckons us to come back.

ABOVE: On the day we left on our nearly 9,200 mile odyssey, I explained to Albie that we'd be gone a while and admonished him for not completing the assigned reading, the book that inspired our venture, John Steinbeck's *Travels with Charley. Photo by Judy Gelman.*
LEFT: Outside of Front Royal, Virginia we stopped to see if these dinosaurs were real.

For the first few days, the weather was too wet and too cold to put the top down. We finally reached warmer weather making our way down the Virginia section of the Blue Ridge Parkway.

ABOVE: The Blue Ridge Parkway is one of America's national treasures, 469 miles of mountain splendor in Virginia and North Carolina. LEFT: Albie with the great explorer Meriwether Lewis near Grinder's Stand in Tennessee, where Lewis took his own life in 1809.

LEFT: Perhaps the greatest journey ever taken across the American continent was Lewis and Clark's from 1804 to 1806. The monument behind Albie marks the final resting place of Meriwether Lewis along the Natchez Trace in Tennessee.

RIGHT: In Tupelo, Mississippi we met "Voz" Vanelli (right) and his friend Jason in front of Vanelli's Restaurant. Voz was one of the most colorful characters we met during our six weeks on the road.

After a day of driving through dangerous torrential rains that were toppling trees all along the Natchez Trace Parkway, the skies cleared in the early evening as we sat along the banks of the Mississippi in Natchez. Louisiana is across the river.

ABOVE: Albie surveys the cemetery at the Grace Episcopal Church in St. Francisville, Louisiana, a lovely little town on the Mississippi River. LEFT: Our older son, Dan, went to Tulane University and now lives and works in New Orleans, a city we have come to love. We spent three nights there, including a stop at our favorite ice cream shop.

JoAnn Clevenger, the proprietor of Upperline, one of New Orleans' best restaurants, originally hails from Alexandria, Louisiana, as Albie does. The day before this photo was taken, I sat down with JoAnn and spoke with her for two hours about what makes New Orleans so magical. *Photo by Dan Zheutlin.*

This photo is from a previous trip to New Orleans, but the woman in the middle, Doreen Ketchens, also known as Queen Clarinet of the Crescent City, made me fall in love with New Orleans years before I ever set foot in the city. I happened upon her playing the most extraordinary music on the street in Portland, Maine just weeks before Hurricane Katrina and we stayed in touch ever since. This is her usual spot at the corner of Royal and St. Peter Streets in the French Quarter.

ABOVE: I had very few "must do" items on our agenda, but one was to stop in Alexandria, Louisiana so Albie could have a reunion with Keri Toth and Krista Lombardo, the two women who saved him from a dire fate. The shelter there puts down close to 90% of all the dogs that come in. Albie stayed alive there for five months before we adopted him. Krista volunteers at the shelter; Keri was our adoption coordinator with Labs4rescue, the organization through whom we adopted Albie. LEFT: The day before we reached Paris, Texas, we met a young man in Louisiana who was from Paris. When asked what we should see during our visit he suggested the Eiffel Tower replica topped with a red cowboy hat. Then he ran out of ideas.

ABOVE: Kurtis Walker of Okemah, Oklahoma owns the property, pictured here, where Woody Guthrie's childhood home once stood. A stop in Okemah was also on our "must do" list, a way of paying tribute to one of my lifelong heroes and America's greatest folk song writer. The day we spent in Okemah was one of the highlights of the trip, a town of friendly and generous people. *Photo by Nyla Walker.* LEFT: Lance Warn and Wayland Bishop of Okemah, Oklahoma in front of a re-creation of part of Woody Guthrie's childhood home, made with wood salvaged from the original, inside the Okemah Historical Society. *Photo by Kurtis Walker.*

Cadillac Ranch outside of Amarillo is an American icon, ten Cadillac car frames buried nose first at a 52 degree angle in the Texas panhandle. The wind was blowing a gale from the North, pinning Albie's ears to the side of his head.

ABOVE: Route 66, the road John Steinbeck dubbed "The Mother Road," and along which hundreds of thousands of people fled the Dust Bowl for California, hardly exists anymore. But it lives on in the popular imagination and in art work like this in the towns, such as Tucumcari, New Mexico, along the route. LEFT: Albie, standing on a corner in Winslow, Arizona, such a fine sight to see.

It had been nearly half a century since I'd last been to the Grand Canyon, but the day we arrived it was completely socked in with fog. But we'd come this far so we waited for hours hoping the fog would break, and it did.

ABOVE: Albie, the international diplomat, greets a tourist from China at the Grand Canyon. BELOW: Another of the iconic murals that adorns building walls in the towns along Old Route 66, this one in Seligman, Arizona.

Albie opened the way for countless conversations along the way. At home he doesn't always welcome the approach of strangers, but on the road his manners were impeccable as these three young girls in Tehachapi, California discovered.

In Tehachapi, California we found more murals that summon the America of another era.

ABOVE: High above Yosemite Valley at Washburn Point I pay homage to my alma mater. *Photo by a complete stranger.* BELOW: Again, in Yosemite, Albie does his part to encourage friendship between America and China.

ABOVE: It might look like Albie is soaking in the magnificence of Yosemite Valley, but he's actually looking for a squirrel that had just darted over the wall. BELOW: Albie, Ollie and me in front of the house where John Steinbeck grew up in Salinas, California. *Photo by Andy Gelman.*

RIGHT: When we reached the San Francisco Bay Area, we spent a few days with my brother-in-law Andy, his wife Ceci, and their dog Ollie. It was hot the day we stopped at the Mission San Juan Bautista after visiting the National Steinbeck Center in Salinas. So Albie and Ollie took refuge on the cool tiles under the portico. BELOW: The trails at Lands End in San Francisco offer some of the most spectacular views available within the limits of a major American city.

Albie gazing at the Sawtooth Mountains along U.S. 20 in Idaho.

ABOVE: Craters of the Moon National Monument in Idaho is an other-wordly expanse of volcanic rock that extends for dozens of miles, the result not of a volcanic eruption, but from lava oozing through fissures in the Earth. Geologically speaking, these lava formations are fairly new: between 2,100 and 15,000 years old. RIGHT: It almost always pays, if you're staying somewhere off an Interstate exit, to drive the mile or two into the downtown of whatever town justified the placement of the exit in the first place. Miles City, Montana has a classic American Main Street with a western flair.

ABOVE: At a Starbucks in Bismarck, North Dakota on a cold and rainy day, we met Louis F., a Marine Corps veteran, who had been biking around the country for more than two years to find out, he told me, "if Americans are still patriotic." Political polar opposites, we nevertheless talked amiably for an hour. RIGHT: State Capitol buildings are a good place to start any visit to a capital city. Some, such as this one in Madison, Wisconsin, are impressive. Others, such as the Capitol building in Bismarck, North Dakota, we found wanting.

It looks like Albie could be sitting near a beach on Cape Cod or the Jersey Shore, but this is actually a beach along Lake Erie near Mentor, Ohio.

LEFT: Our very last stop before heading home was Ogunquit, Maine, where I spent many summer vacations growing up. I had hoped to walk Albie across the footbridge that spans the Ogunquit River to the beach but discovered, to our disappointment, that it's no longer allowed. I think Albie got the joke. BELOW: Albie and me in Half Moon Bay, California. To say I love him would be a vast understatement. Knowing what his fate could have been on any one of the roughly 150 nights he slept on the floor of a cage in a high-kill shelter has made our relationship all the more poignant. *Photo by Ceci Ogden.*

TEN

This Land Is Your Land

B roadway, the main street that runs through the center of Okemah, lives up to its name. It seems about as wide as the westbound half of the Santa Monica Freeway. Downtown Okemah would certainly feel more intimate if the street were narrower. Maybe there's a historical reason it's so wide—to accommodate cattle drives or large farm equipment—I don't know. On an ordinary day this too-big-for-its-britches stretch of pavement would have added to the town's sense of emptiness and desolation, but we had, by sheer luck, arrived in Okemah on no ordinary day.

This farming and ranching town of 3,200 sits right off Interstate 40, about an hour east of Oklahoma City and a little more than an hour west of Sallisaw. Sallisaw is where the Joad family, fleeing the Dust Bowl and the Great Depression for California, begin their journey, one that would have taken them right through Okemah, in John Steinbeck's 1939 novel *The Grapes of Wrath*.

We came here to pay my respects to Okemah's most famous son, America's greatest folk singer and folk-song writer, Woody Guthrie.

John Steinbeck and Woody Guthrie were both extraordinary chroniclers of the Dust Bowl, Steinbeck in prose and Guthrie in song. When *The Grapes of Wrath* was made into a film by John Ford in 1940, Guthrie was in New York City and on the cusp of major celebrity, making his first commercial recording for Victor Records, *The Dust Bowl Ballads*.* According to Guthrie biographer Joe Klein, Victor asked Guthrie to write a song that would capitalize on the film's popularity and thus the song *Tom Joad*, named for Steinbeck's *Grapes of Wrath* protagonist, was written.** Guthrie had lived the Dust Bowl experience and was, therefore, the perfect balladeer to write such a song.

Steinbeck and Guthrie met several times and were kindred spirits and mutual admirers of each other's work. In a 2008 interview, Steinbeck's son Thom told *The Fog City Journal*, a San Francisco-based publication, there was a "spiritual oneness" in the two, especially in their shared concern for the plight of common people, the downtrodden and the marginalized, a

---

* *The Dust Bowl Ballads* included "The Great Dust Storm," "Talkin' Dust Bowl Blues," "Dust Pneumonia Blues," and "Dusty Old Dust," among others. It would be Guthrie's most commercially successful album ever.

** Joe Klein, *Woody Guthrie: A Life* (New York: Knopf, 1980).

theme that defined the works of both men. Anyone who reads Steinbeck's dialogue in his many novels and listens to Guthrie's lyrics or reads his prose (Guthrie authored two books himself, an autobiography and a novel) will also be struck by similarities in the vernacular.[*]

Routing ourselves through Guthrie's hometown of Okemah also meant that we would be traveling clear to the California line on roughly the same route as the Joad family and hundreds of thousands of others who escaped the Dust Bowl for what they hoped would be a land of milk and honey. The Joads followed the famed Route 66 all the way from Oklahoma to California, but that's impossible these days. Only remnants of the old Route 66 remain. Much of it, though still formally designated "66," is one and the same road as Interstate 40. Once we got to Amarillo, just a day's drive from Okemah, we'd also be back on Steinbeck's trail, for he and Charley also paralleled the Joad's route between California and Amarillo, though they did so from west to east.

The Dust Bowl was a staggering disaster wrought by the hand of man and the whimsy of nature. As the Great Plains were settled, farmers stripped the rich topsoil of the natural grasses that literally held the land in place. More than one hundred million acres were affected by over-farming and overgrazing. When a crushing multiyear drought hit, a drought that coincided with the Great Depression, the exposed topsoil turned to dust.

---

[*]   Guthrie's autobiography, *Bound for Glory*, is one of my most treasured books, not least because during a backpacking trip out west in the early 1970s a bear got hold of my backpack one night and left deep claw prints in my paperback copy. Guthrie's novel, *House of Earth*, was finished in 1947, but first published, posthumously, in 2013.

Great clouds of dust, "black blizzards" blown up and carried by prairie winds over hundreds of miles billowed, sometimes nearly two miles high, and rolled over towns, driving fine particles of dirt into every nook and cranny of even the most tightly secured homes. Some of the dust settled as far east as New York City. Nothing grew. Money dried up with the soil and untold human misery ensued. As hundreds of thousands fled in search, literally, of greener pastures, most headed west in overloaded jalopies for California, a land that took root in the popular imagination as so fertile, and so rich, as to be beyond imagining.*

As Albie and I made our way from Oklahoma to California we would be traveling in the footsteps, or more precisely the tire tracks, of countless desperate migrants who passed this way in the 1930s. We were traveling in comfort and style, however, and with none of the worries that weighed them down like the household belongings that made their jalopy springs sag under the weight. In no meaningful way would our journey across this part of the United States be remotely similar to theirs except for the rough outlines of the scenery. But one could, at least, appreciate the immense sadness, hopefulness, and eventual heartbreaking disappointment of their odysseys.

Spirits lifted by rumors that jobs in the rich fields of California awaited any man or woman who wanted to work were crushed by the reality that there were far more people making their way west in hope of finding work than could possibly be employed. This was a deliberate strategy by growers and

---

* *The Worst Hard Time: The Untold Story of Those Who Survived the Great American Dust Bowl* by Timothy Egan (Mariner Books, 2006) is an outstanding natural and human history of the Dust Bowl. The book was honored with the prestigious National Book Award.

middlemen with contracts to harvest the fields to ensure that a massive labor pool of people would work backbreaking hours under a hot sun for next to nothing. And as the destitute "Okies" (a derogatory epithet) would discover, they were looked down upon as barely human, and ruthlessly exploited. They gathered in makeshift encampments of shared misery called Hoover-villes, after the president presiding over the Great Depression. To keep these "undesirables" moving down the road, sheriff's deputies often torched the camps at night.

When Steinbeck's Joad family reached Needles, California, on the Arizona border, they encountered a stranger as they basked in the cool water of a stream near the highway. They assumed he was, like them, escaping the Dust Bowl. But he was headed in the opposite direction, back home to Pampa, Oklahoma.*

"S'pose a fella got work an' saved, couldn' he get a little lan'?" Tom Joad asks the stranger.

"You ain't gonna get no steady work," the stranger replies. "Gonna scrabble for your dinner ever' day. An' you gonna do her with people lookin' mean at you."

Hundreds of thousands found out the hard way that the promise of California was just a mirage. To keep migrants out, the state of California started turning people away at the border, a storyline memorialized by Woody Guthrie in the song "Do Re Mi," one of his Dust Bowl Ballads. (The "do re mi," refers, of course, to money.) The song was a warning to migrants that California might not be the answer to their dreams.

> Lots of folks back East, they say, is leavin' home every day,
> Beatin' the hot old dusty way to the California line.

---

* There is also a Pampa, Texas.

'Cross the desert sands they roll, gettin' out of that old dust
  bowl,
They think they're goin' to a sugar bowl, but here's what they
  find
Now, the police at the port of entry say,
"You're number fourteen thousand for today."
Oh, if you ain't got the do re mi, folks, you ain't got the do
  re mi,
Why, you better go back to beautiful Texas, Oklahoma,
  Kansas, Georgia, Tennessee.
California is a garden of Eden, a paradise to live in or
  see;
But believe it or not, you won't find it so hot
If you ain't got the do re mi.

According to Thom Steinbeck, his father once joked to Guthrie in a letter that if only he'd written "Do Re Mi" earlier, it would have saved Steinbeck the trouble of writing *The Grapes of Wrath*. Woody Guthrie and John Steinbeck captured the struggles and the merciless exploitation of these decent, hard-working Americans as few others ever have, and that, in large part, is at the root of my admiration for both of them.

About six weeks before we started our trip, I e-mailed the Okemah Historical Society to see if they could suggest someone knowledgable about the Guthrie family history in town who might be willing to meet Albie and me and show us around. After a week or so there'd been no reply. I tried a second time, but again no response. So, I called, and a nice, older woman told me I should talk to a society volunteer named Wayland Bishop. I scribbled the name down on a scrap of paper. She took my number and promised to have him call me. More than a week passed and no call, so I called again, and spoke with the same woman. She had given my name and number to Wayland and promised to give him another message. We were about to leave in a week but there was still no word from Wayland Bishop. Indeed, I never did hear from him. I didn't want to make a pest of myself so I dropped it and figured when we got to Okemah I'd just show myself around. Using my fifty-year-old copy of Woody's autobiography, *Bound for Glory*, I'd try to identify some of the spots where Guthrie spent his youth. Before we left home, however, I searched all over for the scrap of paper with Wayland's name on it because I figured I'd ask around for him while we were there, but it was nowhere to be found and for the life of me I could not remember his name.

I'd never set foot in Oklahoma, one of only four states I'd never visited, and all of which we would pass through on this trip. (The others being North Dakota, Wisconsin, and Michigan.) Paris, Texas, where we'd spent the previous night, is only about twenty miles from the Oklahoma border, and we were in the Sooner State before we knew it.

The Indian Nation Turnpike is a pleasant toll road that runs from the Texas border, through lands that once belonged to the Choctaw and Creek Indians, and up to I-40 across broad, gentle, tree-covered hills. Once on I-40, Okemah was just another ten miles or so west.

Frankly, I wasn't expecting to spend much more than an hour or two in Okemah. Wayland's name continued to elude me, and it was a Saturday, when the Historical Society was almost sure to be closed. It would probably be dead quiet in this small town. Woody had grown up in a house known as the London House, as the previous owners were the Londons, and I thought it would be a victory of sorts if we could just locate the place where the house once stood.*

We parked just before we hit Broadway because the street was blocked off with sawhorses and police tape. Something was going on in town; we could see a lot of people milling about. Albie and I walked the block and a half to Broadway and saw that we had, just as we had the day before in Hughes Springs, stumbled onto a carnival with rides and food stands and various businesses and civic groups with their tables and awnings set up along the street. Albie woofed at the ponies walking in small circles with little children perched on their backs.

The action was concentrated at the east end of Broadway; the westerly end, near the fire station, was practically deserted save for a lone woman sitting at a table in front of Warn's, a furniture store, and another woman across the street in front of a business called "Faith (family owned and operated), Fitness (group fitness and self-defense) and Firearms (guns and ammo, gun range)." Many storefronts were empty and the buildings vacant, some apparently for years.

We passed a table staffed by a local school group and asked the kids if they knew where the London House used to be, "You know, the house where Woody Guthrie grew up." They had no idea. It wasn't even clear if they knew who Woody Guthrie was. I thanked them, and Albie and I continued walking down Broadway.

---

* I knew the house had fallen into disrepair by the 1970s. It was being used by local teens as a clandestine gathering place and was ordered torn down by the town.

A miniature schnauzer pulled on his leash, eager to meet Albie. As the two dogs got acquainted the way dogs do, by sniffing one another's private parts, I got acquainted with the couple at the other end of the leash the way humans do, by introducing myself. The man was wearing a badge on his shirt bearing the name of his real estate business and his name: Carl Alls. I told Carl and his wife we'd come to Okemah from Boston to pay tribute to Woody Guthrie.*

"Oh," said Carl, "then you need to talk to Wayland Bishop."

Wayland Bishop! The name I'd written down but lost and then forgot.

"He's right over here. Come on, I'll introduce you."

What luck! We'd been in town all of five minutes and I'd already found the man I would have been looking for had I remembered his name. Without my realizing it, we were standing practically in front of the Historical Society and Wayland was right there, out front on the sidewalk.

"This fella's looking for you," Carl said to Wayland. I introduced myself and Wayland immediately apologized for not getting back to me. He's a tall, trim man in his late sixties, raised in Okemah and now retired there after a career in the tire industry in Oklahoma City. He's been back for ten years.

Wayland invited me into the Historical Society to see a treasure trove of Woody memorabilia on display: record albums, a guitar, family photos, high school yearbooks he had signed, and a partial reconstruction of the London House made from wood salvaged from the original structure.

---

* You really can't make this up. As I was revising this manuscript for the umpteenth time sitting in my local Starbucks, a rendition of Woody's "This Land Is Your Land" started playing over the sound system right at this point in my review of the manuscript. The music endures.

"Woody left town is his mid-teens, but he often came back here whenever he was close," Wayland told me. "He'd be riding the rails or hitchhiking and usually came to a bar owned by his childhood friend, Colonel Martin. That was a nickname. No one knows why he was called Colonel. Woody would sleep in the back of the Colonel's garage, have breakfast with the Martins, and move on. He would just walk off. He just came and went.

"My dad says he thinks Woody never bothered to bathe," Wayland added. "Some folks would invite him for a meal but insist he bathe first while they washed his clothes."

Wayland was the first of many people we met in Okemah who would recall the time the actor David Carradine came to town; he played Woody Guthrie in the 1976 film *Bound for Glory*, based on Woody's autobiography. It was a big deal.

Wayland told us we'd arrived in Okemah on Pioneer Day, a celebration that's the biggest event in town all year except for the annual Woody Guthrie Festival (referred to as Woody Fest), a multiday music festival held on the July weekend closest to Woody's birthday, July 14. The first Woody Fest was held in 1997 to commemorate the life and music of Okemah's most famous native son. Pioneer Day also coincides with a multiyear class reunion for graduates of Okemah High School. This year it included, among others, the classes of 1968 to 1972, and hundreds of people who now lived away were here for the homecoming. I'm a 1971 high school graduate myself, and many of the people out and about on Broadway this day were my contemporaries. Before the day was out Albie and I would practically become honorary members of the Okemah High School alumni association.

❖

Okemah didn't always celebrate Woody Guthrie's legacy; far from it. When the idea first surfaced in the late 1960s that Okemah should recognize Woody's life and music there was powerful opposition. Business leaders and local politicians thought the town's association with a man who embraced aspects of socialism and communism, and once wrote for *The Daily Worker*, a publication of the Communist Party USA, would be a stain on the community; that far from drawing tourists and their dollars, good people would shun Okemah and only hippies and "undesirables" would come to see a Guthrie memorial. Woody's political leanings were so toxic that when he died in 1967, the Okemah Public Library refused a gift of his songs and writings. Woody wanted to be buried in the town where he'd been born but his widow, Marjorie, angered by the library's refusal, had his ashes scattered in the Atlantic instead.

The controversy over Woody's legacy attracted national media attention. A 1972 article in *Rolling Stone* quoted the then president of the local chamber of commerce, Allison Kelly, as saying the paramount issue was whether "Okemah should honor a communist." That same year, a service station owner in town told the *New York Times*, "Woody was no good. About half the town feels that way. I knew him, went to school with him, used to whup him. He doesn't deserve to have his name up there." "Up there" referred to a water tower that had recently been painted with the words, "Home of Woody Guthrie." It still stands today.

But there were others, who were also powerful people in town, and felt Woody had, through song, made a huge impact on the world and ought to be recognized. One was Earl Walker, a leading officer in the Oklahoma/Texas chapter of Kiwanis, who bought the old London House in 1972 for $7,000 with plans (never realized) to rebuild and restore it and turn it into a center for displaying Woody's writings and music. It was Walker who successfully led the effort to get the water board to honor Guthrie on the water tower,* and, thirty years before the first ever Woody Fest in 1997, Walker traveled to visit Woody in the hospital in New York to see if he would approve of efforts Walker and others were making to honor him in Okemah. He did, and gave Walker a signed copy of his autobiography, *Bound for Glory*. Woody died shortly thereafter.

"People fear that putting up a memorial to Woody would attract hordes of motorcycle riders who would cruise through the town and threaten everybody," Walker told *Rolling Stone* in 1972. "But for every motorcycle rider, there would be 50 or 100 other persons who would stop and maybe bring a little business our way."

But Walker's motivation was more than financial. He was, perhaps, just slightly more progressive than many of his neighbors. In 1972, the year he bought the London House, he helped found the Woody Guthrie Memorial, Inc., a nonprofit organization.

"This time," he told *Rolling Stone*, "we are going to get some muscle behind us and make sure we get a memorial to Woody. Woody was no communist, he was an individual who believed strongly in some things. I don't necessarily agree with everything he did, but I don't question his right to do so. Hell, look at what Hannibal, Missouri, did with Mark Twain, and he was an atheist."

"Were it not for Earl Walker," the *New York Times* reported in 1972, "the memories [of Guthrie] might have lain dormant."

---

* There is now a mural and a statue in town that memorialize Woody, as well.

Still, it took more than two decades for Okemah to come around to fully embracing its native son. Wayland Bishop was one of several people we met in Okemah who told me that as the older generation aged and died off and a younger generation came of age, attitudes softened.

"Woody's politics are not important to people here anymore," Wayland told me. "They just know he was for the people. People here were oppressed, and they're still oppressed. They just care about the fact that Woody was for the people and they respect that he became a renowned songwriter, though when he was young and playing the guitar on the street here for change, hardworking ranch folks didn't think that what he was doing was *work*.

"I was a union man," added Wayland, perhaps thinking of Woody's commitment to the working man and the labor movement. "I worked for Firestone Tire and was a member of the Rubber Workers Union, which became part of the Iron Workers. This is a poor town, but when I was growing up in the fifties and sixties, every storefront was occupied. Then the interstate came through in 1963 and later Walmart and it killed all the retail. We don't even have a clothing store in town anymore."

As we talked inside the Historical Society a friendly, nice-looking man in shorts, a T-shirt, and a baseball cap approached us, and Wayland introduced me to Kurtis Walker. Kurtis is the grandson of Earl Walker. Wayland introduced me as "a Woody fan."

"We can tell," Kurtis said good-naturedly. "Like you, people come here, not just from the United States but from all over the world, because of Woody, and they are just looking around trying to take it all in."

Kurtis is an open, gregarious man in his midforties and now owns the lot where the London House once stood, the lot his grandfather bought in 1972. He offered to walk us over there after the Pioneer Day parade that was scheduled for midday.

Albie and I continued hanging out on the sidewalk in front of the Historical Society; it seemed to be the center of a lot of the action. Just in front of us, on the street, Kurtis was one of several volunteers working a table set up to publicize and raise funds for a project to restore three old water towers that stand side by side in town. One is painted with the words "Hot Okemah," another "Cold Okemah," and the third is the one his grandfather succeeded in having painted "Home of Woody Guthrie." Like his grandfather Earl before him, Kurtis is doing his part to honor Woody's memory and better the town.

Wayland and Kurtis kept introducing Albie and me to people, some current residents, others back from afar for their high school reunion, explaining that we were on a cross-country car trip and had come to Okemah because of Woody. And those folks, in turn, introduced us to still others so that before long it felt like we'd met half the people who had ever lived in town in the past sixty years or so. Everyone greeted us with genuine kindness.

Some even heard about us and came over because they had something they wanted to tell us, like 87-year-old Mary Coleman, walking with the help of a cane and wearing a purple cowboy hat, a purple vest, and an ankle-length black skirt. She told me there's an open mic event at the start of every Woody Fest and that she and her 90-year-old brother, Earl "Buddy" Williams, play together, she on guitar (she's self-taught) and Buddy on fiddle and mandolin.

"I can't imagine who wants to hear a nearly 90-year-old woman play," she told me, "but Buddy never misses a note!"

"What kinds of songs do you play?" I asked.

"Oh, 'San Antonio Rose' and other old songs," she replied. "'This Land is Your Land' is my favorite. My mother knew the Guthries, but we lived in the country eight miles from here by Buckeye Creek, so I didn't know them." Almost everyone we met in town had ancestors who knew the Guthries.

"I went to a one-room school there," she continued. "We came here riding the Greyhound bus; nine kids in our family. We sold eggs and cream out of the back of a horse-drawn wagon. You're from Boston someone said?"

"Yes," I answered, "near Boston." Word of our appearance had apparently spread like wildfire.

"My granddaughter teaches at MIT!" she proclaimed proudly. Then she came back to Woody. "Woody was always carrying his guitar, so my brother and I did the same, so we could play whenever. I teach guitar. Have a Gibson and taught all four of my kids music. I'm part Cherokee, you know."

"How much Cherokee?" I asked.

"*Very much!*" Mary replied. "My hair was so black it was blue!"

And with that she started to amble away, but not before turning around to say one more thing. "Thank you!" she called out. "Thank you so much! Come back for the Woody Guthrie Festival!"

Wherever I looked there were old friends, many seeing one another for the first time in years, greeting each other, slapping backs, and embracing. Their warmth and affection for one another were palpable. All had the dust of this town in their bones.

Ed Stokes grew up here, but lives now in Katy, Texas, near Houston. He's a year older than me and had come home for the class of 1970 reunion. He was wearing jeans and a collared shirt and a baseball-style cap. He has a huge smile, an easy manner, and is the kind of guy you can't help but like from the moment he introduces himself and gives you a firm handshake and a laugh that seems to come from somewhere deep inside him. I took him to be a rancher, but he has spent his entire career with Conoco as a petroleum engineer. He lived and worked in Europe for fourteen years and spent considerable time in the Middle East, as well.

As he looked down Broadway he used exactly the same word to describe modern-day Okemah as Wayland Bishop had earlier: "disappointing." He was referring to what's happened to the thriving town of his childhood.

"There used to be ten supermarkets right here on Broadway," he told me. He, too, mentioned the adverse impact of Walmart on the town. Then the talk turned to Woody.

"Used to be Pioneer Day was everything in this town. Now it's the Woody Guthrie Festival," Ed said. Earl Walker's vision of an Okemah that fully wrapped its arms around Woody had come to pass.

"Back in the early 1970s, people here didn't want to have anything to do with Woody Guthrie because he went to New York and became a socialist," Ed, a self-described libertarian, told me. "When Arlo [Woody's son, the singer Arlo Guthrie] came here in the late sixties to try and get the town to honor Woody, the older generation had a lot of bad feelings. But he wrote more than five hundred songs* and had a

---

*   Actually, it was more than a thousand.

great influence on music and affected so many lives. He was world-renowned."

As we talked Ed saw a classmate named Ginny to whom he quickly introduced me. "This here is Peter and Albie," he said. "Traveled all the way from Boston." Ginny is part Creek and part Cherokee and she and Ed spoke briefly in Creek.

"A lot of people here are part Indian," Ed told me after Ginny had gone off to greet some other friends. Many of the people I met in Okemah, like Mary and Ginny, were either full-blooded Native Americans or of mixed white and Indian ancestry and everyone seemed to treat each other with kindness and respect. There's been so much intermarriage over the generations that racial divisions between whites and Native Americans have ceased to be an issue here.

Pretty soon Ed was like my best old friend in this town.

"Hey, Pete, have you met Nokey?" There was also Bubby, Bobby, and Nubbin.

"I don't even know some of their real names," Ed said, his laugh nearly swallowing his words. "And I've known them all my life!"

Back inside the Historical Society there was a table set up with some cookies and soft drinks, and we fell into conversation with three women who were sitting inside. All appeared to be in their sixties or seventies. As usual, it was Albie who caught their eye and started the conversation among us. All had grown up here. In addition to Woody, they told me, Okemah had produced some other notable people. William Pogue became an astronaut and piloted Skylab 4. Larry Coker was once the head football coach at the University of Miami. His sister was one of the women I was talking with. DeLoss McGraw became an artist of considerable renown.

Pat Soledade, like Ed Stokes, was back in Okemah for the reunion. She, too, lives near Houston now. She attended Oklahoma University and later graduate school at Columbia. She joined the Peace Corps in the 1960s partly because the three-week training session was held in New York City and she wanted a look at the bright lights.

"I didn't really intend to go into the Peace Corps," Pat told me. "I just wanted to go to New York City. Imagine coming from here to New York City! I was out all the time."

Pat did enter the Peace Corps and served in Brazil where she met her husband, a Brazilian man, while "dancing on a table during Carnival." They raised their children in Brazil.

All of this surprised me, which tells you something about the biases I brought to Okemah with me. Here was this demure woman in her late seventies from Okemah, Oklahoma, and her life sounded like something out of a Gabriel Garcia Marquez novel. Many of the people I was meeting were more worldly than I expected.

"I first came back to Okemah for my high school reunion in 1990," Pat told me. "The entire town had become decrepit. It was a shock and I didn't come back again for ten years. This is our sixtieth reunion and our class has stayed close. Some of us even travel together."

I asked Pat about the town and its relationship to Woody and she echoed what others had told me.

"Woody Guthrie was *persona non grata* here for a long time," she said. "This county lost a lot of people during the Korean War and people couldn't stand the idea of this left-wing person being honored. But time passes."

The front door to the Historical Society opened and Ed Stokes took a step inside.

"Hey, Pete!" he called out. "Come on, the parade is starting!"

Kurtis Walker had come inside, too, and as Ed headed back out for the parade Kurtis said to me, "You see how friendly people are here. There's no reason to be friendly unless you care about people. People here really care about each other."

It's true. Everyone had a nice word for Albie and for me in Okemah. They also seemed to appreciate that we'd stopped to see their town and that I knew a lot about Woody. I had expected to come into town, walk some relatively abandoned streets, take a few pictures, and leave. By late afternoon we were still there.

Back out on Broadway, Kurtis introduced me to Lance Warn, still youthful-looking at almost eighty years old, who used to own Warn's, the furniture store I'd seen earlier. Warn had been president of the chamber of commerce during some of the years when the controversy over Woody raged in town.

"The older generation, the city fathers, the bankers, they just put the kibosh on it," Lance told me. "They just shut it down. A generation passed, and the younger generation didn't care about Woody's politics. They saw the potential of honoring his legacy and then things really moved." Warn pointed across the street toward the Citizens State Bank.

"There used to be a supermarket next door," he told me, "and between the market and bank there was an alley where my father used to shoot marbles with Woody."

Lance mentioned that up by the fire station there was a section of sidewalk where Woody had carved his name while the cement was still wet nearly a century ago. Kurtis was about to walk me over to the London House property, but I wanted to see if we could find Woody's name in the sidewalk first. Albie and I walked the few hundred yards up to the firehouse and paced up and down the sidewalk but saw nothing. A few of the firemen had a grill going outside and I asked if they knew where Woody had etched his name in the sidewalk. One of them led me inside the firehouse and called for a colleague. A young, solidly built man came to the front. As I explained what I was looking for, he turned and lifted a large piece of old cement sidewalk off a shelf.

"When I was replacing the sidewalk a little while ago I drilled this piece out," he explained.

There, clear as day, was a name: "Woody." It was as if we were looking at the fossil of a small dinosaur. It was thrilling to see it and hold it, this physical link connecting me to one of my heroes.

Kurtis had wandered up and as we began walking back down Broadway toward the London House lot we ran into Kurtis's father, William Earl Walker, Jr. The senior Mr. Walker was dressed as many men usually are in this part of the country—jeans, cowboy boots, cap, and a long-sleeve, button-down shirt—even though it was about ninety degrees. William Walker lives in Moore, which is sandwiched between Oklahoma City and Norman. Moore was familiar because the town was severely damaged with significant loss of life by two F-5 tornadoes, in 1999 and 2013, and both tragedies received national media attention.

Kurtis said we were at the peak of tornado season in Oklahoma (it was late April). No one could remember there *not* being a tornado this late in the season but so far this year, nothing. I've had a morbid fascination with tornadoes since watching *The Wizard of Oz* as a kid and thought it would be awe-inspiring to see one from a distance, but Mr. Walker's harrowing stories of the Moore tornadoes made me reconsider. Kurtis said goodbye to his dad, who was heading back to Moore, and told him he loved him.

❖

As we walked, Kurtis and Albie and I were alone for the first time all day, though we'd been chatting on and off for several hours. Almost immediately Kurtis said something that took me aback.

"I'm like the gay black guy in this town," he said to me in a conspiratorial whisper.

Okay, I thought, what does *that* mean?

"I'm a *liberal*," he added immediately. I breathed a sigh of relief. Not because he was a liberal but because some of the other interpretations of his comment were too dark to contemplate. Kurtis had made an assumption about me, perhaps because I was from Massachusetts, just as I had about him. He'd told me earlier he'd been deployed to Iraq in 2004 as a member of the U.S. Army Reserve (Charlie Company, 120th Engineers), in which he has served for twenty years, and since we were deep in the heart of Trump country I assumed he was pretty conservative. My assumption was wrong. His was right.

"What's it like to be a liberal in such a conservative town?" I asked.

"Well, people know me here. I grew up here, so they don't judge me by my politics," he said. "I have friends that I just avoid politics with; some are tolerant and some are kindred spirits."

We shared our dismay and disbelief over the current president, but the conversation quickly turned to other matters. Kurtis is the divorced father of two, raising the kids pretty much on his own. To make ends meet, in addition to his work in the army reserve, he works part-time for the post office and teaches some basic engineering classes at a local technical school. He's working on opening a pizza place in town.

The lot where the London House, Woody's childhood home, once stood was overgrown and Kurtis said something about needing to come back and mow it. It's not entirely vacant, however. There are remnants of the old stone foundation and some stone steps leading to what was once the front porch. Rising from the middle of the lot is the trunk of an old cedar tree, out of which someone very skillfully carved the words "This Land Is Your Land" on one side and beneath that a few notes on a musical staff. On the other side, from top to bottom, were carved a guitar, the initials "WG," and the word "Okemah."

"Who did that?" I asked Kurtis, thinking it was something official.

He pointed to the house across the street. "The guy who lives over there," he said, referring to a sculptor named Justin Osborn.

There's a vacant lot next to the London House lot and Kurtis owns that, too. It slopes down toward the street Osborn lives on. He imagines building a small amphitheater on it someday where people can play and listen to music. Build it and they will come, I thought to myself.

"What would you need to make that happen?" I asked.

"Money," he answered. "I don't have the money."

As we started walking back toward town Kurtis said, "Come on, let me buy you a beer."

"Let me buy *you* a beer," I said as we arrived at Lou's Rocky Road Tavern. "You've been really generous with your time."

He refused. "That's just not the way it works around here," he said smiling.

Out back of Lou's there's a large fenced outdoor space filled with tables and umbrellas, a bar, and a small stage for performers. I was surprised. It felt more like a hangout for young urban professionals than a place for ranchers, farmers, and dozens of Okemahns home for their high school reunion.

We sat ourselves at the edge of the stage, which sits just a few inches above the ground. Kurtis came back with beers for us and, thoughtfully, a bowl of water for Albie. There were pictures hanging on the stage wall behind us, pictures of people who had performed here, including Jackson Browne and the late Jimmy LeFave. Kurtis pointed to one of the pictures and asked, "Know who that is?" It was a picture of another of my heroes, the folk singer Pete Seeger.

The bar manager, Gary, came over and Kurtis introduced us. He and his partner are openly gay in this very conservative town.

"It's not an issue at all for people here," said Kurtis later. "But it's an evolution and Gary had a lot to do with it. People got to know him for the quality of person he is, not his sexual preference."

Okemah was challenging a lot of my preconceptions.

Sitting closest to us was a table of four, but it was hard to figure out how they were connected, if at all. There was a big guy—a *very* big guy—tall, solidly built, wearing a sleeveless T and sporting a dark growth of beard and a full Fu-Man-Chu moustache, and a woman next to him who seemed to be his companion. Across the table was a very wiry, silent man of indeterminate age. His face was deeply lined and weathered and the beer he was drinking and the cigarette he was smoking appeared to be the millionth in a lifetime of hard living. He had no teeth. When he got up to go to the bar, jeans tucked into his cowboy boots, he wobbled to the point where it appeared he was simply going to topple over. The fourth at the table looked a little less worse for wear than his friend, but like everyone else at the table he was smoking. A cell phone, decorated with a Confederate flag, protruded from his shirt pocket.

When I asked Kurtis if this part of Oklahoma was the South or the West, he didn't hesitate. "The South," he said.

The couple turned in their seats to have a look at Albie. As usual Albie was the conversation starter. They wanted to know his name, how old he was and where we were from. They were boisterous, but well meaning. I doubt I'd have felt that way had I not been with Kurtis who seemed to know everyone here though I only learned later he didn't know *them*.

Somehow the talk came around to my being a writer and the woman, clearly inebriated, said, "It's nice to hear someone who sounds intelligent around here," which certainly didn't reflect well on her immediate company. "We don't get much of that." That brought forth a roar of laughter from her companion whom she'd just insulted, though perhaps unintentionally.

"Yep, we're just a bunch of dumb Okies!" he roared.

"Yup, just bunch of dumb Okies!" she said laughing.

Had I been there alone I would have assumed this was their way of mocking me for what they thought was running through *my* head, and it might have been a signal they were spoiling for a fight. But they weren't.

I muttered something feckless about there being many types of intelligence. It was the best I could come up with on the spot.

"That's true!" said the woman. "There's common sense!"

Though said as a joke, the "dumb Okie" remark seemed to reveal something deeply disturbing. It betrayed a sense of inferiority, of *smallness*, and it troubled me. I would be up half the night that night turning this brief interaction over and over in my head. Though said in jest, it had made me uncomfortable nonetheless. Just by being there, my presence had elicited a harsh self-assessment on their part. Is this what they really believed people like me thought of people like them? And, if so, were they wrong? So much has been written and said about the rise of a con man like Trump being a backlash against the coastal elites condescending to Middle America. Maybe Trump, for all his narcissism and gratuitous cruelty, *was* their voice, even as he shamelessly exploited all their fears and resentments. By giving the middle finger to everyone who ever turned up their nose at a "dumb Okie," perhaps he was, in his perverse way, validating their existence.

Like so many other towns we'd already seen, and others we would see as our journey continued, Okemah is a poor place, a shell of its former self, a town largely left behind and forgotten. I wondered if there wasn't something condescending about my mere presence here, as if these people were just raw material for my book.

Though these thoughts nagged at me, no one we met in Okemah seemed to feel that way or respond to me other than with genuine warmth. Many, like Mary, the elderly guitar player in the purple cowboy hat, conveyed a sense of gratitude that we'd taken the time and made the effort to come to their town, even for a day, to see the place they called home, and to value their stories.

Nothing learned on this trip would be more profound than this: people, no matter where they live, no matter how small or remote their hometown, just want someone *to know them*, to appreciate who they are and where they come from. To be known is to not be forgotten or overlooked. It is to be *somebody*.

And in towns like Okemah, fallen on hard times, the desire to be *known*, to not be invisible, may be especially keen.

Ed Stokes had urged me to stay that evening, to come to the class reunion barbeque being held at the end of Broadway. But this was not my town, and these were not my classmates, and it was only right that we not overstay our welcome. The people of Okemah, in just eight hours, had already showered us with all kinds of generosity. There was much to think about as we continued westward to Norman for the night.

When we arrived at our motel that evening, I had an e-mail from Kurtis. "Stay with us (visiting us and getting to know us) and you'll be an honorary member of the community," he wrote. "It just works that way around here."

ELEVEN

Get Your Kicks on Route 66

That night in Norman I dreamt of tornadoes. We were
in the heart of tornado alley at the height of tornado
season but the only tornado to strike was, fortunately, in
my dreams.

In the morning, Okemah was still on my mind. The
people there had been so hospitable and friendly and fundamentally decent. Our national politics have become so bitter
and so contentious it sometimes feels like we are headed for
a civil war. But one-on-one, most people, whatever their
politics, are civil toward one another, even welcoming. In
just one day I had developed a real soft spot for Woody's
hometown.

Though we'd been gone just two weeks, it seemed like ages since we'd left home. Dinner with Noah that first night in Connecticut, the horse-drawn carriages in Pennsylvania's Amish country, the evening we spent being charmed by Voz Vanelli in Tupelo, all may as well have been years ago. Travel can do that—distort time in peculiar ways.

Few states are more closely associated with the fossil fuel industry as Oklahoma, and the controversial practice of fracking—using water and chemicals under high pressure to fracture rock to access hard-to-reach oil deposits—has destabilized the state, literally. Oklahoma has been shaken by thousands of small quakes caused by fracking in recent years, so many that in Okemah Wayland Bishop told me he had trouble keeping the pictures on his walls level. But Oklahoma isn't just about fossil fuels and the energy sources of the past. Between Tuttle and Minco we saw enormous wind farms that stretched as far as the eye could see, thousands of turbines staked like giant pinwheels across the landscape. In Oklahoma you can see the energy past and the energy future in one sweep of the eyes; fracking wells to your right and wind turbines to your left.*

Just west of Cogar there were subtle changes to the landscape that hinted that the South was gradually becoming the West. The vegetation was scrubbier, there were modest red rock formations, maybe seventy to eighty feet high, and the land opened up a bit and felt more expansive.

---

* President Trump had yet to make his remarkable and fanciful claim that windmills cause cancer.

Beyond Binger, Oklahoma ("home of Johnny Bench"),* it *really* opened up. Trees were few and far between. Where there were copses, they were hard by a creek or riverbed. So sparsely populated was this stretch that the telephone poles, which ran in straight lines for miles, carried so few wires that cross beams were unnecessary; just vertical posts with a couple of phone lines strung between them. This farming and ranching country was dotted with water towers, silos, grain elevators, large corrugated tin sheds, and mobile irrigation systems that looked like fragile truss-style bridges. Other than another wind farm off to the south, it probably didn't look much different back in the days before sustained drought turned this land into a dust bowl. Even now, there seemed to be little vegetation to hold the topsoil in place. One could imagine that with another drought this entire part of Oklahoma could again turn to dust and blow away.

In Sweetwater, we hit our first tumbleweed as it blew across the highway, and when we stopped for gas the wind was so strong it pinned Albie's ears to the sides of his head. No wonder energy entrepreneurs are trying to catch the wind here.

The empty landscape turned flat again, especially as we crossed into the Texas panhandle. To say something, a person or a landscape, is nondescript is, for a writer, a cop-out, for what is the writer's job if not to describe? Yet, as we drove I struggled

---

* Every town with some claim to fame, no matter how obscure, wants to make sure you know it. Bench, of course, was a hall of fame baseball player. Sparta, Tennessee, as noted, was the home of bluegrass musician Lester Flatt, and Okemah of folk singer Woody Guthrie. The town where we raised our kids never lets you forget it's the hometown of Olympic gymnast Aly Raisman. Even the small town where we now live prides itself on being the home of the E. F. Hodgson Company, manufacturer of the first modular prefabricated home. Now *there's* a claim to fame.

to find the words to describe this barren, featureless place. It's almost devoid of trees and as flat as a sheet of ice.

East of Pampa I saw in the distance what seemed like a small rise in the land (a feature!), mottled in color, an odd mix of brown, black, and white. It was a good mile or two before the reason for this peculiar coloring was discernible. We were approaching a massive cattle operation and what we were seeing were thousands of heads of cattle—brown, black, and white—crowded into huge pens. The "rise" was nothing more than a wall of cattle that, from a distance, gave the illusion of a solid, slightly elevated land formation.

Never have I seen a town as forlorn and desolate as Pampa. Countless buildings were abandoned and gone to seed. Vacant motels and gas stations sat rusting among weed-covered lots and abandoned cars and RVs, and rusty metal barrels were strewn along the roadside.

As we traveled down Highway 60 a freight train, easily a mile long, passed us going in the opposite direction on tracks that paralleled the highway. Out here you get a better sense of how freight moves around the country on massive trains and a never-ending stream of tractor trailers.

An hour later we were in Amarillo. With apologies to the good people there, Amarillo is, to put it mildly, one of the most hideously ugly places I've ever seen, and my hometown is just thirty minutes from Newark, New Jersey, a place not known for its natural wonders. It's your classic, tacky commercial sprawl on a pancake-flat, nearly treeless plain. Amarillo: such a pretty name, though.

But Amarillo did have the virtue of being the place where we would pick up the world famous and historic Route 66, "the Mother Road," as Steinbeck dubbed it in *The Grapes of Wrath*, which runs (or, more precisely, *ran*) from Chicago to Los Angeles. Though Route 66 has mostly been abandoned and replaced by Interstate 40 in these parts, there are short sections of the original blacktop you can still drive. And many of the main streets in towns along the way still bear the designation "Historic Route 66." As in Okemah, the new interstate diverted traffic—the lifeblood of many towns along Route 66—away from downtowns that could then only be reached by exiting the new highway.

A couple of years ago the Amarillo Public Library invited me to give a talk about *Rescue Road*. During that visit I'd been downtown and was astonished by how deadly quiet it was, even in the middle of the week. My hosts took me to lunch along a thirteen-block stretch of the old Route 66, and it was there that Albie and I returned for an early dinner.

You would think that since this old section of Route 66 is just about the only real point of interest in Amarillo (something local folks would surely take issue with), the city would have made some effort to make it an appealing place to spend some time and some money, but you'd be wrong. The streets were strewn with litter, there were several empty storefronts among the souvenir shops and low-end restaurants, and enough motor-cycles roaring up and down the main drag to make you want to stick your head in a meat grinder for relief.

Albie and I took a table on the outdoor patio of a cheap Mexican restaurant to soak up the atmosphere. There was a noisy group of six at the picnic table directly in my line of vision to the street. One man, well over three hundred pounds in my estimation, sat with his T-shirt hiked halfway up his back and the waistband of his shorts roughly halfway down his rear.

Every couple of minutes he let out a bizarre growl. I could hardly wait for our food to arrive. Occasionally, when the din of the motorcycles subsided for a brief moment, it allowed the subtler sounds of squealing car tires and pickup trucks stripped of their mufflers to be heard.

Some places cannot be adequately captured in photographs. No still image of the Grand Canyon, for example, can do justice to the scale and grandeur of the place. The Kalalau Valley on the Hawaiian island of Kauai has to be seen to be appreciated, as does Yosemite Valley, the magnificent work of photographer Ansel Adams notwithstanding. The reality of these places is vastly more impressive than any representation of them. Other places—oh, let's see, the Eiffel Tower in Paris, Texas, leaps to mind—are equally unimpressive in photographs *and* in reality.

What then to make of Cadillac Ranch just off Interstate 40 on the outskirts of Amarillo? After a noisy meal of mediocre Mexican food Albie and I headed off to find out.

In 1974, a group of hippies from San Francisco, an art collective calling themselves the Ant Farm, alighted in Amarillo and planted ten Cadillac car frames, nose first, into the Texas panhandle at a nearly 52-degree angle, an angle that purportedly corresponds to the angles of the sides of the Great Pyramid of Giza in Egypt. The Ant Farm's silent financial partner was an eccentric Amarillo billionaire, a gadfly with a troubled history named Stanley Marsh 3 (not Stanley Marsh III, but Stanley Marsh 3).

This distinctively American Stonehenge has achieved iconic status and almost everyone passing through Amarillo makes a pilgrimage to see it. You've no doubt seen pictures of this unusual work of art and it is indeed impressive in pictures, mostly because cars are big things and seeing them "parked" this way, stuck in the ground nose first, is rather novel, unless you still have teenagers just learning to drive. Yet, this is one of those rare places where the real thing doesn't do justice to the photographs.

Sitting in an empty field in the middle of a vast plain and dwarfed by the huge Texas sky, Cadillac Ranch seems smaller and less imposing in real life than in pictures. But at least in real life, you can interact with the visual spectacle before you.

The thing to do here is to pick up one of the dozens of cans of spray paint visitors have left behind and make your own mark on the Cadillacs, so densely covered in layers of paint over the decades that the tires look like round, psychedelic blobs.

The day we were there was not the day to try that, however. The gale blowing from the north was so strong that when we faced into the wind Albie's ears were, as in Stillwater, pinned inside out to the sides of his head. If you tried spraying the Cadillacs with the wind at your back and missed, the paint would likely have landed somewhere in Mexico. If you'd have sprayed paint *into* the wind it would have blown right back in your face. That didn't stop people from trying, of course.

Because weather was a major factor in our travel plans I was always checking the forecast for the places we planned to be a few days ahead of time, and the forecast as we left Amarillo was cause for concern. The day we expected to reach Grand Canyon a few days hence looked to be cold and snowy and we had been planning to camp there. It looked more favorable for the days following so I considered arriving later than planned. But that alternative ran headlong into a second concern. Though we were still a few days away from our expected transit of the Mojave

Desert between Needles and Barstow, California, the long-range forecast for Needles was for temperatures to exceed one hundred degrees, and reach as high as one hundred nine degrees, for a week straight. When the air temperature is between ninety and a hundred degrees, the road surface can be between one hundred forty and one hundred fifty degrees, hot enough to buckle or turn gooey, and our car sits a mere twelve inches above the ground and would be close to that scorching heat.

The last thing we needed was an overheated engine or a flat tire while crossing the desert. The pavement would be too hot for Albie's paws and we might not be able to run the air conditioning if we broke down. So, I started to consider making that drive at night, or taking alternate routes that would mean reluctantly bypassing Grand Canyon, in my opinion the singularly most spectacular sight in America. I was loath to do that since I very much had my heart set on seeing it again after more than five decades and who knew if there'd ever be another chance? Poring over the maps, I considered a route through southern Colorado and Utah, but the choice of roads was limited, and travel would be painstakingly slow. That idea had two other strikes against it: it would again take us off Steinbeck's route, which we were trying more or less to follow, and off the Joad's route from Oklahoma to California. Our best bet was to take our chances with the weather at Grand Canyon and move faster than planned across New Mexico and into Arizona to beat the heat to the Mojave. We'd stay one night in Santa Fe instead of the two I had booked, drive in one day from Santa Fe all the way to Flagstaff, Arizona, our jumping off point for Grand Canyon, and get past Needles while the forecast there topped out at a mere ninety-nine degrees. One of the reasons we started this trip in mid-April was to avoid such extreme weather, but here we were facing the prospect of cold and snow at Grand Canyon and blistering heat in the Mojave.

The wind that had whipped us in the face at Cadillac Ranch the evening before hadn't abated the next morning as we left Amarillo, which explains why this part of the country, like Oklahoma, is also littered with massive wind farms, unimaginable in Steinbeck's day. Some people find the giant turbines a blight on the landscape (and worry about their impact on migratory birds); others find them whimsical. When it comes to energy there is no free lunch. But, truth be told, central Oklahoma and the Texas panhandle are pretty desolate anyway. It's not as if we're desecrating a national treasure such as Yosemite Valley with these windmills, at least not here.

Outside of Amarillo, as we did in the South, we passed a few churches with signboards carrying messages. But here they had a more practical angle: "Pray for Rain," several proclaimed, something the Joads would surely have understood.

About fifteen miles east of the New Mexico border the impossibly flat, seemingly endless plain ended abruptly and gave way to a more contoured landscape of dry arroyos and low-lying mesas and buttes, and the grass, such as it was, yielded to vast expanses of sagebrush. It was the most dramatic and sudden change in landscape of the trip thus far. It was as if we had suddenly been deposited in a new place, the way it feels when you fly somewhere.

When traveling by plane we can't see the subtle ways the landscape changes, the way the Blue Ridge Mountains, for example, gradually yield to the southern flats, or the way the wooded hills of southeastern Oklahoma imperceptibly become the more barren flatlands around Okemah. By car you can appreciate these changes, and the often peculiar names of the places you pass through, such as Deaf Smith County, the last county in Texas before reaching New Mexico. Erastus "Deaf" Smith was a partially deaf scout and soldier who served in the Texas Revolution in the 1830s and the first person to reach the Alamo after its fall. Lest you be overly impressed that I knew this because I am fantastically well-read, I didn't. I looked it up.

If you've seen the animated movie *Cars*, an homage to Route 66, you are familiar with the distinctive look of the vintage sports cars depicted in the film—long in hood, aerodynamically smooth and rounded and, typically, painted in bright colors with racing stripes in an accent color. As if on cue, just as we entered New Mexico and started looking for remnants of the old Route 66 we could drive, a dozen Dodge Vipers traveling together flew past us at high speed. It was if the animated cars in the film had sprung to life. There was some sort of rally or convention of Viper aficionados underway somewhere in the area; some of the cars were from as far away as Florida. My favorite was one from Texas because the license plate simply said, "HOLD EM." (Get it? "Texas" along the top of the plate and then "hold 'em.")

Cars, the film, also explored the ruin of the once vibrant towns along Route 66. One of those real-life towns is Tucumcari where Albie and I stopped for a walk. Route 66 still runs right through the town, it's the main drag, but most traffic flies by on Interstate 40. As in Pampa, Texas, many of the empty lots were overgrown with weeds and the empty husks of old gas stations were slowly deteriorating in the desert sun. A few cheap motels, the Buckaroo and the Palomino, were still in business, just barely, it seemed.

The main attraction here, as it is in all of the small towns along the old 66, is nostalgia for the Mother Road. Souvenir shops carry all manner of Route 66 ephemera: replica road signs, shot glasses, T-shirts, and license plate holders, all adorned with the iconic "Route 66" insignia.

Albie posed for some pictures in front of a large mural painted on the side of a brick building in Tucumcari, a mural depicting the glamour of the road as it existed in the mid-twentieth century, cars passing cacti and road signs that said, TUCUMCARI TONIGHT and GET YOUR KICKS ON ROUTE 66. One of the motels in town had elaborate murals painted onto the façade that incorporated the doors to the motel rooms, murals depicting characters dancing the Lindy Hop or the jitterbug, characters that appeared to be straight out of *The Great Gatsby* with their classic cars and champagne glasses. These murals, which appeared in towns all along the old Route 66, became one of my favorite parts of our passage, iconic American folk art, worth the trip in and of themselves.

We were bound this day for Santa Fe and the farther we got into New Mexico the more quintessentially Western the scenery became. Mesas off in the distance, tan expanses of grass dotted with sage, scrub pine, and tumbleweeds, nearly as light as air, blowing across and along the highway. Freight trains snaked along the tracks that paralleled the highway.

What makes car travel for the easterner so novel, and a little discomfiting here in the vast empty spaces of the West, is that places of human habitation can be so distant from one another. Back East we mostly travel town to town to town, but it's not unusual in these parts to go thirty, forty, or fifty miles between human settlements during which the road itself is virtually the only sign of human presence. Even Santa Fe is "apart," about fifty miles off Interstate 40 on Highway 285, and until you reach the outskirts there's not a single town to be seen.

Once we exited the interstate onto 285 and were no longer traveling eighty miles an hour, I pulled over and put the top down. (At eighty the turbulence in the car, especially in the back seat where Albie was riding, can be too much.) As is typically the case here in the high desert, the sky was perfectly clear and the temperature a comfortable seventy degrees. At midday we cruised into the heart of downtown Santa Fe and parked.

Downtown Santa Fe is touristy and upscale, filled with boutiques and shops selling Native American art and jewelry, but it's a lovely place with a central square to walk about. The buildings are mostly traditional adobe pueblo style, which felt at once charming and a little contrived. Even the new, multilevel parking garage looked like it was designed by architects from Fred Flintstone's hometown of Bedrock.

But downtown was blessedly quiet; none of the motorcycles and hot rods that plagued us from Tupelo to Amarillo. As we sat at a sidewalk table at a Mexican restaurant all we could hear were the sounds of birds chirping and people conversing at a normal level. A gentle desert breeze riffled the leaves on the trees and all around us trees and flowers were in bloom. It was extraordinarily, impossibly pleasant. Santa Fe is also very dog-friendly; there wasn't a store or coffee shop where Albie wasn't welcome and everyone, it seemed, had put out a water bowl by their front entrance.

Albie and I had been with one another nearly every minute of every day for more than two weeks now. We'd driven all the way from Massachusetts to Santa Fe, and all that time I thought we were on this trip together. That night, in Santa Fe, I realized I was mistaken. We were actually on separate trips . . . together.

Our hotel was up in the foothills not far from downtown, with a direct view of the Sangre de Cristo Mountains, which run north-south along Santa Fe's eastern flank. Just before bed I debated whether to take Albie outside to give him one more opportunity to relieve himself before settling down for the night—debated because I was beat and ready to sleep. But it had been a while, so we went for a short walk.

Outside there was a barely perceptible, faint white glow behind the mountains across the valley to our east. The night sky was moonless, and I wondered if the glow was the moon about to rise. If so, it was bound to be a spectacular sight in the clear night sky. Gradually the glow grew brighter and brighter and expanded until a slim line of solid white appeared above the ridge line.

Those moments when the moon rises and the sun sets, as they reach or breach the horizon, are the most awe-inspiring because you can see them move or, to be more precise, you can see the Earth's rotation bring them into fuller view or make them disappear. Once above the horizon and transiting the sky the sense of movement slows to imperceptibility.

The moonrise was utterly breathtaking in its silent beauty. It felt as if we were inside the works of an intricate watch, only the watch here was our solar system. Here we were, just Albie and me, watching the rotation of the Earth itself, a breathtaking moonrise, a miracle of the universe unfolding right before us.

Except Albie was completely oblivious to this astronomical spectacle. As much as I wished he could share this exquisite, almost spiritual moment with me, he could neither appreciate the visual beauty of the moonrise nor grasp the basic cosmology required to understand the gradual appearance of a white sphere in the night sky and the workings of the solar system. Without that knowledge, what to me was a moment of sublime, transcendent beauty was for Albie a nonevent. As I watched in awe as the moon hung itself in the night sky, Albie turned and faced the other direction, utterly disinterested in the spectacle unfolding *behind* him. But maybe he was indulging some new intoxicating and unusual desert scent, wondering why I was staring at the sky instead of putting my nose to the ground as he was.

As much as he had been a true and loving and uncomplaining travel companion, and as much as I will always treasure the memory of our adventure together, he simply wasn't capable of sharing some of what made the trip such a joy for me. It's not a fault, it's a limitation, one dogs make up for in myriad ways. But we won't, not now and not two years from now, look at each other and say, "Remember that night in Santa Fe? Wasn't the moonrise amazing?"

Albie had been happy wherever we'd been to pose for pictures—at Cadillac Ranch and in front of the Route 66 mural in Tucumcari, for example—but he had no way of knowing *why* I'd chosen those spots, or *why* ten Cadillac cars were sticking up out of the Texas plain. He didn't realize how lucky we were to chance to stop in Okemah, Oklahoma, the day that we did, why Woody Guthrie mattered to me, why Elvis mattered to the people in Tupelo, or what distinguished Asheville from Nashville. He may have known we were no longer home, but he had no idea how far we'd traveled or why, or if we were ever going back. In short, there was a limit to what Albie and I could share. This didn't make him an inadequate travel companion in any way. I loved being with him, but we were not, alas, having the same experience. I was, in some ways, traveling alone but not quite alone. Just as Albie was unable to share much of what I was experiencing, I was unable to share much of what he was experiencing and *how* he was experiencing it, and we couldn't talk about it.

The next day, we happened to wake up for our morning walk just as the sun was rising in nearly the exact spot where the moon had risen the night before. The moon still hung high in the deep blue sky to the west. Here we were, man and dog standing on planet Earth with the sun rising over the mountains to the east and the moon still in transit across the sky to the west. It felt as if we were bit players in a giant celestial time piece. As I got lost deeper and deeper in the profundity of my own thoughts and the cosmic grandeur of it all, I looked over at Albie. He was squatting over a carefully selected sagebrush.

TWELVE

Grand Canyon Sweet*

I wished we could have stayed another day in Santa Fe as we'd planned, because one day was hardly enough to explore this lovely town in the high desert surrounded by mountains. But the heat forecast for Needles and the Mojave was getting more extreme every day. Now the high temperatures were predicted to be one hundred and ten with no relief in sight. We had just three more days to beat the heat. And to think I had originally planned to make this trip in the summer!

But for now, as we crossed New Mexico at the very end of April and the very beginning of May, the weather was exactly as I'd hoped, especially for Albie's comfort: clear and in the sixties.

---

* A play on *Grand Canyon Suite* by American composer Ferde Grofé, composed between 1929 and 1931.

As we approached Gallup we were driving through a landscape that had launched a thousand Westerns: flat, scrubby land dotted with sage bumping up against massive table-flat mesas of red rock. It was easy to imagine John Wayne or Clint Eastwood astride a horse, squinting into the sun here.

When I say high desert, I do mean *high* desert, for just east of Gallup we crossed the Continental Divide at 7,000 feet above sea level. I was last in Gallup about fifty years ago and had no specific memories of the place. We parked downtown on the main drag (old Route 66 again) and took a walk around. Unlike many of the towns we'd seen, Gallup actually seemed *alive*; there were a lot of people out and about, many of Native American descent. Shops selling Native American crafts abounded.

We stepped into a coffee shop where Albie was welcome, and I chatted with the young woman making my iced mocha, who also happened to own the place. She was a self-described "military brat" who'd grown up mostly in New Mexico and Virginia and returned to Gallup five years ago.

"I love it here," she told me. "It's the town that time forgot. There's no Starbucks [a big plus, I suppose, for a coffee shop owner] and none of the tourist trap things you find in other places."

This struck me as not quite right since downtown was chock-full of shops catering to the tourist trade, and I was sure the Gallup I was in fifty years ago was smaller and quieter than the one we were in now, even if I couldn't summon a particular memory of it.

I mentioned that we were making haste across the Southwest because we were determined to see the Grand Canyon and get across the Mojave before the extreme heat arrived.

This elicited a comment from a well-worn gentleman sitting at the counter listening to our conversation.

"You sound like you're from the 19th century," he said to me. "Cars don't overheat anymore." His tone betrayed no playfulness; he sounded as if he were challenging my manhood.

"Is that so?" I thought, but I didn't say it out loud. There was no point in getting into an argument with a perfect stranger in a coffee shop in Gallup, New Mexico, about the state of automotive technology. Instead, what I did say was, "I'm actually from the 20th century and I can't take a chance with a dog in the car. If we get a flat or break down the pavement will be too hot for his paws." It didn't make me sound any more masculine that I was concerned about Albie's tender feet.

"I've driven into California at Needles dozens of times," the long, tall stranger in jeans and cowboy boots said, as if he were again suggesting I was a wimp for not giving it a go.

At this point, there were two conversations. The one we were actually having and another that was taking place entirely inside my head.

"OK, wise guy," I thought, "give me your phone number and if we break down I'll call you and you can drive 450 miles and come pick us up."

Cars have indeed improved since the 19th century from whence he insinuated I had come—after all, the first automobile wasn't built until around 1890—but cars can still overheat for many reasons, a busted radiator hose or a deranged thermostat are two that come to mind. I've listened to "Car Talk" on National Public Radio for years and I know there's no end to what can go wrong with a car. We could run over a nail and get a flat. The air conditioning could develop a vacuum leak leaving us with no way to cool the car. The fuel pump could fail. It's almost a hundred and fifty miles across the desert from Needles to Barstow and I wasn't going to drive it when it was a hundred and ten degrees outside, especially when someone else was depending on me to keep him safe. I had nothing to prove to a stranger in a coffee shop in Gallup, New Mexico.

A short while later we crossed into Arizona and stopped in Winslow where, of course, my main mission was to take a few pictures of Albie standing on a corner. "Take It Easy" has been one of my favorite songs for decades. As we set up for a picture, a small, elderly Native American man whose wizened face was strikingly weathered from sun exposure walked slowly past us staring straight ahead carrying two hot dogs, one in each hand. Like the elderly man we glimpsed making his way toward his house in Connecticut our first day on the road, I wondered what life he had led out here in the desert. From the looks of it, it had been one tough row to hoe and it likely bore little resemblance to a life lived in suburban Connecticut. His was one of those faces I glimpsed but for a moment, but can still recall, many months later, quite vividly.

We lingered in Winslow only long enough for a few pictures. Just a mile or two west of town we got a faint glimpse of what had haunted the Dust Bowl refugees. The air all around Winslow was a hazy reddish-brown. Strong winds had kicked up a lot of desert dust, nothing nearly on the scale of the miles-high clouds of dust that rolled over and buried towns in Oklahoma and Texas in the 1930s, but enough to obscure the blue desert sky. This was not, apparently, an unusual phenomenon, for road signs west of Winslow warned drivers to beware of blowing dust.

Once clear of the dust, far in the distance, more than sixty miles away, I could make out the silhouette of Arizona's highest mountains straight ahead of us. The San Francisco Peaks rise thousands of feet straight out of the flat desert, the highest being Humphreys Peak at 12,633 feet above sea level. Winslow is below 5,000 feet so the peaks are dramatic. Being able to see more than fifty miles in all directions around you is such a novel experience for an easterner. It's simply astonishing how vast and sparsely populated so much of the West is.

Something I did remember from my travels here half a century ago is how dramatically the landscape and the weather change as you climb the Coconino Plateau on the approach to Flagstaff where we would spend the night. Land that can barely nourish a single tree suddenly becomes densely forested and within ten minutes the temperature dropped nearly twenty degrees, down into the upper fifties.

Warm and sunny in Winslow gave way to a chilly rain in Flagstaff, a bustling city of 71,000 inside the Coconino National Forest. (When I was last here Flagstaff was a quiet town with little more than 20,000 people.) Flagstaff feels like a Rocky Mountain ski town, something out of *Twin Peaks*, and not the kind of place you normally think of when you conjure images of Arizona.

Flagstaff was to be our jumping-off point for the Grand Canyon, a little more than an hour north. I had hoped Albie and I would camp there: it's why I'd packed a tent and a sleeping bag. Alas, after days of worrying about the wall of heat about to suffocate the Mojave, the forecast for the canyon for the next day was still a high of forty-four with wet snow.

When I was in my mid-teens, in the late 1960s, my parents signed me up with an outfit called Outdoor Travel Camps, based in Killington, Vermont. For two summers I hiked, backpacked, and rafted through the mountains, deserts, and canyons of the West, and was I ever smitten. Having grown up in suburban New Jersey, I was awestruck by the vast, empty landscape, the otherworldly rock formations, and the grandeur of it all. We hiked across snowfields in the Rockies, camped deep in the Tetons, backpacked through the Sierras, and floated in rafts between sheer canyon walls on the Green River in Utah. Those experiences made me passionate about conserving wild places and protecting the environment, a passion still with me today.

But no place rivaled the Grand Canyon. Twice I hiked from the rim to Phantom Ranch at the very bottom of the canyon, a hike that begins well before the break of dawn in summer because of the heat. I shook scorpions out of my hiking boots in the morning and watched the sun set early over the canyon rim from a mile below. There was, back then, a far less traveled part of the Grand Canyon few visitors saw, many miles west of Grand Canyon Village. To reach the ancient town of Supai in those days, you had to drive about fifty miles down a dirt road from the town of Peach Springs to the trailhead, and then hike eight miles down and through Havasu Canyon to the village. Just beyond are Havasu Falls, a series of waterfalls that put you in mind of Shangri-La. The water flows over deposits of travertine that make the water aquamarine blue. Today, you need to reserve a campsite here online; the word has gotten out since 1968.

So, I was very much looking forward to seeing the Grand Canyon again, even if I was no longer adventurous enough to hike to the bottom, and, perhaps less able than I was at fifteen, to hike back up. And Albie, with his gradually progressing arthritis, certainly wasn't up to it. But I just wanted to walk along the rim trail and stare for a few hours at one of Earth's grandest sights, and certainly its grandest canyon, and share this natural wonder with Albie, who would experience it in his own particular way. I didn't think he'd appreciate the view, but perhaps in his own doggie way, he'd find something new and exciting to appreciate, such as the smell of the pinyon pines or the great sense of empty space that is the canyon itself.

Unfortunately, nothing about the forecast had changed. Indeed, on the morning of our drive up to the canyon I had to clear some wet snow that had covered the car overnight. Whatever had accumulated on the ground had already melted. My previous trips here had all been in summer; it was now May 2. I had seen pictures of the Grand Canyon in snow and they were spectacular, so perhaps we'd be treated to views of the canyon partly dressed in white. (Snow never reaches the bottom, where the climate is markedly different than at the rim; the elevation difference is, after all, a mile.)

Once we hit the highway, snow showers alternated with bursts of tiny frozen pellets of hail. The mountain peaks around us wore new blankets of snow. We turned off Interstate 40 and onto the two-lane road leading north to the canyon. My hopes for the weather rose and fell with every small change in elevation across the gently undulating Coconino Plateau. One minute there was no snow, then, after gaining a few feet in elevation, we were surrounded by snow on the ground and covering the trees, then, dropping back down a few feet, bare ground and snowless trees again, so exquisitely sensitive was the snow line to slight changes in elevation.

We arrived at the entrance to Grand Canyon National Park expecting the crowds to be sparse. It was early May and it was cold. We were wrong. (Well, Albie probably didn't have any thoughts about whether there'd be crowds, but at this point our separate identities were merging into one, despite our cognitive differences.) Though no doubt even more crowded in summer, the slushy parking lots and walking paths were mobbed. For the first time since I'd walked Albie in twenty-seven-degree temperatures along the Skyline Drive in Virginia I put my winter parka on. And for the first time in nearly half a century I was just yards away from taking in the sight that had so captivated me as a teenager. Albie sat patiently in the back seat while I slipped his harness over his head and then alighted into the slush. We walked past the cars and tour buses for the first overlook we could find. And there we stood, at the very edge of the great Grand Canyon, one of the true wonders of the world. We could see absolutely nothing.

A thick fog completely filled and obscured the canyon. You could sense it, this great crevice in the Earth, and you could hear the great silence, but you could not see it. And because of the heat coming to the Mojave we couldn't linger another day in the hopes the weather would improve as the forecast suggested it would.

I looked at Albie and spoke to him, explaining my plan . . . our plan. "Albie, we're gonna wait all day if we have to, but we're not leaving. Maybe it'll get better." He looked at me as I talked as if to say, "Whatever you say. You're the boss!" He's nothing if not agreeable.

For the next couple of hours, we walked along the South Rim Trail, really a paved walkway. Many of the tourists were from Asia, traveling in large, luxury buses. Several of them wanted to meet Albie, shake his paw, and have their picture taken with him, and he happily obliged.

The farther we got from the parking area the fewer people we encountered until we were utterly alone with the great yawning invisible silence of the canyon literally at our feet. I hadn't brought waterproof shoes and my Vans and socks were thoroughly soaked from walking through the slush. As the stubborn fog persisted, my disappointment grew. It was entirely possible we'd come all this way and would never see the canyon. Occasionally, a patch of blue sky would suddenly open above us, but they were just teases. The fog lingered in the canyon and the sun wasn't burning it off.

We soldiered on soaked and disappointed for nearly two hours when the fog and the canyon began playing an elaborate game of peekaboo. For a few seconds, we could see down the canyon wall for a hundred feet or so, enough to whet our appetite and raise our hopes, only to have the fog roll back in and again obscure the view. This continued for about a half hour during which we briefly had one glimpse all the way across the canyon to the North Rim. By now we had walked back to the parking lot, but I wasn't ready to give up. As I put on dry socks and shoes, tiny pellets of hail started dancing off the windshield. Albie and I shared some cheese slices.

Two night earlier, in Santa Fe, I had the epiphany that Albie was utterly indifferent to what we *saw* on our trip. The magnificent moonrise over the mountains mattered not at all to him. As desperately as I was hoping the skies would clear so we could see the canyon, it wouldn't matter to Albie one way or the other. He had no way of appreciating how the Colorado River had over the eons carved this canyon into the Earth. He could not be awestruck by it. He enjoyed our wet walk along the trail because he liked eating the snow, smelling the juniper bushes and pinyon pines, and seeing the occasional squirrel darting about. Grand Canyon? What canyon? I had to beg his indulgence for a few hours more to satisfy myself that we'd done our best to see what we, or I, had come to see.

"We're going to stay until dinnertime," I told him. He didn't disagree.

Rather than continue walking in the slush I decided to drive the South Rim road toward what was surely a misnomer today: Desert View, about twenty-five miles east of Grand Canyon Village. It was like fishing. If you aren't having any luck in one spot, change spots.

We weren't even two miles down the road when the canyon suddenly came into full, take-your-breath-away view. I pulled into the first overlook I could find and hustled Albie out of the car. With snow on the rim and any flat surface it could cling to a few hundred feet below the rim, the canyon never looked as stunning as I saw it at that moment. Snow squalls swept through under dark clouds which only added to the drama. Weather makes the canyon seem more alive than seeing it on a clear, sunny day when only slowly shifting shadows slightly change the view. It's static. But today it was all drama.

We took in the view from several different overlooks, sometimes with hail smacking us in the head. I so wished Albie could appreciate what we were seeing. Clouds, fog, shadows, and snow showers raced through the canyon as breaks in the overcast allowed the sun to illuminate large sections of it at the same time. Occasionally, you could see a huge illuminated section of the canyon *behind* the snow showers or a curtain of light fog would suddenly drop down from the sky. The wildness of the weather made for quite a show.

Of course, human stupidity always seems to be part of the show, too. People scrambled past barriers and signs warning them of the danger to clamber onto narrow pinnacles, seeking the most dramatic picture of themselves they could muster. Even the slippery wet snow wasn't a deterrent.

All afternoon we played cat and mouse with frozen, pellet-ized snow, sun, and fog; views opened and views obscured. Our patience had paid off, at least for me.

En route to Kingman, where we would spend the night, I stopped just before we rejoined Interstate 40 in Williams, Arizona. Albie had been so patient as we waited out the weather, he deserved a special treat: a plain McDonald's hamburger which he consumed in about three seconds. On a whim, we pulled off the highway in Seligman, one of those Route 66 towns orphaned by the interstate. The attraction of these towns is quite genuine; you can get a taste of the old Route 66 and imagine what it must have been like in its heyday. Here we again met many Asian tourists, and again Albie patiently posed for pictures with them. I can only assume dogs are not common pets in parts of Asia, or at least not large dogs like Albie, especially in cities where people live in small dwellings, because he sure was a hit. Because he'd been such a good ambassador, he not only got to have a hamburger this day, but now a vanilla ice cream cone as well, also polished off in about three seconds.

Between Seligman and Kingman, the roadside scenery became quite dramatic: jagged mountain ranges and huge boulders, and every which way you looked you could see for fifty miles or more. Through breaks in the clouds, enormous draperies of sunbeams hung from the sky and brushed the ground, brilliantly lighting parts of the landscape as others sat in shadow. To our right a dust devil danced a jig and spun reddish dirt a couple of hundred feet in the air.

As we drove this stretch across the Arizona desert I felt like we'd really hit our stride. The strangeness of the road, away from home and the familiar routines, made our days seem surreal at times. It took a while for me to truly appreciate that we really were on this glorious trip. Tomorrow we'd cross the California state line, meaning, yes, we really had driven this little red car clear across the United States.

I was determined to enter California at Needles, just as the Joads had, my little, inadequate way of paying homage to the hundreds of thousands of Dust Bowl refugees who had passed this way in desperation nearly a century ago. Needles is where the Joad men bathed in the Colorado River, on the edge of their soon to be dashed dreams.

Most affordable motels in small cities and towns across America are clustered near exits off the interstate. There, side by side with all the familiar fast-food joints, these little villages of sleeping and eating franchises welcome weary travelers looking for a decent night's sleep and something to fill their bellies. They're all pretty much the same, which is why it often pays, once you've unloaded your bags, to drive another couple of miles into town, the *real* town.

There was something very appealing about little downtown Kingman, Arizona, where we walked at twilight as the sun set in the western sky. It wasn't bustling, to be sure, but there were a few inviting eateries spread along Main Street (old Route 66 yet again) with retro art deco–style signs that looked to be original. The grounds around the multi-columned Mohave County Court-house and city hall were handsome and the buildings themselves simple but attractive. It was clean, mercifully quiet, and peaceful.

"We're going to California tomorrow, Albie," I said. He cocked his head slightly. I knew it meant nothing in particular to him, but I liked talking to him anyway. "Let's get some sleep."

THIRTEEN

California Dreamin'

W hy do some towns, such as Okemah, Oklahoma, and Pampa, Texas, die or become shells of their former selves, while others, seemingly in the absolute middle of nowhere, grow and prosper? The answer is probably as varied as the towns themselves.

On our way south along Arizona Route 95 toward Needles we made a slight detour and drove across a bridge spanning the Colorado River into Laughlin, the town at the pointed southern tip of Nevada. And if you stood at the very southern tip of Laughlin you could easily throw one baseball into Arizona and another into California.

I'd never heard of Laughlin, and it took me by surprise. It's a tiny version of Las Vegas, seemingly in the middle of nowhere, with large casinos, riverboats sitting in the Colorado, brand-new manicured parks filled with flowers, and a modern pedestrian bridge, part of the Colorado River Heritage Greenway and Trails, that offers views of the river and Laughlin's sister city on the other side, Bullhead City, Arizona. Everything looked brand new, as if it had been laid down in the last couple of years. As we walked, a Suncoast 737 glided past on approach to the Laughlin airport. This rapidly growing city at the edge of the Mojave is a destination.

Here in the middle of the desert, a place as unlike home in New England as one could imagine, reality interrupted when Judy called me about a billing problem with our health insurance. When Judy and I are home together, there isn't a phone call, text, or tweet that doesn't seem to demand her immediate attention, whether we're driving somewhere, having dinner, or taking a walk. Yet, when I'm traveling, and it was true thus far on our trip, when *I* call I'm lucky if she answers. Usually I talk to voice mail. And when I do get through I'm most likely to hear, "I'm just walking into my mother's, can I call you later?" or "I'm just getting the dogs out, can I call you later?" or "I'm just going out to meet [fill in name of any one of Judy's several hundred close friends], can I call you later?" There had, on this trip, been no conversations that began, "I just wanted to hear your voice" or "I miss you" or "Just checking in to make sure you guys are OK." I might be driving through a barren stretch of desert feeling slightly homesick when I'd get a text that read, "Did you move the baking pans?" or "Where is Salina's medication?" or "Jamba hasn't pooped in two days." Not even an opening salutation! Maybe it's a sign of a mature marriage—like our agreement that this year's anniversary gift to each other would be new gutters for the house—that our communication was mostly transactional, such as this one about the health insurance bill. Don't get me wrong, Judy is a caring, generous (to a fault), and sentimental person, a good wife and mother, and I love her very much, but it would be an understatement to say she doesn't wear her heart on her sleeve (as I often do), and she certainly doesn't put it in writing, not even into a text, and rarely into a phone call.

In any event, since I was the primary policy holder on our health insurance (I'm on Medicare now), they insisted on talking with me. It was odd, to say the least, to be standing in Laughlin, Nevada, in the desert, Albie by my side, trying to unravel a mundane billing issue back in Massachusetts, and it reminded me of how nice it was to be divorced from all of the day-to-day tasks that demand attention at home.

With the health insurance issue resolved (we owed them $32), we crossed back into Arizona and continued down Highway 95 toward Needles. There was construction everywhere. New houses and strip malls were going up for miles and miles around, joining others recently built. We passed a brand-new hospital and new schools and new parks. The place was booming. Not that I've ever been there, but it seemed like an American version of Dubai. There was even a boat dealer with gleaming white boats and yachts for sale, boats that would have looked at home in Nantucket Harbor, but odd here in the middle of the desert even if the Colorado River was nearby. The sprawl continued all the way to Needles some thirty miles south of Laughlin.

I thought back to towns such as Okemah and Pampa, towns on the decline, and marveled that here in the middle of the desert a new metropolis was being born. This wasn't an area reinventing itself. It was *being invented*.

❖

As we approached Needles, I was quite aware of the absurdity of my determination to track the Joad family route here and across the Mojave. Our circumstances could not have been more different from those faced by the Joads, and the countless thousands they represented in Steinbeck's novel. They were driving for their lives, broke and desperate, in a jalopy barely up to the journey. We were on a pleasure trip in a BMW convertible and I had three credit cards with generous credit limits in my wallet. No one was looking to exploit us, run us off their land, or treat us like vermin. Still, I wanted to see the landscape they did and summon Steinbeck's unforgettably heartbreaking account.

Needles is a small place and we were through it in just a few unremarkable minutes. Tomorrow the heat would descend and stay for a week or more. We'd made more haste than we'd planned across the Southwest to beat that heat and as we drove the one hundred thirty miles across the Mojave I wasn't sorry. The land was devoid of trees and almost any sign of human life, save for the passing cars and trains. The land rises and falls gently so that in some places you can see the traffic, like a marching army of ants, making its way along Interstate 40 for miles off in the distance. And you can see the freight trains snaking their way across the desert, too. It was as if we had entered a world in miniature, all human presence dwarfed by the vastness of it all. What a journey it must have been in an old jalopy with no money and all your belongings piled high and strapped on back, barely clinging to your humanity and your hope.

As we approached Barstow I wondered when the Dust Bowl refugees first glimpsed the rich, verdant fields and valleys of their imaginations, the Land of Plenty they had heard rumors about. We saw some irrigated and cultivated fields starting about fifteen miles east of Barstow, but Barstow is still very much a desert town. We'd have to wait.

A short way beyond Barstow we passed an exit sign for Twenty Mule Team Road. Now, if you're about my age, that almost certainly will ring a bell. It rang my bell, but I couldn't quite remember why, and for Albie, of course, it rang no bell at all. I know because I looked over my right shoulder and asked him. He was lying with his front legs stretched out in front of him with his head in between. He raised his eyebrows ever so slightly as if to say, "Can't you see I'm resting here? When do we eat?"

Then we passed another sign, for the town of Boron, and it hit me: "20 Mule Team Borax." But what the heck was 20 Mule Team Borax and what did it have to do with Boron? I couldn't recall. So, I pulled over and looked it up on my phone.

From 1952 to 1970 there was a popular television show called *Death Valley Days*, sponsored by a brand of laundry cleaner, still made today by Dial, called 20 Mule Team Borax. Indeed, just beyond the exit for Boron was another exit for Borax Road. Borax, or sodium borate, is a compound of the chemical element boron, and it won't surprise you to learn that near the town of Boron is a large boron mine where they harvest the raw material for 20 Mule Team Borax. It was all quite bemusing; a little boron blast from the past.

A few days earlier, as I was plotting out our travels ahead, I decided we would stay in Tehachapi our first night in California. Neither Barstow nor Bakersfield appealed. All I knew of Tehachapi, located between the two, was the lyric from the Little Feat song, "Willin'":

I've been from Tucson to Tucumcari
Tehachapi to Tonopah
Driven every kind of rig that's ever been made
Driven the back roads
So I wouldn't get weighed
And if you give me weed, whites, and wine
And you show me a sign
I'll be willin' . . . to be movin'

Tehachapi turned out to be a very nice surprise. No weed, whites, or wine for us, but it had perfectly manicured parks with thick green lawns, cozy cottages on flowered lots, and a pleasant downtown. The main park was a perfect place for Albie and me to stretch our legs and make some friends; it was filled with families scampering on playground equipment or sitting at picnic tables. A little towheaded five-year-old with hazel eyes named Kylee was the first of many to stroke Albie's head; within five minutes he was basking in the attention of a gaggle of young girls who were utterly taken by his good looks and gentle manner. Goodness, he was being so much calmer and approachable on our trip than at home and I was again truly grateful for that. He might not have been able to appreciate the Grand Canyon in the same way I did, but he was definitely making the most of this adventure in his own way, even if the end result was just more belly rubs.

A young couple in clothes that would have been in place at the turn of the 20th century stood on the grass next to a portable stand with some religious literature. We passed them twice walking the footpath around the park and simply nodded at one other. Thankfully, they didn't try to rope me in to a discussion of theology. Thus assured that they weren't aggressive proselytizers I said hello on our third pass. They were warm and friendly, and as we talked they made no attempt to turn Albie and me into Jehovah's Witnesses. They seemed astonished we'd driven all the way from Boston and told us they liked living in Tehachapi, which they described as "quiet and churchy." Apparently so, since about a half hour later as I sat on a bench with Albie next to me on the grass, we were approached by a second couple who were also spreading the Word, but with a little more determination. The young man was dressed in a dark suit with a black shirt and a white tie. I told him he looked like he'd walked off the set of *The Sopranos*. He laughed, but when I asked, he admitted he had no idea what I was talking about. Wanting to be polite, I accepted the pamphlet his companion offered, but I also knew I'd be tossing it at the first opportunity.

Just off the main street Albie and I found a decent looking "Mediterranean deli," as it described itself, with an outdoor patio and took a table outside. It was a perfect evening, warm but not hot, with a cloudless sky and a dry gentle breeze.

So many of our conversations, long or short, with people on this trip started with one of four questions, all related to Albie. May I pet him? What's his name? What kind of dog is he? And, finally, how old is he? I never quite understood why people were so curious to know his age. So, it was a bit novel when the man at the next table, dining alone, simply said, "That's a nice-looking dog."

His name was Shady (pronounced "Shad," he told me) and he hailed from southern Egypt. I was surprised to meet someone from southern Egypt in this small California town, and over our respective meals we talked. Thirty-six years old, he had recently finished training to be a pharmacist in Los Angeles. He'd been in the United States for four years with his green card and had taken a job a few months earlier at a pharmacy in Tehachapi, a town where he knew absolutely no one, though his brother lives in Bakersfield, about forty-five minutes away. His mother and sister are still in Egypt. He lives in a house he found on Craigslist with three other guys he doesn't know and though he said he'd met a few people in town I had the sense it was a pretty lonely existence for him in this small California town.

He always wanted to come to America, he told me, because there is very little opportunity in Egypt. Like so many people, born here and not, Shady was pursuing his own American dream.

"If you don't mind my asking," I said, "are you Muslim?" I was curious to know what it might be like for a Muslim in this "churchy" town.

"No, I'm a Christian," he told me. Given the anti-immigrant sentiment that has gripped America in the Trump era, I wondered if he'd encountered any of it. It was good to hear he had not.

After we'd wished each other good luck and gone our separate ways I thought about what it must be like to be so far from home, trying to make your way in a foreign land, and almost never seeing a face familiar from your past. His brother is the only person in America who knew him more than four years ago when he came to the United States, and no one he ever sees in Tehachapi has known him more than a few months. Though Albie and I were strangers here, too, we weren't making a life here, and we'd seen people we'd known for years in New Orleans and would again, both family and friends, in a few days when we reached the Bay Area. We were traveling *through* here, not living here, and we would, in a few weeks, be back where everyone knows our names. That's a much different kind of "alone" than Shady was experiencing. He was a man without context here, in a country not his own. What, then, does it mean for him to "be home?" Can a room in a house shared with three strangers met on Craigslist ever feel like home? How long, if ever, would it take for a man from Egypt to feel like this small town in California was his home?

Earlier in the day, as we drove past Barstow, my iPhone, which was playing songs from my music library randomly, alighted on Eric Clapton and Steve Winwood's 2009 version of "Can't Find My Way Home," the one I added to my playlist when I had pre-trip dreams of being unable to *get* home. It must have been that and my conversation with Shady that worked their way into my subconscious that night. It was also our first night in California, which meant we had driven about as far from home as we could get and still be in the continental United States. Our sparse hotel room smelled strongly of disinfectant, nothing homey about it, adding to the sense of isolation.

First, I dreamt I was trying to drive home but couldn't. No matter which way I turned we were unable to get closer. Then I dreamt we'd lost the car, parked it somewhere and couldn't find it. I dreamt I wanted to go back to college, Amherst College where I went as an undergraduate, but realized I wouldn't know anyone when I got there.

You can't go home again. That's what all those dreams seemed to be saying. And what if we couldn't? What would life be like forever on the road trying, futilely, to get back home? It was terrifying.

In the middle of the night I awoke with a headache, the first of the trip. The overpowering odor of the disinfectant was the first thing I noticed, and I felt very, *very* far from home. When I was talking with Shady the previous evening and he asked me how old I was, I could hardly believe the words that came out of my mouth. "I'll be sixty-five in November," I said. Here, in the middle of the night with a splitting headache in an antiseptic motel room on the other side of the continent I wondered, "Why is a man my age driving across the country with his dog?" I was homesick.

When we had arrived in Tehachapi the day before, I e-mailed back and forth with an old friend and colleague, Bill Monning. Bill, a native Californian, was a lawyer with the legal department of the United Farm Workers of America (UFW) in the 1970s and 1980s, working closely with Cesar Chavez and Dolores Huerta, the cofounders of the UFW. He was later directing attorney with the legal aid organization California Rural Legal Assistance. One of Bill's primary efforts was litigation to seek compensation for farmworkers for illness and deaths caused by exposure to pesticides in the fields. A little over a decade ago, Bill entered politics, first winning a seat in the California State Assembly, then in the state Senate, representing a coastal district that stretches from just south of San José all the way to just north of Santa Maria. He's now the California Senate majority leader.

Bill and I were trying to work out the timing for Albie and me to spend the night with him in Sacramento. When I told him we were in Tehachapi he wrote that we should plan a stop just fifteen miles down the road in Keene, at the place Cesar Chavez called "La Paz" (or more fully, "Nuestra Señora Reina de La Paz"), now the site of the Cesar Chavez National Monument, where Chavez and his wife, Helen, were laid to rest. This small national monument is a property with a Spanish-style building purchased by the UFW and became the political and spiritual center of the farmworkers' movement.

I had been looking for the place where the Joads might have finally glimpsed the green, fertile valleys of their dreams and, fittingly, it very well might have been in Keene, for it is here that State Highway 58 descends into California's Central Valley, the richest farmland in the world. Just before the road reaches the valley floor, we turned off to visit La Paz, which Albie and I had to ourselves, save for a groundskeeper, that morning. It felt like a tiny Garden of Eden. Wisteria hung from trellises, the flower gardens were carefully curated, and the graves of the Chavezes were set in a small lawn bordered on one side by a granite wall with a fountain, above which was a frieze showing workers in the fields marching forward. It was profoundly peaceful. On the granite wall was a quote, in Spanish and English, from the American-born son of Mexican immigrants who dedicated his life to the farmworkers' cause: "It is my deepest belief that only by giving our lives do we find life." It was all very moving. The bountiful fields of the Central Valley are where countless dreams have crashed and many have lost their lives.

As you drive the Central Valley, which runs for hundreds of miles, the basic, immutable and cruel laws of nature and economics stare you in the face, the very same laws that so daunted the Joads. It's a place where water, earth, and a steady supply of hands have to cooperate to bring forth the bounty. For the migrant workers who toil under the hot sun harvesting grapes and lettuce, dates and oranges, pecans and pistachios, life is lived on the margins. For the growers, dependent on having enough hands at precisely the right time, life can be good. As we made our way up the eastern side of the valley there was the occasional McMansion, lavishly landscaped, sitting among the fields as if it had been dropped down, complete with a yard, from outer space. They looked preposterous here, these little estates that would have been more at home in the suburbs of Atlanta or Nashville or New York.

As we made our way from Bakersfield toward Porterville the road was lined with oil derricks that looked like a herd of davening* mechanical dinosaurs. Through Visalia, Exeter, and Orange Cove, all the way up the valley, orange groves extended in every direction, and in the distance to the east the snow-laden Sierra Nevada mountains provided the backdrop.

That we were in the Central Valley at all was unexpected because until just two days earlier I had planned to drive up the Pacific Coast Highway through Big Sur and Monterey and then inland to Steinbeck's hometown of Salinas. So much of Steinbeck's work—*Cannery Row, Of Mice and Men, Tortilla Flat, East of Eden*—is set in these places. It's a drive I'd made several times before, but never in a convertible, and it was to be the automotive highlight of the entire trip. California. The Pacific Ocean. Albie in the back and the wind blowing through what's left of my hair.

A couple of years ago a landslide near Big Sur closed the Pacific Coast Highway, but I didn't know that it had not yet reopened.** I only found out when my brother-in-law, Andy, with whom we planned to stay in the Bay Area, e-mailed to tell me. It was just as well, though still a little disappointing. In *Travels with Charley,* Steinbeck didn't drive along the California coast, but through the Central Valley. Since we were hewing to Steinbeck's route with some modifications, it was more fitting. It also meant

---

* *Davening* is part of the prayer ritual of orthodox Jews who, while praying, repeatedly rock back and forth from the waist up, their heads bobbing up and down, as if to take a sip of water from a water fountain.

** It reopened in mid-July, a couple of months after our trip.

we would be within shouting distance of Yosemite National Park, so we decided to head there, not a bad consolation prize. To my surprise, even in early May, every campsite in the park was booked, but that turned out to be a small blessing because we otherwise would never have met Jon and Lois Moroni.

I didn't know what to expect when I booked a room for the two of us at the Restful Nest, a bed-and-breakfast in Mariposa, high in the Sierra foothills and about an hour from the western entrance to Yosemite. Well off the beaten path a few miles from town, Jon and Lois's house sits on acres of splendid isolation with views of distant mountains. They're both in their late seventies and diabetic, and Jon suffers from neuropathy in his feet that gives him an awkward gait. Yet, they tend to the house and the grounds, which include an in-ground pool, with loving determination. They have several guestrooms, but Albie and I were the only guests the first of our two nights there, and Jon and Lois invited us to have dinner with them. It had been weeks since we (or, rather, I) had had a home-cooked dinner so I was delighted by the invitation and the warmth it implied. Albie was welcome, too—they *loved* Albie from the moment they laid eyes on him—and he made me proud by lying quietly at my feet throughout.

There were only three of us, but enough food for ten: pasta puttanesca, fresh asparagus, and plenty of red wine. All thanks to the kindness of strangers who, within an hour, felt like family.

Jon and Lois, refugees from the fast pace and tumult of Los Angeles, had looked all over the west for a bed-and-breakfast to buy and had bought this place twenty-one years earlier. Jon spoke with an accent I couldn't identify and was too polite to ask about, but he solved the mystery when he told me he'd been born in France to a very poor family and orphaned after the Second World War. At age thirteen he was adopted by a middle-class family in L.A. and came to the states speaking not a word of English. We spoke of family, of our kids, and, of course, about dogs; Jon and Lois showed me pictures of dogs they once had and told me their B&B is dog-friendly because dogs are much better behaved guests than young children. We touched only lightly on politics—Jon told me he was more "red than blue" though he decried the great concentration of wealth in this country. "It's what leads to revolution," he said. Just when I thought I'd had my fill (of dinner), Lois insisted the three of us finish a newly opened pint of Häagen-Dazs ice cream.

Everything about Jon and Lois spoke to the basic decency of most people everywhere and the simple but powerful effect of breaking bread with strangers. By the end of a single meal it felt like we'd come to stay with long-lost cousins, and our cozy room had the feel of staying at grandma's. Indeed, Jon and Lois have thirteen grandchildren and great-grandchildren.

Breakfast the next morning, again in Jon and Lois's living quarters in the large house, was enough to sink a ship. After the fresh fruit and peach cobbler, I thought breakfast was over. Then came the frittata, sausage, bacon, and potatoes. Jon and Lois were intent on making sure not only that we felt at home, but that I should never go hungry again, which is why, as Albie and I were about to head up to Yosemite, Lois handed me a cooler bag packed with more peach cobbler, fruit, and a frozen bottle of spring water, to drink when the ice melted.

It had been decades since I'd been to Yosemite and even now, in early May, it was overrun by visitors, many of whom, especially those from China and India, seemed more interested in Albie than the impossibly beautiful valley before them.

Yosemite's magnificent waterfalls can dry up in late summer, but the snow melt of spring makes them especially prolific. After driving to the classic viewpoints—Tunnel View and Washburn Point high up above the valley—we settled into a spot in the valley by the river across from El Capitan, the massive, sheer granite rock face that is a Holy Grail for rock climbers.

I was unaware that the previous June a climber named Alex Honnold became the first person to scale El Capitan without ropes, safety equipment, or assistance—free solo—and he did it in just under four hours, an astonishing feat that would become the subject of an Oscar-winning documentary by that name: *Free Solo.* But when I saw the film a few months after our visit to Yosemite I had a far better sense of just what a mind-boggling accomplishment it was, for the scale of the thing is hard to comprehend.

The top of El Capitan is 3,600 feet above the valley floor and it's so massive that it's nearly impossible to spot a rock climber with the naked eye. Albie, as is his wont, lay down briefly in the river, shook himself off, and then settled down by my side as I scanned the rock for signs of a climber. It took a few minutes, but I eventually spotted a tiny bright orange dot about three-quarters of the way up. With the aid of binoculars, I located the orange dot again and saw that it was a caddy of some kind for conveying rock-climbing equipment. A little farther up the wall I spotted him (or her): a climber painstakingly making his way up and across the rock face toward the summit.

There are people my age still capable of a climb like that, but even as a young man the thought of clinging to a sheer rock wall thousands of feet above a valley floor was far beyond my risk tolerance, though the view, if one had the time or presence of mind to enjoy it in such circumstances, must be amazing. There are many things I will never do in my life: jumping from an airplane is one and climbing El Capitan is another.

Scaling El Capitan is more than a test of physical strength and endurance; it requires an unimaginable Zen-like focus and mental toughness, as anyone who has seen *Free Solo* can attest. The drama of watching this tiny speck of a human being thousands of feet above the valley floor was almost too much to bear. It had, no doubt, taken many hours to get within shouting distance of the summit, but at the rate he was progressing there were many hours yet to go. We had all day and settled in hoping to share, at a distance, his moment of triumph.

To keep track of the climber when I momentarily put the binoculars down to tend to Albie or to take in the extraordinary beauty all around us, I chose natural shapes and lines in the rock face to keep me oriented to the climber's position. After forty-five minutes or so, the climber seemed to be reversing course and was making his way back down toward the orange shuttle he was hoisting up behind him. I assumed he was getting crampons or other equipment needed to progress, and for a few moments I put the binoculars on the ground to make some notes. When I resumed my vigil, the climber was gone. Simply gone. I knew from a distinctive line in the rock exactly where he'd been. I scanned up and down and across. Nothing. My heart skipped a beat and I assumed the worst. At any moment I expected to hear the sirens of emergency vehicles, but there were none. He must have abandoned his quest and belayed quickly down the face of El Capitan until he was below the line where trees obscured the view. Lest this seem alarmist, less than a month later two experienced climbers fell to their deaths on El Capitan.

After we returned from our full day in the park, Jon and Lois invited us into their living room where Albie feel asleep at Lois's feet. Jon brought forth a bottle of sherry.

Later that evening, Albie and I walked the ten-acre property just as the setting sun was illuminating distant peaks to the east. It was dead silent save for the sounds of the birds. We sat for a bit at the pond at the edge of the property as the evening deepened. Six years earlier Albie had been lying in a small chain-link enclosure with a concrete floor for most of five months. Now we stared miles and miles off in the distance with nothing to keep us hemmed in. The world seemed infinitely large and tranquil and full of promise. He may not have been able to appreciate the physical beauty of these places we were visiting in the same way I was, but I like to think that somewhere, somehow, he knew he was as free as the birds, unseen, singing in the trees around us.

In the morning, after another impossibly generous breakfast, shared with a couple from Wales who had checked in the night before, we said goodbye to Lois, who gave me a big hug, and Jon, who handed me another package of fresh fruit and water for our drive to the Bay Area. We're not likely to ever see Jon and Lois again, but for two days they treated us as family and reminded us of the power of kindness.

We drove back down the foothills and into the Central Valley and stopped for gas in Los Banos. As we pulled out onto the main drag about two dozen bikers clad in leather and denim jackets bearing the name of their motorcycle club in Oakland roared up beside us at a traffic light. We had the top up and the windows closed because it was hot and the air conditioning was on. A couple of the bikers started gesticulating at me and yelling. Oh, good Lord, I thought, what do *they* want? We don't want any trouble. I stared straight ahead, pretending not to notice and hoping they'd just move on, but they persisted. I reluctantly lowered the window and one of the bikers lifted the visor on his helmet. I braced for the worst.

"Your gas cap!" he yelled. "You forgot to close your gas cap!" The gas cap was dangling by the plastic tether attached to the car. I waved my appreciation and, relieved, realized that once again my stereotypes, this time about bikers, had gotten the best of me. As the first few riders blew past when the light turned green, several more, unaware I'd already been tipped off, pointed and shouted, "Your gas cap!" all trying to be helpful. There are many exceptions to be sure, but most people, given the chance, just want to be helpful to others.

As we made our way west toward Mountain View, where we would spend a few days with my brother-in-law Andy and sister-in-law Ceci and their adopted terrier mix Ollie, a worry that had been with me all along intensified. Albie doesn't always get along with other dogs, and if he didn't take a liking to Ollie, or at least tolerate him, it was really going to throw a wrench in our plans. Ollie's a little fellow, too, and no match for Albie were Albie to get ornery.

Andy was actually at our house in Boston visiting Judy when Albie and I arrived in Mountain View, and Ceci and Ollie were just coming back from a walk as we pulled up. Though Albie and Ollie didn't exactly play together during our stay, they got on fine and I was deeply relieved that Albie rose to the occasion. He proved to be a perfect houseguest, possibly even better than me.

Being off the road for five days was welcome. We were with people not only familiar, but family, in a house I've known for nearly thirty years. Both Andy and Ceci are great cooks, too. We were home away from home and it felt good.

The day after we arrived, Ceci and I took the dogs to Half Moon Bay and sat on the beach. Seeing the Pacific Ocean, dipping our toes in it, made tangible the reality that we really had driven our little car clear across the continent. The country can seem impossibly big, but if you put your mind to it, and had another driver, you could make it from coast-to-coast by car in a few days; we'd been gone just three weeks, but it seemed longer; much longer.

It was a breezy day on the coast; the sky was a faultless, cloudless blue. Albie waded into the Pacific and lay down at the water's edge. A few hundred yards off shore a gray whale spouted.

Albie has always been very attached to me, but with all his familiar reference points three thousand miles away and having been alone together now for all this time, he had become even more so. I take his happiness and well-being seriously and, somehow, I think he knows that. But for me, too, Albie had been my constant these past three weeks. As we posed together for Ceci to take a picture with the Pacific as a backdrop, I put my arms around his ruff and gave him a hug that I hoped would convey all my gratitude and happiness for his being in my life.

Midweek, we made the overnight trip to see my friend Bill Monning, majority leader of the California State Senate, in Sacramento. The legislature was in session, which is why we met him in Sacramento instead of Carmel, where he and his wife Dana make their home. Bill and I first met in 1987 when he was hired as the executive director of a nonprofit I was working for, International Physicians for the Prevention of Nuclear War (IPPNW).* At that time, Bill and Dana, who'd been accepted to Harvard Medical School, had moved East from California with their two young daughters for work and school, respectively. Bill's devotion to public service, the public interest, and the pursuit of social justice is deep and formidable.

In the state Senate, Bill has championed the state's death with dignity law, a soda tax to help fight childhood obesity, and, most recently, efforts to guarantee that all Californians have access to clean drinking water. It may seem surprising, but close to one million people in the state, mainly poor and marginalized people in farming and rural communities, lack consistent access to clean water. Pesticides, fertilizer run-off, and animal waste combine to pollute local drinking supplies. In some ways, this last passion brings Bill's work decades ago with the United Farm Workers full circle.

Dogs aren't permitted inside the majestic state Capitol building, but after dinner, when everyone but the janitorial staff had gone home, Bill used his key card so we could go inside and see his spacious office, one befitting the powerful position he holds in state government. What I so admire about Bill is that for him power's only purpose is to make life better for the people of his state, especially those who have little power themselves. The business of government is detailed, often tedious, and relentlessly demanding for those who take it seriously, as Bill does. He is the same deeply dedicated guy I knew back in 1987. Despite all the trappings of power evident

---

* In 1985, about six months after I started working there, IPPNW won the Nobel Peace Prize. I wish I could say there was a cause and effect relationship between the two, but clearly there was not.

in his office, Bill is all about the little guy. It was clear in the warm way he greeted the janitors we passed who were sweeping and polishing the floors.

We took a few selfies in Bill's office, Albie beaming happily, and then a few of Albie and me in front of the statue of a California grizzly bear, the state symbol, directly outside the governor's office.

In addition to his relentless work ethic, Bill has always been a relentless optimist. But as we talked about the current state of national politics, for the first time in memory I heard a note of pessimism in Bill's outlook. Everything we both believe in—social and economic justice, civility, environmental protection, health care for all—had been under assault for over a year. I half-joked that the country seemed like it might be headed for another civil war.

"Yes, and they have all the guns and we only have the pot!" he said jokingly, but with some seriousness. "The future of the country and our planet are at stake," he added. "We're so divided but the need to work together has never been greater. Climate change should be uniting everyone, but we have a president who claims it's a hoax. Mass shooting are commonplace, yet we can't even get sensible gun control. The list goes on."

Bill's morning starts very early so the next day we had a bagel together at a nearby café before Albie and I took off to return to the Bay Area. While Bill went in to order I took Albie for a quick walk. Sacramento has a serious homeless problem and we came upon a man with his knees drawn under his chest lying face down in some bushes. It was impossible to tell if he was just asleep, had overdosed, was inebriated, or all of the above and I wondered if we should call 911. I can't tell you why I didn't, but I have wondered ever since if that was a mistake. We live in a rich country, but our social problems run deep, and it was evident, in different ways, wherever we went.

It's hardly news that San Francisco is perhaps the most beautifully situated city in the continental United States. So, on our way back to Mountain View, after battling midday traffic across the Bay Bridge, we drove out to Lands End, the network of parks and trails on the city's northwest corner. The views of the Golden Gate Bridge, the Marin headlands, and the ocean hundreds of feet below the cliffs are almost too beautiful to comprehend, even more so for the fact that they lie within the limits of a major metropolis.

But as beautiful as it was, the way I've long felt about the Bay Area during dozens of visits over many years was shifting. It used to seem like an intoxicating paradise—the glorious hills, the moderate, sunny climate, the to-die-for views of bay and ocean. But this time it seemed like a restless, relentless, frenetic place, dense with cars that, when free of the frequent traffic, moved at a whiplash-inducing pace. It all seemed more harried and more congested than I remembered, with the area's three major cities—San Francisco, Oakland, and San José—blending into one giant megalopolis. Not that we could afford to live there even if we wanted to. Gainfully employed people are living in their cars because even a modest home on a small lot in and around Silicon Valley can cost millions. For the first time in all my visits to this part of the country, I didn't entertain fantasies of living here. New England, winter aside, seemed more and more pleasing the more we drove around the country.

The day before were to leave the Bay Area to begin the long trip home, my brother-in-law Andy, who had returned from Boston, and I drove with Albie and Ollie to Salinas, about an hour from Mountain View. Dogs aren't allowed in the National Steinbeck Center, a museum devoted to the life and work of John Steinbeck, so Andy was going to keep an eye on both dogs while I made my visit.

There was no way a trip across the United States inspired by *Travels with Charley* was not going to include a visit to Steinbeck's hometown. In part, I wanted to see *Rocinante*, the pickup truck and camper that conveyed Steinbeck and Charley back and forth across the United States. But it was more to pay my respects to the writer who penned two of my top three favorite books of all time: *East of Eden* and *The Grapes of Wrath*.* His ability to plumb the depths of the human soul, his direct, muscular writing style, and his ability to deliver a sense of place, whether Oklahoma in the grip of drought and the Depression or a Salinas whorehouse in the early 1900s, is, for me, both glorious and intimidating.

The center is an impressive place mostly organized around several of Steinbeck's most famous works. But it was *Rocinante*, restored to a shine, that captivated me most. A dark green 1960 model GMC pickup with a V-6 engine and a white-sided camper mounted in the bed, *Rocinante* was much as I imagined. You can't touch her or sit inside, but the back door is open, so you can gaze inside its cozy, wood-paneled interior. Toward the front is what appears to be a Formica table bolted to the floor at which Steinbeck poked away at his typewriter as he and Charley traveled. There's a built-in fridge, a stove, a sink, and several cabinets for storage. Steinbeck wrote of cleaning his clothes by hanging a covered bucket with his laundry from a pole in his

---

* The third would be William Styron's *The Confessions of Nat Turner*.

little closet and letting the motion of the truck do the work of an agitator. I imagined Steinbeck, Charley, and their laundry being jostled to and fro on some of the rougher roads they traveled. It made me feel that perhaps Albie and I were cheating by traveling in a convertible sports car.

As I stared through the plexiglass barrier and into the back of *Rocinante*, a little *Twilight Zone*-like fantasy unspooled in my head. Steinbeck, with a few days of gray stubble lining his face and seated at his typewriter, motioned for me to come in and as I stepped forward the plexiglass behind which *Rocinante* sat melted away. Charley, lying at Steinbeck's feet, lifted his head momentarily, looked at me, gave his signature "*Ftt,*" and lay his head back down and closed his eyes. I took a seat across from Steinbeck as he poured two cups of inky black coffee and we talked, about writing, about life, and about his journey nearly sixty years ago that had inspired my own. Then, a security guard, one still of my imagination, knocked on the glass and told me I couldn't sit in there. I looked across the table and Steinbeck was gone, and then to the floor, and Charley was gone, too. It all lasted just a few seconds, but they were sweet.

I met Andy and the dogs outside about an hour later and we walked over to the house where Steinbeck grew up, a neat Victorian that features in *East of Eden*.

On our way back to Mountain View we stopped at the Mission San Juan Bautista to eat some sandwiches we'd bought in Salinas. The mission sits just yards away from the San Andreas Fault, the fault that promises to someday deliver "the big one," a massive earthquake, to central California. I defy anyone to stand on that spot and *not* think about whether this might be *the* moment when the two tectonic plates slowly grinding against one another in opposite directions for decades suddenly give way to a brutal reorganization of the landscape.

It was dry and hot, and Albie and Ollie enjoyed lying on the cool stones under the long, arched portico that runs the perimeter of the mission. As beautiful as the golden hills of California are, they are golden in summer because the grasses that cover them are scorched and I found myself missing the lush green blanket of New England in spring and summer. New England suddenly seemed so very far away and so long ago. Traveling as we were—in no particular hurry to be anywhere on any particular day—was still playing tricks on my mind when it came to my sense of time.

The morning after our first night on the road, we paid a brief visit to a woman named Jody Proct and her three-legged rescued Lab, Magnolia, in Norwalk, Connecticut. I'd met Jody at a book talk I'd given months before and she saw one of my first Instagram posts about my trip with Albie and knew we were in her neighborhood. It was just four weeks ago that we'd seen Jody and Magnolia, but it may as well have been two years ago. It felt like I hadn't seen Judy, Salina, and Jamba in ages either. In the scheme of a lifetime, in my case sixty-four years, four weeks is a mere blip, yet it seemed we'd been on the road for eternity. Even stops we'd made less than two weeks earlier along old Route 66 in Arizona seemed as distant as memories of childhood. It's been said that dogs don't have a sense of time, that whether you go out for four minutes, four hours, or four days, they can't distinguish. I'm not convinced this is true, largely because when we've been away for a few days and the dogs have been in the care of a dog sitter it takes an unusually long time for them to settle down when we come home. But I had no idea how Albie was processing the passage of time on our trip, if he was processing it at all.

And, so, after five days in the company of friends and family in the Bay Area and in Sacramento, people I'd known for decades, the trip home began.* We were four weeks into a six-week trip, and just past the halfway point mileage-wise.** The road home promised to be a very long one.

We spent the first night after leaving Mountain View in Redding. On Mother's Day morning, before heading up into eastern Oregon, Albie and I drove from our motel near the highway into downtown Redding, which, in a few weeks, would be ravaged by the massive Carr Fire, one of several enormous forest fires that tormented California in the summer of 2018. Since it was early on a Sunday morning the streets were deadly quiet.

In front of the old city hall building, now a community arts center, we met a woman organizing her belongings. She called to mind the woman of the streets in *Mary Poppins* selling bird feed to passersby for "tuppence a bag." She wore a floppy gray hat, several layers of shirts, a baggy turquoise parka, and a long skirt.

Her name was Jean and she'd arrived in Redding the night before by train from Los Angeles. She slept on a bench at Shasta College a few blocks away until she was rousted by a security guard who told her to move on. Jean was very articulate, laughed easily, and was enchanted by Albie.

As well-spoken as she was, much of what she told me didn't quite make sense. She'd come to Redding because she was

---

* In addition to my brother-in-law and sister-in-law and my friend Bill Monning, we spent time with my nephew Nicky and Sam, a close friend of my son Dan's since kindergarten, then living and working in the Bay Area.

** Somewhere between Tehachapi and Mariposa we passed the halfway mark of our eventual 9,187 miles.

convinced there were people here who could help her, people affiliated with an anti-immigrant organization in Redding she'd read about in the newspaper in L.A. Why she thought this was completely unclear, but she added that she didn't want to insult me in case I was a Communist or a socialist. She told me she'd grown up in Queens, New York (her accent betrayed her New York roots), and when I told her I had grown up in New Jersey she said, "So you understand, we're all some shade of liberal." She said she had some sinus-related ailment caused by people pointing their iPhones and iPads at her. She was quite coherent, if a bit off and given to conspiratorial thoughts.

Jean, in her late sixties, has no family and never had children. When she asked, I told her I was married and had two grown boys. With no trace of shame, which I admired, she spoke of some of the most intimate details of life on the streets.

"I hope you don't mind my asking," I said, "but living on the streets, where do you take care of your basic hygiene?"

"Most of the coffee shops keep their bathrooms locked now," she told me, precisely to keep the homeless from using them. "I'm not an animal. If I have to defecate I shield myself and pick it up with a bag and dispose of it." She pointed to Albie. "That's how we do it for dogs," she said.

But the comparison itself was heartbreaking. How does one maintain any sense of dignity having to use the streets as a toilet?

When I asked where she would go next, she wasn't sure, but figured it would be back to L.A. "I have stuff in storage there," she told me, "and a post office box where my social security check is delivered."

"Do you need some money?" I asked, though it was obvious that anyone in Jean's circumstances could use some money.

"I'm not a panhandler," she replied, "and I don't want to get inside your wallet. I don't want you to think that's what this is about. I don't drink or take drugs."

"Well," I answered, "you didn't ask. I offered." With that she accepted a five-dollar bill.

As we started to say our goodbyes, I told her even though she didn't have kids I hoped she would have a happy Mother's Day.

"And a happy Father's Day in June to you!" she replied.

There was a Starbucks a couple of blocks away and as Albie and I walked up there we saw another homeless woman pushing her belongings in a shopping cart. Her face was deeply weathered and lined and brown as a hazelnut from the sun. She looked far worse for wear than Jean. There are so many people like this roaming the streets for so many reasons—mental illness, addiction, poverty—hollowed out souls who lurk in the shadows and live on the margins. Most of the time we look away because it makes us uncomfortable; many among us wish the powers that be would simply make the problem disappear, just as the security guard at Shasta College made Jean disappear from the campus that morning. Albie, of course, cannot make judgments about people's circumstances, which may be why meeting a dog that cannot and will not discriminate against you based on your circumstances, your race, or your religion, must be refreshing for a woman such as Jean and perhaps a lesson for us all. We underestimate the resourcefulness it takes to survive on the streets and the humiliations that must be endured daily, and for that reason alone Jean had my esteem.

When we got back in the car, I circled back to the spot where we had met Jean intending to wish her one more farewell, but she was already gone, vanished as quickly as she had appeared, however briefly, in our lives—vanished back into the margins and the shadows.

California's lightly traveled northeast corner, its *quiet* corner, was a welcome departure from the frenzy of the Bay Area. We drove up and over pine-forested mountains and across expansive green valleys that offered breathtaking views of Mount Shasta dressed in snow practically to its base; through tiny towns such as Adin, Canby, and Davis Creek, many with populations under one hundred.

As the road turned north at Alturas the land gradually became less vertical and more horizontal, the dense forests yielding to a paler, sparser landscape, bluer and grayer than the rich green of the forests. We were still about 5,000 feet above sea level, as we had been through some of the mountain passes, but it was flatter, a sign that we were approaching the high desert country of eastern Oregon.

Just south of the Oregon border the road hewed to the eastern side of a wide valley and to the left was a massive, grayish flat, miles across and many miles long. Try as I might I couldn't figure out what we were looking at. It wasn't cultivated land and it didn't look like water. Puzzled, I pulled over, took out the road atlas and discovered we were looking at Goose Lake, but it appeared to have no defined edges. Where the lake ended and the land began was impossible to tell; the lake blended seamlessly into fields with grazing horses and cattle. Goose Lake is thirty miles from north to south. The northern end is in Oregon and it doesn't seem to end so much as it appears to simply, imperceptibly peter out. It was otherworldly and unlike anything I'd ever seen.

Later that night, when we'd arrived in tiny Burns, Oregon, I did a little research. Goose Lake is a "closed basin" meaning it retains water but has no outflow to other water bodies. It's heavily alkaline, thus its grayish appearance. Nine times since 1851 the lake has completely dried up, which is why NASA designates it as an "ephemeral" lake. Ominously, four of those nine times have been within the last decade: in 2009, 2013, 2014, and 2015. Can anyone say climate change?

Over the previous four weeks, Albie and I had driven across some barren landscapes, places where human settlements were separated by tens of miles. But nowhere we'd been, or would go, rivals eastern Oregon for sheer, unnerving isolation. One no longer needed to imagine what the land looked like hundreds or even thousands of years ago. You only needed to look out the car window.

PART THREE

. . . and Back Again

FOURTEEN

North Up to Oregon*

About a half hour after we crossed the Oregon border, near Valley View, the landscape changed dramatically. We were driving on a tree-lined, two-lane road, came around a bend, and suddenly found ourselves staring at the leading edge of a formidable mesa that stretched for miles. The trees yielded immediately to sagebrush, announcing our arrival in the high desert. It was among the most abrupt transitions in the landscape we'd seen or would see.

At a fork in the road, we turned in the direction of our destination for the evening, Burns, and a sign proclaimed: "Last

---

*   From the Woody Guthrie song, "Pastures of Plenty." The lyric goes as follows: *California, Arizona, I harvest your crops/Well its North up to Oregon to gather your hops/Dig the beets from your ground, cut the grapes from your vine/To set on your table your light sparkling wine.*

Gas for 90 Miles." Even the Mojave was more touched by the
hand of man. Indeed, the traffic on I-40 across the Mojave
seemed like the morning commute into Manhattan compared
to the desolation of the next ninety miles—we could have
counted the number of cars and trucks we saw on two hands.
All around was a sea of sagebrush until the road hugged the
shore of another alkaline lake on the other side of which were
great expanses of flat rock. It would not surprise me to learn
that this is where they shot the scene where Charlton Heston's
spacecraft crashed in the original *Planet of the Apes*. For ninety
miles the only man-made structures were the occasional fence
to confine livestock, a few corrugated tin storage sheds, a state
highway maintenance garage, and a small café at Wagontire which,
from what I could tell, *was* the town of Wagontire.

If you're a political junkie, as I am, you are probably well
familiar with electoral maps that show America, county by
county, to be a mostly red country with small pockets of blue,
and looking at that map you would, depending on your political
persuasion, be vastly reassured or ready to go into hiding. But
Harney County, Oregon, where we now were, offers some
perspective.

Harney County is deep, deep red America. It's home to the
Malheur National Wildlife Refuge, the federal property occupied in early 2016 by a small band of armed anti-government
extremists led by Ammon and Ryan Bundy, sons of the infa-
mous Nevada rancher and Sean Hannity hero, Cliven Bundy.
As the standoff continued, the tiny town of Burns, the nearest
town to the refuge, was itself besieged by national media who
had come to cover the story. During the siege, which lasted six
weeks, one of the occupiers was shot and killed by authorities
as he reached for a weapon. Though some of those eventually

arrested pled guilty to federal charges, the Bundy brothers, who led the armed occupation, ostensibly to protest federal ownership of public lands, were acquitted on all charges in what ought to be exhibit A in the case establishing white privilege in America. Imagine a group of armed black men taking over a federal building and occupying it in defiance of federal and state authorities for six weeks. How would that have ended?

In any event, Harney County comprises more than ten thousand square miles of land, larger than all of Massachusetts. Roughly seven *million* people live in deep blue Massachusetts. A little more than seven *thousand* people live in Harney County, and sixty percent of them live in the five square miles that comprise the adjacent towns of Burns and Hines. On an electoral map, Harney County is red and Massachusetts, of comparable size, is blue, but Massachusetts has eight hundred seventy-five times the number of people, which explains why so much of the country the places where few people live in vast empty spaces, is colored red. To put an even finer point on it, there is less than one person per square mile in Harney County. Manhattan is 73,000 times more densely populated but on an electoral map Manhattan's twenty-three square miles are just a tiny speck of blue while Harney County's 10,228 square miles is a solid chunk of red. But as Ammon Bundy and his merry band of heavily armed right-wing extremists proved, some people in Harney County can be just as dense as those in Manhattan.

We arrived in tiny Burns, Oregon, a little after 4:00 P.M. The main drag was what you'd expect, a McDonald's (our only dinner option for that night), a few discount stores, some boarded-up storefronts, a small strip mall, and almost no activity. It was, after all, Mother's Day Sunday. Old trailers, rusted lawn mowers, and broken-down pickups littered the lawns of the small single-story houses, many surrounded by chain-link fences.

As Albie and I walked the streets behind the seedy motel where we were staying the night, I thought of something JoAnn Clevenger, the New Orleans restaurateur, told me a few weeks before about people from all walks of life rubbing elbows in the Big Easy: that familiarity, far from breeding contempt, fosters understanding. When you live in a tiny town like Burns, profoundly isolated, 92 percent white and 4.7 percent Latino, who is there to challenge your prejudices and offer you another perspective? It's no coincidence that red America is overwhelmingly rural, sparsely populated America.

The next morning, as Albie and I again walked the streets of the dispiriting neighborhood behind our motel, there were a few more signs of human activity than there had been the evening before.

A handful of sleepy-eyed kids with their backpacks emerged from houses on their way to school. We exchanged "good mornings" with a young mother and her son, who appeared to be about twelve or thirteen and a bit awkward in his black-framed glasses, and a blond-haired daughter a few years younger.[*] Our lives are filled with thousands upon thousands of such cameo appearances by people whose lives intersect with ours for the most fleeting of moments, never to be seen again. Yesterday it was Jean, the homeless woman in Redding. Back in Natchitoches it was the young waiter who steered us to the Eiffel Tower in Paris, Texas. Along the Natchez Trace it was the park ranger with whom we discussed the fate of

---

[*]   This was my assumption anyway, that she was the mother of the two children.

Meriwether Lewis. Now, more than four weeks into our journey, we'd had countless such encounters, some even more brief than this one.

After we'd said "good morning" to this young mom and her two children I began to wonder about them. The son hardly appeared to be a rough and ready rancher type in waiting as one would have expected in a rugged ranching town. Was he dreading going to school on this May morning? Would he be bullied there? Will he stay in this town all his life and work on the roads or the ranches? Does he daydream about the places that lay beyond the extreme isolation of his tiny town? Will he graduate from high school? Go to college? Will he live to a ripe old age and have children of his own? Every one of these people who have cameo roles in our lives has a story, a life to be lived, heartaches to bear, and questions to ask and answer. And we know nothing of what has been and what will be for almost all of them, which is why, until and unless they prove otherwise, they deserve our courtesy and kindness, even if it is just to say, "Good morning."

Out here in what's called the "Oregon Outback" I was also struck by how similar *and* how different the lives we lead are. We get up, get kids ready for school, fill our cars and trucks with gas, go to the market, send Mother's Day cards, blow out birthday candles, and share Thanksgiving turkey. But a life lived here in the isolation of Burns, running a small motel or herding cattle on the ranchlands, is a very different life than the one lived by the software engineer in Silicon Valley, the cancer specialist in Houston, or the investment banker in New York. I wondered what I ultimately had in common with the young mom with two kids doing what I had done so many mornings when our kids were in school. The basic outlines of life were familiar, but the rich details within those outlines were likely much, much different.

About a half hour east of Burns the terrain again turned dramatic. Hills of massive boulders lined the highway and rivers ran through valleys, but still virtually no signs of human life other than the road itself. "Towns" were little more than an RV park in one case and a roadside café in another. For the most part it would have looked exactly the same to those pioneers who trekked west on the Oregon Trail, forbidding yet beautiful. If you had a time-lapse video—say, an aerial view of New York City over the past one hundred and fifty years—you would see incessant activity: the rise of great skyscrapers, the tearing down of old neighborhoods to make way for new, excavation of great tunnels, and the building of great bridges and sports stadia and airports; millions of people going about their daily business, first on horses and in carriages and later on buses, in cabs, and in subways. You'd see the dynamic flux of a great city constantly changing, the arrival of countless immigrants aboard huge ships docking along the west side of Manhattan, or dream seekers arriving by train from the Midwest. If you had a similar time-lapse film of this part of Oregon over the past *thousand* years it would practically look like a still photograph with the occasional traveler, whether by wagon or car, passing through. Time stands almost still out here.

Boise, Idaho, is farther from any other major metropolitan area than any city in the continental United States. I'd never been there and really didn't know what to expect.

When we arrived in the midafternoon we headed directly to the state Capitol; almost every magazine photograph of Boise

THE DOG WENT OVER THE MOUNTAIN

I'd seen shows a majestic building set against large, wheat-colored hills, and in my experience state capitol buildings are usually a good way to get oriented in a capital city.

It was a magnificent spring day, sunny, clear, and about seventy degrees. The Capitol grounds were beautifully landscaped with flower gardens and deep green lawns all around. Within the grounds Albie and I found a bench in a small, circular, memorial park dedicated to Cecil Andrus, the progressive, conservation-minded former governor who served as Jimmy Carter's secretary of the interior. Thanks to Andrus some of the nation's most treasured wilderness has enjoyed protection from the forces of development and greed. Across from where we were sitting was a pedestal with a bust of Andrus on top. On the bottom I was surprised to see that the memorial we were enjoying had been dedicated just a few days before. Perhaps even more surprising here in deep, deep red Idaho, one of the most Trumpian states in the country, was this inscription beneath the bust of Andrus:

> Now we must look ahead. We must prepare ourselves
> to fight and win new battles, to press the great and
> just cause of improving the human condition. Our
> calling is to assure a full place at the center of society
> for those who, too often, live on its edges. Our mis-
> sion is to use the power we possess and the good
> that government can do to carry the fight against
> ignorance, disease, poverty and intolerance.

My goodness, whatever became of *that* Idaho, the progressive bastion that sent Andrus to the State House and a liberal icon such as Frank Church to the United States Senate just a few decades ago? That was also the sentiment of a young employee of the state education department named Mark who was perusing some of the markers that memorialized Andrus's legacy to Idaho. We said hello to one another and I remarked that this memorial was brand new.

"Yes, the area's been roped off for a few months, so I wanted to see it," he said.

"Are you from here?" I asked.

"Born and raised," he replied. I ventured a cautious comment about the inscription under the bust of Andrus.

"That seems very progressive for Idaho," I said. He shook his head in dismay.

"I don't understand what's happened to this state," he said. He told me how friendly a place Idaho is, but that he had recently had two encounters where people were rude, as if these were black swan events, so rare as to be practically unique. One involved a skier who cut him off on the slopes and muttered something about his skiing too slow. Wow, I thought to myself, he wouldn't survive a day in Boston or New York. But it was his sense that something was shifting beneath his feet that struck me; that we were all losing something, a basic decency, that held us together. We shook hands, and Mark wished us a safe journey and headed back to his office.

I took the time to read the various displays about Cecil Andrus and one seemed especially relevant given the Trump administration's hostility to public lands, its evisceration of the Bears Ears National Monument in Utah (a gift to mining interests) its desire to open virtually all U.S. waters to oil exploration. We forget that conservation of land, water, and air was once a very conservative value. During Andrus's tenure as governor, large swaths of wilderness in the state were protected, including the Sawtooth Mountain Wilderness. One of the plaques in the park bore this quote from Andrus:

> You and I will be dead and gone, but future genera-
> tions will come here and see the Sawtooths with snow
> on it, the beautiful lakes that we have here. Future
> generations are entitled to benefit as we have. The
> good Lord didn't put us here to change what we have.
> We were put here to enjoy it, but to also make certain
> that we didn't alter or destroy it.

Boise continued to surprise wherever we went. There were huge well-manicured parks and the Anne Frank Human Rights Memorial situated right behind the Boise Public Library. The memorial comprises two semicircular walls of granite divided by a waterfall that flows into two moats in front of the granite. On the panels are inspirational quotations about human rights, peace, freedom, and social justice from Anne Frank, Martin Luther King, Gandhi, Jimmy Carter, and comedian-activist Dick Gregory, among others. There's even an image of Cesar Chavez among the farmworkers on whose behalf he toiled so hard. The names of major donors to this memorial are etched into some of the benches and I recognized one: David and Mary Peterman. Mary, formerly Mary Zheutlin, is a second cousin I had never met and with whom Albie and I would be staying for the next two nights, along with her physician husband, David Peterman, and their two Labs, Maya and Scout. Mary, I would learn over dinner that night, chaired the effort to create the memorial; second cousins and kindred spirits.

All of this—the memorial to Andrus and this moving human rights memorial—surprised me, and I wondered what other surprises Boise would have in store for me. Downtown was filled with outdoor cafés and coffee shops; it was like a slightly smaller version of impossibly hip Portland, Oregon. Albie and I stepped into a wine store; never arrive for dinner, especially with family you've never met, empty-handed.

Albie and I spent two days with Mary and David and Maya and Scout. Just as I was pleasantly surprised that Albie and Ollie had gotten on well during our stay in the Bay Area, Albie seemed to enjoy having more canine companionship. We walked the hills just behind Mary's house with the dogs and talked and talked and talked about our related families.

As we age, more and more of we baby boomers seem to be taking more and more interest in genealogy. This is hardly surprising. With our time slowly dwindling there is an urge to find our place in that great circle of life, to see where we fit in the larger scheme of things. There were no revelatory family secrets, just tidbits of information that filled out, for both of us, a little more of our family trees. Mary's late father, Bert, and my father were first cousins, both raised in Jersey City, and had been in medical school together at Johns Hopkins in the 1940s. I'd met Bert many years ago and knew my dad was very fond of him. My dad was one of eight children of whom six were boys; Bert had just one sibling, a sister, and Mary described her father's relationship to my father and uncles as more brotherly than cousinly. How odd, it seemed, that Mary, just a year older than me, and I had never met (I'd met two of her three siblings), but then again, she's lived most of her adult life in Boise and I've lived mine in Boston. But sharing stories of our families gave our meeting a sense of familiarity and connectedness and intimacy it would not otherwise have had. With each memory shared and tidbit of information offered we were able to add little pieces to the larger jigsaw puzzle.

Since returning from my trip with Albie, many people have asked me what the biggest surprise was, and the answer is Idaho, and not just Boise. The state was more spectacular than I had thought.

In keeping with our commitment to stay off the interstate wherever feasible, we followed Highway 20 across the wider, southern part of the state from Mountain Home to Idaho Falls. Looking at a map there was no way to know that the line representing Highway 20 would take us through some of the most breathtaking scenery of the entire trip. Within just a few miles we were surrounded by snowcapped peaks and shimmering blue lakes set in verdant valleys that edged up against the foothills. The high desert had met an alpine wonderland. The sky was immense and lavishly adorned with a mix of cumulus and stratus clouds.

We stopped near an old grain elevator by the side of the road and stood staring at the Sawtooth Mountains that Cecil Andrus had done so much to preserve. It was still and utterly silent. "In wildness," Thoreau once wrote, "is the preservation of the world."

Here along Highway 20 in south-central Idaho is a literary monument of sorts, one Mary's husband David told me about. In the tiny town of Picabo, hometown of Olympic skier Picabo Street, is the Silver Creek Store, a general store that specializes in hunting and fishing gear and houses the local post office. The store is now in the hands of the son of founders Leonard ("Bud") Purdy and his wife, Ruth. Back in the day, when Ernest Hemingway used to spend much of his time, when he was away from Key West, living and hunting in these parts, he and the

Purdys became close friends and hunting and fishing partners. On display in the store are signed books, letters, photos, and even rifles Hemingway gave the Purdys. Steinbeck was our touchstone for this journey, but the opportunity to gaze upon tangible evidence of Hemingway's life was an added bonus.

Hemingway and Steinbeck, great writers of the same generation, did not know one another, but Steinbeck publicly and privately praised Hemingway's work, even as Hemingway disparaged his, perhaps jealous of Steinbeck's success with *In Dubious Battle* (1936) and *The Grapes of Wrath* (1939), a time when Hemingway was unproductive and being criticized for not tackling major social issues in his writing.

I chatted briefly with the fellow behind one of the counters and explained that Albie (who was waiting for me in the car; it was cool enough) and I were heading back home to Boston. He then asked a question that took me by surprise.

"Are you taking 20 all the way?"

It never occurred to me that we could. I had assumed Highway 20 was a state road. When I looked it up I learned we were on U.S. 20 and that U.S. routes ending with a zero signifies a coast-to-coast highway. We were on a precursor to the Interstate Highway System; indeed, U.S. 20 runs from Newport, Oregon, right to Kenmore Square, near Fenway Park, in Boston. It's the longest highway in the United States, 3,365 miles. I was familiar with a Highway 20 in the Berkshire Hills of western Massachusetts, I'd driven on it many times, but it never occurred to me it was part of a coast-to-coast route. If we'd had more time, it would have been tempting to follow this road all the way home, but our six weeks were rapidly evaporating.

About fifteen miles east of Picabo, the highway entered terrain that was distinctly different than what we'd been passing through, an otherworldly landscape of ancient lava fields, dark brown and red piles of rock many dozens of feet deep, some extending for more than fifty miles to the south. At Craters of the Moon National Monument we pulled in to walk among these strange rock formations. These massive lava fields didn't result from a volcanic eruption, however. There's no vestige of a volcanic cone to be found, nor was there ever one. These fields were formed by lava that seeped out of great fissures in the Earth thousands of years ago.

The isolation of eastern Idaho made it a logical place for the U.S. government to research and develop nuclear weapons and nuclear energy, a legacy reflected in various ways throughout the region. At Pickle's Place, a restaurant in the tiny town of Arco, they feature an "Atomic Burger," and we drove through Atomic City before passing the sprawling Idaho National Laboratory (INL), thirty miles west of Idaho Falls, which occupies more than nine hundred square miles of land, an area three-quarters the size of Rhode Island. INL was the site of the largest nonnuclear explosion ever detonated. Since 1949 more nuclear reactors have been built here, more than fifty, than anywhere else on Earth. The landscape here bears little resemblance to the one we had driven through earlier in the day; no regal mountain ranges topped with snow or rivers flowing gracefully through green valleys, just brownish flats.

Just outside Idaho Falls, Highway 20 veers north and for many miles we had dramatic views of the western side of the Grand Tetons in Wyoming, heavy with snow and alternately bathed in sunshine and partially obscured by low lying clouds. Straight ahead the sky was a deep, dark purplish black and lightning bolts shot through the sky. In fields far away, massive curtains of rain fell even as we stayed dry. In the East you rarely get such a perspective on the weather for the simple reason that the view rarely extends for forty or fifty uninterrupted miles as it does here and throughout much of the West.

When I was last in West Yellowstone, Montana, the western gateway to Yellowstone National Park, it was a tiny place. That, too, was half a century ago and, needless to say, it's changed. It was stunning, and not in a good way, to see there's even an IMAX theater there now. Albie and I took a walk in the cold drizzle among countless other tourists poking their heads in souvenir shops, restaurants, and little museums.

We'd been gone now for over a month and even though Albie had had some canine companionship in Mountain View and Boise, I sensed that our routine was wearing thin for him, as it was for me. But I knew we were headed home, and he didn't. As I'd learned in Santa Fe and again at Grand Canyon and Yosemite, he was unable to appreciate the scenery which made the trip so interesting for me. Seeing how the terrain changes (sometimes gradually, sometimes suddenly), the play of light and shadow and weather on the land, the features that make some of it a feast for the eyes and some an eyesore, the remarkable variety of vegetation, rock formations, mountains, deserts, and plains, all of it are what kept me interested across the miles. Albie didn't have that. Mostly, when he wasn't snoozing in the back seat, he seemed to watch *me*. When we were staying with family, even if I went out to the car to fetch something, he followed me to the door and watched. In our motel rooms he seemed to be monitoring my movements to make sure I wasn't going to leave him behind.

I also knew ours was a temporary departure from the comfortable life we knew; he didn't. To his eternal credit, not once did he balk, resist, or show the slightest sign of disaffection. But it was starting to feel like we were going through the motions. I tried to keep those feelings at bay, though, for the more intense I allowed the longing for home to be, the slower time would pass and the more torturous the long drive back would seem. And we were, after all, only in Montana.

I'd planned to drive the famous Beartooth Highway, "the top of the world" as it's called, which straddles the Montana-Wyoming border. Its sixty-eight miles are widely considered one of the most spectacular drives in America. Alas, every spring those sixty-eight miles have to be cleared of twenty-plus feet of snow and the highway would not reopen until Memorial Day, two weeks hence. We settled for driving through Yellowstone which, of course, isn't a bad consolation prize. *

West Yellowstone was encased in a thick fog the morning we drove into the park. Not that it mattered to Albie, but it seemed like a dispiriting replay of our visit to Grand Canyon where we waited for hours for breaks in the fog. We paid the entrance fee and within a few minutes we were in the Wyoming part of the park (the vast majority of Yellowstone in is Wyoming; small slivers are in Montana). And just like that, the fog burned off, the sun glistened on the rivers and the grasses, pure white mists drifted through the valleys, and bison lumbered along the roadway. We pulled into a turnout to take it all in.

Why is the preservation of our natural treasures even remotely controversial? They are so rare and so magnificent, and if you aren't emotionally moved as you gaze at all the majesty of a Yellowstone, a Yosemite, or a Grand Canyon—if you are not awed—check to see if you have a pulse.

---

* Parts of Beartooth Highway are in Yellowstone.

Though Albie had proven immune to the manifest beauty of many of the places we had visited, that seemed to change, miraculously, at Yellowstone, though I don't know why. At our first stop, along a river with snow gilded hills across the river valley and eddies of fog dancing along the mountain peaks, for the first time Albie seemed enchanted by the view. He stood staring for a good long time. Was it a fluke? Can a dog "see" and appreciate natural beauty after all? Can they take pleasure in it? Had I been mistaken about Albie's inability to enjoy the sights? There's no way to know, but Albie, for the first time, really seemed to be taking in the view on that crystalline morning.

A short while later we shared the most exquisite, if fleeting, moment of our entire journey together. We parked the car at Gibbon Falls and started down the walkway that runs along the edge of the canyon through which the falls cascade. To keep visitors safe, a stone retaining wall, about three feet high, runs along the walkway. You can hear the falls before you see them, and a refreshing mist thrown off by the tumbling waters permeates the air. Albie couldn't see over the wall, but he seemed excited and seemed to know something lay just beyond the barrier. To my surprise he stopped, put his front paws on the stone wall and stared down at the falls. His nose twitched, his tail wagged, and he seemed to be smiling. I squatted down and put my left arm around his ruff; I had his leash firmly in hand but wanted to be sure he didn't get carried away. As I did, my head was against his and for several minutes we remained like that watching the water tumble over the rocks and letting the fine mist settle over us. And I spoke to him as I might have to my sons when they were little.

"Isn't that beautiful, Albie? What do you think? Do you hear the water crashing on the rocks? Do you feel the mist?"

We were, at last, sharing the pleasure of this exquisite sight. At least that's what I want to believe, and in that moment, I felt intensely close to him as you would a child experiencing wonder and awe for the first time. Whether it was the sound of the rushing water, the refreshing smell of the mist, or the physical beauty of the scene that prompted Albie to lift himself up on the wall to see what lay on the other side I don't know, but I felt we had achieved a kind of perfection together. We had driven thousands of miles for this and it was worth every one. I love him so—it seemed we were joined together in some transcendental way that would outlast our physical presence together.

We exited Yellowstone at Gardiner, Montana, and headed north toward Livingston. The scenery around us was still breathtaking. But the first inklings that the trip was running out on us, that the best lay behind us, began to surface. From here on out we were going to be driving through less dramatic country; the northern prairie and industrial Midwest lay ahead, and the tug of home started to insinuate itself more strongly with each passing mile.

As I said, if you travel long distance on the interstate you quickly learn that most places of accommodation and restaurants are clustered near the exits which are often a couple of miles from whatever town justified the placement of the exit in the first place. Whenever we stayed in such places we made it a point, even if time was short, to drive into town just to see what we could see and it often paid dividends. It's how we met Joan, the homeless woman in Redding, and discovered the lovely parks and pleasant streets of Tehachapi and the retro charm of

Kingman. If you don't venture the few minutes into these towns you might think they comprise only chain motels, gas stations, and fast-food restaurants. Some turn out to be duds, but many are minor revelations.

The evening we arrived in Miles City in eastern Montana we drove the mile and a half from our highway motel to downtown and found a classic American main street with a Western flair. There were saddleries, clothiers specializing in Western wear, and several bars with vintage neon signs: The Bison Bar with a bison outlined in red light, the Montana Bar with a map of Montana also in red light, and the Trails Inn Bar which featured a neon cowboy atop a bucking bronco. This wasn't reproduction nostalgia, it was the real thing.

As luck would have it we had, yet again, stumbled into a town on the eve, or in the throes of, a major event. "Bucking Horse," an annual festival held in Miles City the third weekend in May for the past sixty-eight years, features music, food, and a rodeo. Folks were out and about setting up tables, a few vendors were up and running, and Main Street was cordoned off, so we were able to walk right down the middle of the street and admire the classic all-Americanness of it all.

On Main Street, a young boy of about seven or eight wearing a Little League cap and uniform was standing behind a card table with his sister and mother. He appeared to have stepped out of a Norman Rockwell painting and was all smiles. In his hands was a sign announcing the sale of raffle tickets to help his mom pay her way for a choral performance her local choir was giving in Europe. He looked at me eagerly, hoping I'd buy a raffle ticket, and I offered him some advice.

"Turn the sign this way," I said as I gently took the sign in my hands and turned it right side up, much to his amusement.

He laughed and rolled his eyes, not at me but at himself. He appeared positively tickled. Tickets were twenty dollars and the prize, which I wouldn't be around to collect if I won, was a freezer full of steaks. *Very Montana*, I thought.

"We're from Massachusetts," I told him, "and we won't be here for the drawing." Whereupon he reached out and earnestly tried to hand me the pouch with all the money they'd collected so far. He was adorable and the gesture kind; maybe he thought Massachusetts was a poverty-stricken place, I don't know. But I thanked him, told him the money was for his mom, and made a contribution without buying a ticket. I appreciated his generous spirit, though. We could use more of that in America.

FIFTEEN

Running on Empty

It had been a while since I'd had a proper American breakfast and the next morning I was determined to find one that would include an omelet, home fries, bacon, toast, and pancakes. Steinbeck had noted in passing that he and Charley had driven through the improbably named town of Beach, North Dakota, a small hamlet of about a thousand souls, and the first town in North Dakota heading eastbound from Montana along Interstate 94. Needless to say, there is no beach in Beach; it was named for Warren Beach who supervised a group of railroad surveyors who worked in the area in the 1880s. We'd stop in Beach and find that traditional breakfast I was craving.

A few miles before we crossed the North Dakota line Judy called to report that there were animal noises, scratching, in the ceiling above the kitchen sink. These were the kinds of problems I so enjoyed being away from on the road. There's no end to what needs to be attended to in a house and the simplicity of being on the road with only Albie and the car to worry about had its benefits. Normally, attending to this kind of household problem falls to me, and Judy didn't want to call a pest control person without a consult. But it hardly seemed like this was happening in *my* house anymore. Gone just five weeks, but it felt like a lifetime. Why is this my problem? But it was indeed *our* problem.

It was a cold, rainy, gray morning and little Beach felt desolate. This is a farming and ranching town; grain elevators sat along the railroad tracks that took the fruits of Beach's labors to markets far away. We parked in the center of the tiny town, in front of the Buzzy Cafe. Albie waited in the car while I went in for breakfast. In a room off the main dining room about a dozen gray-haired people had gathered for what seemed like a community meeting of some kind. In dress and appearance, they looked exactly like what you'd expect a group of older Americans in a North Dakota ranching town to look like. It was portrait of aging, white Middle America.

Earlier that morning, in Houston, there'd been yet another mass school shooting and the TV above the cash register was tuned to Fox News. Watching the television, I turned my ears to those paying their bills and catching a glimpse of the unfolding horror. These mass shootings have become so common they've practically become background noise, like the weather or sports report. I was eager to hear the reaction.

"Yeah," said an older man sarcastically, talking to the TV. "Let's make sure we don't arm the teachers," as if that were the obvious and logical answer to the mayhem. "Maybe we should homeschool all of them." He walked out in disgust.

For the first time I noticed the framed poster on the wall next to my table was a studio photo of John Wayne in full Western dress, a pistol drawn into shooting position.

A stout woman looked up at the TV and laughed inappropriately. "Yup, there goes another one!" she said, smiling. "Mental problems!" And then she, too, walked out. Beach may not have been the farthest we'd been from home, but it sure felt that way. At least the breakfast was everything I'd hoped for.

For a long stretch outside of Beach there were some beautiful canyons, buttes, and mesas, but the rugged "West" soon petered out and became the less dramatic Midwestern plains. Though it's just across the river from Bismarck, where we planned to stop for a long walk, we made a brief visit to Mandan for two reasons. First, the Mandan Indians, for whom the town is named, played a significant role in Lewis and Clark's great expedition. A short distance north of Mandan, Lewis and Clark wintered over in 1804–1805 in an encampment they named Fort Mandan. Stopping here seemed like a bookend to our visit, just a few days into our trip, to Lewis's burial place along the Natchez Trace. Second, though he said nary a word about it other than to note they'd stopped there, Steinbeck and Charley had been here, too. It was one of many "what the heck" stops we made along the way. We found a grassy field adjacent to a racetrack (still closed for the season) where Albie could tend to some business. It was past the middle of May, but a chill, damp wind was blowing under slate-gray skies. The buds on nearby trees looked to be struggling with the decision of whether to close back up until June or to try to spring forth. *Poor trees*, I thought, *sentenced to a lifetime in central North Dakota.*

In the past week or so we'd seen some impressive state Capitol buildings in Sacramento and Boise and since I wasn't sure if there were any other points of interest in Bismarck that's where we headed when we left Mandan. No matter how inglorious a state capital may be—Trenton and Harrisburg come to mind—it's usually worth a visit to the Capitol building because they are a point of pride and typically either majestic, as California's was, or lovely, as Idaho's was.

The Capitol grounds in Bismarck were marked by a large granite slab that announced, "North Dakota Capitol." We turned off the main road onto an access drive and we crept along slowly trying to find the Capitol building which, I was sure, would be readily identifiable, as almost all of them are, by a dome. I thought we'd found it, a small sand-colored building with a small domed roof but it turned out to be the state library. To our left was a massive lawn, probably two football fields in length, but unadorned with any gardens, plantings, or indeed *anything* of visual interest save for a few trees and a monument to some pioneers who had, for some unfathomable reason, decided to stop when they reached this place. If there was a landscape architect involved in the design here I hope they sued him or her for malpractice.

The vast, sterile lawn sloped gently upward toward a building I was certain could not be the Capitol but which, of course, was. It looked like two buildings stitched together, an architectural Frankenstein. Part of it was about four stories high, light brown in color, that resembled the department of motor vehicles building in Lodi, New Jersey, where I got my driver's license in 1970. Positioned in front and right of center and attached to this low-slung building was a rectangular structure, slightly tapered at the top, about twenty stories high. It was so bland

and uninteresting it could have been an apartment building in the Bronx. Together, the whole thing looked like something Stalin might have built in a far-flung provincial capital in Uzbekistan to serve as the Soviet sub-ministry of ingot production. Was it supposed to be reminiscent of the grain elevators that are such a staple of the North Dakota landscape? Whatever it was, it was, hands down, the most unimpressive, nay ugly, Capitol building I'd ever seen, and *I've actually been* to the capital of Uzbekistan. Maybe it would have looked better on a warm sunny day. Most things do, but since it was still cold and gray we left knowing we would probably never get the chance to find out.

It was drizzling when we pulled into a Starbucks just before the entrance to the interstate. I was just going to grab something for the car and then we'd be on our way.

Parked in front of Starbucks was a medium-sized hybrid bicycle (a cross between a road bike and a mountain bike) hitched up to one of those child trailers, which was stuffed to the gills with personal belongings. A blue tarp was strapped over the trailer with bungee cords which also secured a water jug, a gym bag, a hand broom, and other assorted odds and ends. Mounted to the trailer were two flagpoles around which, tightly wrapped, were an American flag and another flag I couldn't identify. On one flagpole a little stuffed purple unicorn (or maybe a squirrel, it was hard to tell) and a plastic toy that looked like Donald Duck had been affixed. On the back of the trailer was written, "Traveling Vet: Anything Will Help." I had a feeling I might be lingering a little longer than planned. This looked like an interesting story. It was plenty cool enough for Albie to wait in the car, so I went in alone thinking it would be pretty obvious whose bike it was.

I ordered my usual, took a seat, and scanned the other customers, but not a single one looked as if they'd be remotely connected to the contraption sitting by the parking lot. About five minutes passed and just as I was about to leave, a large, broad-shouldered man emerged from the restroom and took a seat at the table next to me on which he had left his laptop. He was about six feet tall and was wearing a U.S. Marine Corps cap, camo shorts over black leggings, hiking boots, and a heavy grayish-green hooded sweatshirt. He had a couple of days of gray stubble on his squarish, strong-featured face and steel gray eyes. He appeared to have been out in the weather for quite some time. I knew the answer but asked anyway.

"That your bike outside?"

And that's how my hour-long conversation with Louis F., a marine combat vet a couple of years my senior, began.

He hit the road two and half years ago in Florida, where he was living, and had been riding ever since, on a mission, he said, "to find out if Americans are still patriotic."

Louis had been waiting in line at a coffee shop one day behind an Afghan war vet in uniform. As he described it, the young woman taking orders got into an argument with the vet and accused him of killing women and children in Afghanistan.

"I wanted to reach across the counter and throttle her," Louis told me in a deep, resonant voice that reminded me of actor Sam Elliott's, but with more than a hint of his native Tennessee. I tried not to betray my discomfort at the image of this large, powerful man with his hands around a young woman's neck. He didn't throttle her, of course, but that encounter was the catalyst for his remarkable odyssey.

"So, what are you finding?" I asked.

To show me how encouraged he was, Louis told me a story, which he found inspiring and reassuring. He was riding across Texas when he spied an elderly man struggling to wield a chain saw and stopped to help. As they spoke, the man asked Louis if he had any interest in joining an armed militia he was part of.

"I told him I had other things to attend to," Louis told me, "but I said maybe if I come back. How many of you are there?"

"Thirty-two thousand," answered the man, taking Louis by surprise.

"In Texas?" asked Louis.

"No," said the man. "Just in these three counties."

What Louis found inspiring and encouraging I found appalling and dismaying. These were people like the Bundys who had occupied the wildlife refuge back in Harney County, Oregon—armed right-wing extremists. Though I was horrified, I found myself liking Louis in spite of myself. He was friendly and easy to talk to and rarely have I had the chance to talk with anyone like him.

"You know, the reason no one has ever invaded the United States is because people have guns and know how to use them," he said. Somehow that didn't seem quite right to me; we do have a massive navy, army, and air force, after all.

"Did you hear about the school shooting in Texas this morning?" I asked.

"I did. It's not the guns; it's bad parenting," he said. There are lousy parents all over the world, of course, but in no other country are there mass shootings on anywhere near the scale as in this country, a thought I kept to myself. There was no point in debating Louis; I was more interested in hearing what he had to say.

Between his southern accent and gravelly voice, I sometimes had trouble following him and thought he had said early in our conversation that he'd once been a police officer. I asked him about that, but I'd misunderstood. He had investigative experience in the military but had never been a police officer.

"Oh, I couldn't be a police officer," he told me. "I understand the Constitution requires due process and a trial by a jury of your peers. But if I came upon a scene with six people dead on the ground and an armed suspect running for his vehicle, I'd kill him right then and there. Not gonna waste one taxpayer cent on that guy. Those people dead on the ground? That's his judge and jury and they said 'guilty.'" Louis clearly was a disciple of the Dirty Harry school of law enforcement.

The subject moved on to my trip and Louis seemed charmed by my own mission, to rediscover America with Albie.

"You know," I said sheepishly, "I'm looking to answer some of the same questions as you, but kind of from a different political point of view."

Louis grinned wide and kind, straightened up, and leaned back in his chair. "I know," he said almost wearily, as if to say it was perfectly obvious I was of a different political persuasion. All the time we'd been talking he'd sized me up easily.

As we talked, Louis was waiting for his old laptop to perform a software update and it had been taking hours; he travels without a phone and his three adult children worry about him.

"Where do you go from here?" I asked.

"Northern Maine, then back to Florida," he replied. "Been on the road since November 2015. Mind if we step outside so I can have a smoke? And I wanna meet that dog you're traveling with."

How a man can ride thousands of miles on a bike and smoke is beyond me. In a light-hearted way I suggested he was working at cross-purposes with himself. He laughed. "I know."

We walked over to my car and I felt a little embarrassed. Here was this tough as nails ex-marine smoking and riding a bike around America and Albie and I were in a BMW convertible on a six-week lark. I was a little mortified.

"You guys," Louis said smiling and referring to Albie and me, "are just too cute!" The word "cute" and Louis seemed utterly incongruous.

"I'd like to make a contribution to your travels," I said, motioning toward the words written across the back of his little trailer. He didn't refuse the ten-dollar bill I extended.

"You have anything to read along the way?" I asked. I'd opened the trunk and pulled out a copy of *Rescue Road*, the first of two books I'd written about rescue dogs. I'd brought a few copies along to give as gifts and had one copy left. "I know you don't want to carry more than you have to." Louis took the book in his large, weathered hands.

"You wrote this?" he asked, surprised. I assured him I had, and that Albie had been my inspiration. He thanked me for the book. And with that we exchanged e-mail addresses, shook hands, and wished each other well.*

Louis's vision of America and mine coexist, uncomfortably and perhaps impossibly, in the same country. In so many ways,

---

* Louis and I stayed in touch by e-mail for a short while. A few weeks after we'd met, and Albie and I were back home, I e-mailed Louis to see where he was. Having driven across the rest of North Dakota and all the way to New England since meeting him I could imagine what a slog he had ahead on a bike. To my surprise he was in Rhode Island of all places and headed to New York City. He'd hitched a ride, with his bike, on a truck and had dispensed with the idea of going to Maine.

his view of America is incomprehensible to me, the antithesis of all I learned in college and law school, all I have read over decades about American history, and everything I was taught growing up. Much of what he said appalled me, frightened me, and, had I read it on Facebook, would have enraged me. Yet, here in a coffee shop on a cold rainy day in Bismarck we both were able to look beyond the politics and have a civil conversation. He wasn't out to change my mind nor me his; there was no tension, no anger, and no disrespect. Perhaps it was because we were, for now, both engaged in similar, but hardly identical, journeys of discovery into the country we both loved. I wouldn't want to live in Louis's America any more than he would want to live in mine and yet we both do. As ironic as it may be, as long as we live here, I *have to live* in Louis's America and he *has to live* in mine. Though Louis's politics were anathema to me, I genuinely liked him, and he seemed to genuinely like us, too. Maybe there is hope that despite the widening fractures in our politics, we won't end up killing each other over it, or perhaps more to the point, Louis won't end up killing me over it.

As we continued east through the rain and chill to Jamestown, North Dakota, where we would arrive in a couple of hours, I kept thinking of Louis pedaling along at a snail's pace. It would likely take him a few days to get where we would be in a few hours. You have to admire that kind of grit.

It was sunny but cold when we woke up in Jamestown for what would be our last Saturday on the road. A strong gusty wind swept across the prairie; not the best morning for Albie to stubbornly refuse to do his morning business. The motel was right next to the interstate entrance and when I read the sign, "94 East: Fargo," home seemed awfully far away. Practically half the United States is farther away from Boston than Fargo is, but few places *sound* or *seem* farther away. I wished there were a way to magically transport us home, perhaps a pair of ruby red slippers whose heels I could click together three times.

Before we left Boston, I discovered that according to the tentative schedule I'd outlined we were likely to be in Fargo the same weekend friends from home, John and Myra Anderson, would be visiting John's sister in Fargo. And so it was that we met at John's sister's house where, for the second morning in a row, I enjoyed pancakes. John and Myra were flying home the next morning, which only made the 1,600-odd miles we had yet to travel seem all the more formidable and interminable.

As we rolled through the flats of western Minnesota toward Minneapolis I could sense we were now truly running out of gas, not literally, but figuratively. It seemed unfair to give short shrift to the states of the upper Midwest, but with every mile, home loomed larger and larger. We were just passing through.

We spent the night in Eau Claire, Wisconsin. Wisconsin was pretty enough, more eastern than western, well forested with farms nestled among gently rolling hills.

The racism he witnessed in New Orleans in 1960 drained the life out of Steinbeck's journey with Charley. A different kind of spectacle put the final dagger in ours. Our transit of Wisconsin was marred by an absolutely extravagant amount of roadkill lying along the shoulder of the highway. I don't know if there's a national roadkill competition among the states, but Wisconsin has the championship locked up. It was like a macabre zoo for dead and decaying animals: racoons, groundhogs, squirrels, and foxes were standouts in the small animal category; deer had a lock in the large animal division. Many carcasses had clearly been there for weeks or more, decaying grotesquely. We passed several deer whose bodies were in an advanced state of decomposition, or even missing altogether, save for the heads. It was nightmarish and ghoulish and for the life of me I couldn't fathom why the state of Wisconsin couldn't do a better job of clearing the death and destruction from the roads. Albie, asleep in the back, was lucky not to share this horror show with me.

At one point we hit traffic and the car ahead of me had a Wisconsin license plate, the kind states charge extra for to fund special programs. It had an image of a wolf and the words "Endangered Resources" along the bottom. Endangered resources? No shit! You people are slaughtering those resources with your cars with what appears to be reckless abandon! If the state of Wisconsin commissioned me, which it most surely won't, to come up with a new state motto to put on their license plates, it would be: "Wisconsin: America's Roadkill Capital."

To try and breathe a little life back into our adventure, we planned to stop in Madison, a city I'd heard so much about but had never seen. People rave about Madison, home of the University of Wisconsin, whose downtown is located on a narrow isthmus about ten blocks wide between two large lakes. I'd seen pictures of people eating under colorful umbrellas at outdoor cafés along the waterfront and college towns tend to be hip, lively places, drawing energy from their youthful populations. Albie and I would, I thought, spend the better part of the day there soaking up the spring sunshine and walking along the lake shore. Except that the day was cold, gray, and wet and went downhill from there.

An outdoor festival with some excellent bluegrass musicians was in progress in a plaza near the magnificent state Capitol building (this is how it's done, North Dakota), but it was sparsely attended because of the weather and had the dispiriting feel of people trying to have a better time of it than they were. We walked from the edge of Lake Mendota to the edge of Lake Monona, but our hearts weren't in it. We got back in the car and headed toward Chicago. Along the way, the carnage that was a prominent feature of Wisconsin highways continued. If we had to look at one more desiccated dear carcass, I thought I'd scream. I ended up screaming.

The highway for about twenty miles on either side of Janesville was under construction, causing a major traffic jam. The road was rough, the weather gloomy, and the driving exhausting. It felt as if the trip had finally, and irrevocably, slipped away from us. It was, for all practical purposes, over.

The journey slipped away for another reason, too. Albie had indulged my late midlife fantasy long enough. The concerns that occasionally gnawed at me about whether this trip was fair to him now stood front and center. We needed to get back to the yard where he could run, untethered to me by his leash, with Salina and Jamba. Between the uncooperative weather and lack of adventure at our recent stops, I knew he needed more stimulation than he was getting. As uncomplaining and agreeable as he'd been I couldn't shake the feeling that I'd been a little selfish. As much as I was ready to be back home, I wanted him to be back home even more. I knew exactly what Steinbeck meant, and how he felt, when he wrote about the final leg of his journey with Charley:

> My own journey started long before I left, and was over before I returned. I know exactly where and

when it was over. Near Abingdon, in the dogleg of Virginia, at four o'clock on a windy afternoon, without warning or goodbye or kiss my foot, my journey went away and left me stranded far from home. . . . The road became an endless stone ribbon, the hills obstructions, the trees green blurs, the people simply moving figures with heads but no faces. . . . It is very strange. Up to Abingdon, Virginia, I can reel back the trip like film. I have almost total recall, every face is there, every hill and tree and color, the sound of speech and small scenes ready to replay themselves in my memory. After Abingdon—nothing. The way was a gray, timeless, eventless tunnel, but at the end of it was the one shining reality—my own wife, my own house in my own street, my own bed. It was all there, and I lumbered my way toward it.

We hadn't planned it this way, but I was feeling self-satisfied that we would be going around Chicago on a Sunday. No weekday rush hour traffic to contend with. We had sprung free of the construction traffic in southern Wisconsin, to my considerable relief. But the next hour and then some, as we circumvented the Windy City, was the most harrowing of the entire trip, and that includes the terrifying, nausea-inducing Tail of the Dragon in Tennessee. It was as if we were in a small boat in a gently flowing stream and were suddenly thrust into a raging river. Traffic on the tangle of highways around Chicago, always dividing, merging, looping around, and intersecting, roared along in a manic, wild, reckless, heedless, headlong rush. I've never seen people drive with such abandon or with so little regard for their own safety and the safety of others and that's saying something since we live near Boston. It was utter madness as we were swept along, my hands gripping the wheel and trying to follow the instructions of my GPS through the spaghetti-like tangle. Now, you might think, "Oh, he's just getting old and more timid behind the wheel," but I assure you that's not the case. It was like being in *Mad Max* for well over the hour-plus it took us to bypass Chicago (we never even glimpsed the skyline).

When we crossed into Indiana I thought the madness would subside, but it didn't. To add to what was already a dismal day, industrial northern Indiana was ugly (not unlike the industrial wasteland around Newark Airport) and an acrid chemical smell permeated the air. I set the climate control to "recirculate" to keep the fumes at bay. It felt like we'd been surfing class five rapids in our little boat for an eternity. When the mad rush finally subsided east of Gary, we stopped at a rest area so Albie could tend to some business and I could regain my composure. It was still cold, windy, and dank, perfectly miserable weather in a perfectly ugly place.

Albie has an endearing habit when he's feeling a little unsettled or frightened of lifting both paws up, so I can hold him under his arms or hold both his paws in my hands. It's his way of making sure I have his full attention. And he did it now, there in the parking lot of the rest area of this godforsaken place.

"We're gonna be home soon," I told him. "Promise."

For the past five weeks I had largely avoided talk of politics, though there were exceptions. Kurtis Walker, the confessed liberal in Okemah, Oklahoma, and Louis, the right-wing cyclist in Bismarck, were two of them. Here, at a rest stop in frigid, industrial northern Indiana, the air smelling of poison, a thick-bodied man, his hair cut in a modified Mohawk and a surly expression on his face got out of a pickup truck. He wore cargo shorts and a dark blue T-shirt. In bold letters across the front it said: "TRUMP: FUCK YOUR FEELINGS." My little respite from the insanity of our times was most definitely over. That T-shirt seemed to sum up perfectly the dismal state of our politics here in a most dismal corner of America. It had been an ugly day in every way, from the decomposing roadkill in Wisconsin to the decomposing state of our politics summed up on a T-shirt.

We spent the night in a motel near the airport in South Bend, Indiana. After a day of harrowing interstate driving I was determined, despite my eagerness to get home, to spend at least part of the next day back on secondary roads and to try and extract some pleasure from the miles that lay ahead.

South Bend is just a few miles south of the Michigan border and Michigan was now the only state in the country I'd never been in. The childlike fascination many of us have with checking off the states was still there, even at age sixty-four, so I was looking forward to completing the quest to set foot in all fifty states. Within ten minutes of leaving the motel, we were in Michigan and turned east on Highway 12, which skirts through farmland just north of the Indiana line. We actually set foot in Michigan when we stopped to gas up the car in the curiously named town of White Pigeon which, I should note because the town does, is home of the Michigan High School Athletic Association Boys Golf State Championship Teams of 2003 and 2014 (Division 4).

In the great interstate roadkill competition, which seems to be dominated by states of the upper Midwest, Michigan was giving Wisconsin a real run for its money (small game division only). I'll spare you the details save to say that the roadway was littered with small critters who came to their ends under the wheels of cars and trucks. It wasn't quite as extravagant as the carnage in Wisconsin, but impressive, in a sad way, nevertheless.

At Sturgis, home of the Michigan High School Athletic Association Boys Bowling State Championship Team of 2012, we turned south to reach the great and mighty asphalt river known as Interstate 80. Past Cleveland we again followed secondary roads near the shores of Lake Erie and ended up again on U.S. Route 20, the very same Route 20 we'd been on across Idaho. It was mostly a slog, traffic lights and gas stations and fast-food restaurants, but I resisted the temptation to get back on the interstate. The congestion eased east of Ashtabula and when we crossed the state line into Pennsylvania I couldn't help but marvel that just two days ago we were in North Dakota and now we were back in the Northeast. Well, technically, perhaps, but the very first house inside the Pennsylvania line was flying a Confederate flag.

That night, in our motel room in Erie, I talked to Albie, but I had more to say than usual. The trip had been dragging for me for the past few days as I am sure it had been for him. As I rubbed his belly and kissed his face I thanked him for being so patient and for being such a good traveler, told him he was a great guy, no, the *best* guy, and that we really would be home soon, the day after tomorrow, in fact. He listened patiently, as always, and when I was done he took a deep breath and lay his head on the bed with a sigh.

Our trip, it seemed, was destined to end as it had begun, with persistent, heavy rain. It's only about a dozen miles from Erie to the New York state line. I toyed with the idea of stopping at Niagara Falls, which I'd never seen, but it would have been utterly pointless as we seemed to be driving *through* the falls all the way to Buffalo and beyond. It was exhausting because the rain was so heavy it required complete concentration behind the wheel. I had not remembered at the time, but a few months after we had returned home, while perusing parts of *Travels with Charley* again, I found this:

> It rained in New York State, the Empire State, rained cold and Pitiless. . . . Indeed the dismal down-pour made my intended visit to Niagara Falls seem redundant.

Though separated by more than five decades, our trip and Steinbeck's had many parallels.

It was tempting to make a big, final push to get home that night, to put this trip away and tuck ourselves into our own beds. But several weeks earlier, I'd made a promise we had to keep, and so we had miles to go before we could sleep. To keep that promise we went a bit out of our way and spent our last night in the lovely, but wet village of Bennington, Vermont.

SIXTEEN

Coming Home˙

About a week into our trip, back in Maryville, Tennessee,
my cell phone rang. It was Wini Mason, a very dear old
family friend. Wini was ninety-four then, and she knew my
mother when both were young girls growing up in Brookline,
Massachusetts. They remained the closest of lifelong friends and
Wini still grieves for my mother, gone more than ten years now.
The families were so close I was named after Wini and Paul's
first son, Peter Alan. Paul, Wini's husband of seventy years, was
ninety-nine at the time Wini called and has since celebrated his
one hundredth birthday. They live independently in a house
they have owned for more than sixty years overlooking the

---

*   There are at least a dozen songs by this title, including songs by John
Legend, Roy Orbison, and Keith Urban.

dunes in the seaside community of Ogunquit, Maine. It was originally their vacation house, but they've lived there year-round now for decades.

Growing up, my brother, Michael, and I both knew that if "something happened" to my parents (a euphemism, of course) we would go to live with the Masons. They were our legal guardians. We always called most of our parents' friends "Mr." and "Mrs." but Wini and Paul were always Aunt Wini and Uncle Paul. They are the closest I've had to a second set of parents.

Nearly every summer growing up, our family spent two weeks in Ogunquit. Many of my fondest and most wondrous memories of childhood were formed there. I learned to ride a bike on the street in front of Wini and Paul's house. There were always kids to play with, even if some, like the Mason's three children, Peter, Jimmy, and Wendy, were all a bit older than we were. Many Mason cousins also came as did family friends from Montreal. On the beach, once we all spread our towels and chairs out, there might be twenty or more of us passing the sunny, rocky days along the Maine coast together.

When Mike and I were really young, before they started renting cottages, my parents rented two rooms in the Seaview House in Ogunquit, a simple two-story house built by Meredith ("Meb") Young and run by his wife, Ethel. During the summer, the Youngs slept on beds they set up on a porch adjacent to their kitchen in the back of the house. All the other rooms were rented to vacationers.

To keep us from disturbing other guests in the morning, Ethel entertained us in the kitchen and made us breakfast. She was a gentle, kind, gray-haired woman, but firmly in charge. Meb was a wiry Mainer who worked at the Portsmouth Naval Yard about a half hour south in New Hampshire. Meb was a man of few, but always well-chosen and usually dryly humorous, words, always spoken in a classic Down East accent.* One summer we arrived, and it was obvious from the way his lips were pursed that all of Meb's teeth were missing. My father and I were sitting with him at the picnic table in the Young's backyard, but my father was too polite to say anything. After a couple of minutes of small talk there was a pause and Meb looked straight at my father, a small, wry smile forming at the corners of his mouth: "In case ya had-unt noticed, I had all mah teeth rah-moved."

To get to the beach from Wini and Paul's or the Seaview House, we took a short walk and went over a footbridge, maybe fifty or sixty yards long, that crosses the Ogunquit River, which is actually a tidal estuary. The bridge has been rebuilt at least a couple of times in the past fifty years or so, but we used to spend countless hours on that bridge using drop lines to catch crabs in the river. We'd bring our buckets, find some mussels in the river or clinging to the bridge supports, crack them open and run the hook on our drop lines through the flesh. When the tide was low the bridge was about twenty feet or so above the water and you could see when a crab had climbed onto your bait. The challenge was to gradually hoist the crab up and into your bucket before it let go and dropped back into the water. When the tide was high the water was too deep to see the crabs on the bottom. You

---

* Though the term "Down East" refers to all of coastal New England and parts of maritime Canada, it is most often used to refer to the Maine coast. The farther up the Maine coast you go toward Canada, the farther "Down East" you are going. The term goes back hundreds of years. When ships sailed from Boston to ports in Maine, which are to the north and east of Boston, the wind was at their backs, so they were sailing downwind. Hence the term, "Down East."

just kept dropping the line, let it sit for a couple of minutes, and draw it up hoping for the best. They no longer allow diving from the bridge, but in the old days Peter and Jimmy Mason and other "bigger" kids, typically teenagers, routinely dove or jumped into the river from the bridge at high tide.

Right at the start of the bridge, on the "landward" side, there was, and still is, a small shack that served steamed hot dogs on buttered, grilled buns and the best and most uniquely flavored hamburgers I've ever had. They also had a lemon-lime soda I craved all year long. As recently as a few years ago members of the same family, the Littlefields, ran the place and the recipes never changed. I have told many people, and meant it, that I would rather sit at one of the picnic tables next to "The Stand," as we called it, eating a steamed dog with mustard and onions and a burger with the same, than eat at the finest restaurant in New York. For dessert, a frozen Milky Way bar.

Often, on the evenings when we weren't having dinner at the Howard Johnson's in Wells (like most HoJos, no longer there), someone would call in an order to a lobster pound in Wells for lobsters, steamers (steamed clams), and fried clams. My dad and I might drive up to Wells to pick them up while Wini and my Mom and various other adults would make salad and corn. Then, as the adults talked well into the evening, or played bridge, the kids would play games—jacks was a favorite, or hearts—staying up well past our usual bedtimes. It all felt so safe and secure and warm and wonderful.

When we got a little older, or more to the point, as Peter and Jimmy Mason got a bit older, became teenagers, there was more mischief. They'd get some firecrackers somewhere and after dark we'd walk down near The Stand, closed for the evening, or cross the footbridge into the dunes, and they'd set off the firecrackers until some agitated neighbor would call the police, "the fuzz" as the Mason boys called them, and we'd scatter, feeling very grown up and a little bit like outlaws.

It was in Ogunquit that we were allowed to go to the movies by ourselves for the first time. We saw *The Guns of Navarone* at the Ogunquit Theater (which is still in town) in 1961, and, when it came out in 1965, the Beatles' movie *Help!* three nights in a row at the same theater.

On those countless days and evenings we spent with the Masons, Wini would always get mad at us boys if we didn't put the toilet seat cover down when we'd finished using the john. To this day, whenever I visit them I come out of that same bathroom and say to Wini, "I forget, do you want me to leave the toilet seat up or down?" And she always grits her teeth in mock disapproval, says, "Don't be fresh!" and gives me a playful swat on the arm.

The point is that Ogunquit is freighted with some of my happiest memories of childhood, of my parents, once young and now gone. Wini and Paul are my link to both. They have known me since birth and I have never known the world without them.

When Wini called while Albie and I were in Tennessee, she didn't know I was taking this trip. As we talked it occurred to me that it would be entirely fitting that this odyssey end in Ogunquit, and I promised Wini that Albie and I would come see them in a few weeks. It would be our last stop before heading home at last.

And so, despite a nearly overwhelming desire now to get home, Albie and I drove from Bennington to Ogunquit to spend the better part of the day with Wini and Paul, and to revisit a place that remains, and always will be, such a meaningful part of my life.

❖

The hills and dales of southern Vermont were covered in thick fog when we left Bennington, but the sun quickly burned it off and we drove across the southern part of the state, and New Hampshire, too, under clear blue skies with the convertible top down. When we left New England nearly six weeks before, the trees were still bare, and we had driven across a lot of desert, farmland, and plains since. It was easy to forget just how densely forested the vast majority of New England is and how luxuriantly and lavishly green it is in spring. The electric greens of spring fade a bit as summer progresses, as the new leaves on the deciduous trees mature and blend more seamlessly with the evergreens. But today, the bright greens, especially in the brilliant sunshine, stood in stark contrast with the dark.

The grand scenery of the West—Grand Canyon, Yosemite, the Pacific headlands around San Francisco, Yellowstone, the Grand Tetons—is more dramatic and jaw-dropping, but it's *so* big and *so* grand that you can often feel like you're gazing at a movie screen. The scale of it all can leave you feeling like a spectator, and a small one at that. The natural beauty of New England, the older, well-worn mountains, the slivers of beach along low-lying dunes on Cape Cod, or the rocky coast of Maine dotted with small towns and fishing villages, is more intimate; the land and seascapes are on a more human, more relatable scale. Without carrying a backpack deep into the backcountry, these are landscapes you feel more *part of* than *apart from*.

Knowing Albie needed a walk when we arrived in Ogunquit, we didn't go straight to Wini and Paul's, but to the footbridge that spans the Ogunquit River. Over the years, this once sleepy seaside town has drawn ever larger crowds and with it has come all that's needed to support the tourist trade—more motels, more restaurants, more mini-golf—more *everything*. It was a couple of days before Memorial Day, so the hoards had not yet descended. There were just a few cars in the beach parking lot, where they now charge $25 to park starting on Memorial Day weekend.

It was disappointing that right smack in the middle of the entrance to the footbridge was a new sign: "No Dogs: $100 fine." My plan had been to walk Albie across that bridge for old time's sake and I was tempted to take my chances, but a pass-erby told me, somewhat chagrined, that they strictly enforce the no-dogs rule. But just to be in that spot was enough. More than half a century ago we filled buckets with crabs on this bridge; now it was on my bucket list to see it with Albie and we'd done it.

We took a couple of pictures and then we walked a bit, past the old Seaview House where my brother, Mike, and I had often stayed as children with our parents. As we passed, we saw a compactly built, older white-haired man working in the driveway. We waved to each other and Albie and I walked on, but not far, before we turned around. I remembered that Meb and Ethel had one child, a son, Bob. There used to photographs of Bob's children, Meb and Ethel's grandchildren, on the console television set in the living room of their house. Meb and Ethel had both died many years ago and I wondered if that was Bob who had just waved to me. We walked up the driveway and the man put down his work gloves and came to greet us. He looked to be well into his seventies.

"Are you Meb and Ethel's son?" I asked.

"I am!" he said, smiling now. "I'm Bob."

I introduced myself, we shook hands, and I told him how we used to stay at the house and how his mother had entertained us as young children in her kitchen. Bob didn't remember us, but there was no reason he would have. He lived and worked in and around Groton, Connecticut, most of his adult life. Now that he was retired he'd moved back to this house, where he'd grown up, and was still running it as a guesthouse in summer. We chatted for a few minutes; he sounded exactly like his father. It seems such a simple, incidental thing, but I was thrilled to talk to Bob and make this connection to a long ago past, to these fragments of memory that, when stitched together, form the fabric of my life.

Wini and Paul and I spent the afternoon *kibitzing*, as my mother would have said. I brought them up to date on our kids, and vice versa, though Wini and Paul have grandkids and great-grandkids to talk about, too. Wini, as she always does, spoke of how much she missed my mother and wondered aloud, as she had to me many times before, why my parents had divorced in the early 1980s. They were very fond of my father, too. Wini recalled when she first met my father, while my mother was still at Radcliffe and my father was doing a pediatric fellowship at Boston Children's Hospital.

Wini asked if we would be staying for a bite to eat for supper and I told her my heart was set on a lobster roll.

"We could order some and I'll pick them up," I suggested.

"*If* I pay for them!" Wini said, chiding me.

"No, *I'll* pay for them," and I phoned the same lobster pound up in Wells where we used to order lobsters and steamers fifty years ago.

After we finished our lobster rolls, Albie lying patiently at my side the whole time, I helped clear the table. When we used to come here for vacation we thought one of the coolest things was that our parents would set up an account at The Stand and we could go in, order our hot dogs and burgers and frozen Milky Ways, and "charge it." The Masons, too, had an account and just to make trouble we'd often say, "Charge it to the Masons."

Over all these years our charging stuff "to the Masons" has been a running joke between Wini and me, like putting the toilet seat down after using the loo, but one I never tire of playing my little role in. "All right, Wini," I said. "I paid for the lobster rolls, so I never want to hear again about what I owe you for charging all that stuff at The Stand!"

Wini, always a community activist, was off to a committee meeting to discuss some town issue or other . . . at ninety-four! I gave her a big hug, so she could go get ready for her meeting, and Paul walked us out to the car. Albie, for the thousandth, and next to last time, hopped in back without complaint. As we backed out, Paul waved, and I waved back thinking what a long and remarkable life he and Wini have had together, and what an incredible vitality they have well into their nineties, though they have their ailments and have slowed down considerably. Earlier, I had asked Wini the secret of their longevity and she said, "Genes." But really, I think they are each the secret to the other's longevity.

As we drove off I thought about what a steady presence these people have been in my life, like the North Star—always there when you look up at the night sky. But when people are ninety-four and ninety-nine, you can't help but wonder, "Will I see them again?" And I thought back to the very first day of our trip when I briefly glimpsed the elderly man with a walker making his way up *his* driveway in Hamden, Connecticut. An old man in his driveway. How soon might that old man be me? Given how time seems to pass ever faster was we age, sooner than I might like to think, which is why I was glad I didn't wait any longer to see my country, or Wini and Paul, again.

It was nearing 6:00 P.M. We had an hour and half yet to drive, but one final stop to make. We drove down to Perkins Cove, a cozy little harbor filled with dinghies and fishing boats and lobster traps, cedar-shingled restaurants and shops, and a wooden drawbridge across the inlet so the boats can pass as they go to and from the sea. A little narrow peninsula, not even a hundred yards wide in some places, separates the cove from the ocean.

I took a seat on a bench overlooking the ocean side, Albie, as always, close by my side. The evening was warm, the light golden, and the ocean unusually calm. How many times had I sat in this very spot and watched the ocean lap up against these craggy rocks? Then I looked down at Albie. Every time I think I couldn't love him any more than I do, I do.

As we soaked up the view and took in the preternaturally serene evening my mind wandered back across the decades and over the past six weeks. We had more than 9,000 miles behind us and just ninety to go; I had nearly sixty-five years behind me and an unknown number, but far fewer, to go. Neither of my parents made it to eighty; my dad died when he was just seventy-three. And Albie, too, now about nine, was closer to the end than the beginning. All of these journeys were slowly ebbing away.

Then Judy called, snapping my attention back to the present. Suddenly all those miles, and all the powerful memories stirred up by the day, caught up with me. I wanted to lie down and take a long nap. As I started to tell Judy where we were my voice cracked and I fought back the tears welling up in my eyes. So much of my life had passed, some of the best of it right here at this very spot and others nearby. I felt grief for my parents, for all the time that had now passed, for innocence lost. On those summer evenings in Ogunquit long ago my parents were less than half the age I was now. So much in life had changed, so much had *happened*, since the days when, as children, we spent our summer vacations here. But the view? It hadn't changed at all.

Albie, dear, sweet, earnest Albie sat quietly by me for about another half hour before I mustered the energy to stand up and ready myself for the drive home. I gave Albie a long, long hug and thanked him for being with me, for being so patient over so many miles, miles that were, no doubt, far more interesting for me than they were for him. This gentle old soul, once lost in the woods of central Louisiana and now part of who I am and will forever be. An enormous surge of gratitude that fate had brought us together washed over me. Then we walked over to the take-out window at Barnacle Billy's and I bought him a vanilla ice cream cone.

And that is how the travelers came home again.

Acknowledgments

First, of course, I am deeply indebted to the love of my life, my partner in crime, my soul mate, my better half, and my best friend . . . Albie. No, maybe that was supposed to be my wife Judy. In any event, my thanks first and foremost to Albie and Judy; Albie for being such a faithful, ever-patient and genial traveling companion over all the miles, and Judy for never hesitating to encourage me to take this trip and for holding down the fort with Salina and Jambalaya, our other two rescue dogs, while we were away. I like to think she was glad when we got home, however. The other dogs certainly were.

To all the people mentioned in this book, each and every one, thank you for being a part of the journey. A few deserve special mention: Voz Vanelli in Tupelo, JoAnn Clevenger in New Orleans, Kurtis Walker and Wayland Bishop in Okemah, Oklahoma, Andy Gelman, Ceci Ogden, and Ollie in Mountain View, California, Bill Monning in Sacramento, California, Jon and Lois Moroni in Mariposa, California, Mary and

David Peterman in Boise, Idaho, Louis, the wandering Marine Corps veteran we met in Bismarck, and Wini and Paul Mason in Ogunquit, Maine.

I am eternally grateful to Krista Lombardo, Keri Toth and Labs4rescue without whom Albie might never have left the shelter in Alexandria, Louisiana alive. Our reunion with Krista and Keri as we traveled through Louisiana was short but oh-so sweet.

This is the seventh book I have worked on with my outstanding agent Joelle Delbourgo. Through several rounds of feedback, she made sure I kept improving on my execution of the proposal for this book until it was ready for prime time.

This is my first book with Pegasus Books, a smart, nimble, independent press based in New York that punches well above it weight. Thanks a million to Associate Publisher Jessica Case, whose enthusiasm and gentle but insightful touch ran from start to finish, to Maria Fernandez for the interior design, Mary O'Mara for her careful copyediting, Daniel O'Conner for his meticulous proofreading, and Spencer Fuller of Faceout Studios for the stunning cover design. The result is a far better book than I would have written if left entirely to my own devices.

During our travels, Albie and I relied heavily on the travel web site BringFido to help us find pet-friendly accommodations and restaurants. After the trip I wrote them to see if they might help sponsor my book tour and they quickly said "yes," enabling me to undertake a more ambitious book tour than would have been possible without them. I am most grateful for their enthusiastic support.

Finally, I thank my car for its flawless performance over 9,187 miles. It didn't break down, not even once, and we were often a long, long way from help if it had.